TARTS & PIES

CLASSIC & CONTEMPORARY

TARTS & PIES

CLASSIC & CONTEMPORARY

PHILIPPA VANSTONE

GRUB STREET • LONDON

Acknowledgements

I would like to thank my husband Richard for his support, my parents for encouraging me to take an interest in food as a child and Jan for her help testing some of the recipes. Allan Collier for giving me the opportunity to learn my craft and being a great teacher. Liz Cooper for her advice on recipes over the years. Anton Edelman and Neville Campbell for employing me in their kitchens. Lastly but most importantly thanks to Anne Dolamore for publishing my work.

This paperback edition published in 2008 by
Grub Street
4 Rainham Close
London
SW11 6SS
Email: food@grubstreet.co.uk
Web: www.grubstreet.co.uk

Text copyright © Philippa Vanstone 2006, 2008
Copyright this edition © Grub Street 2008
Photography shot in Natural Light by Michelle Garrett
Designed by LizzieBDesign

The right of Philippa Vanstone to be identified as the author of this work has been asserted by her in accordance with the Copyright, Designs and Patents Act 1988.

A CIP catalogue for this book is available from the British Library Cataloguing

ISBN 978-1-906502-08-9

Printed and bound in India

CONTENTS

INTRODUCTION

Thinking back to my childhood, an interest in food was probably sparked by family holidays to France; shopping excursions to village markets and meals out in local restaurants being the main activities. But it wasn't until I graduated from studying Home Economics that I developed a yearning to cook for a living. I was drawn to the sweet side of food preparation because I felt it offered more scope for creativity. Starting with the basic ingredients of flour, sugar, butter and eggs and adding a few more such as chocolate, nuts, fruit and cream, seemed to me to open up limitless possibilities. And even though later working in professional kitchens gave me the opportunity to learn about more than just the sweet side of things, I chose to specialize in pastry and desserts. And so I embarked on my journey of food discovery.

This book comprises recipes acquired on my travels through numerous basement kitchens of London's hotels and restaurants as well as a few recipes given to me by friends and colleagues. There are adaptations of French classics, a few New World favourites and some old fashioned British ones too.

Sadly sweet tarts and pies have not been overly popular of late. Without a doubt this is due to their high fat and carbohydrate content. Despite this, as in fashion, there are some classics that don't date and the same can be said for tarts and pies. Apple pie will change with the seasons to accommodate blackberries in autumn, cranberries in winter and raspberries in the summer. Year in and year out pumpkin and pecan pies are popular at Thanksgiving whilst lemon and chocolate tarts remain perennial. I'm keeping my fingers crossed that people will return to producing more food in the home and become less reliant on ready-processed convenience foods and that in turn they may choose once in a while to bake a homemade tart or pie for their friends and family.

I'd like to think that occasionally you will dispense with the ready-made pastry and opt to make your own instead – with the exception of puff pastry, which does require more time, the other pastry recipes are really quite straightforward. With chapters on different key ingredients I hope there will be something here for everyone.

A BRIEF HISTORY OF PASTRY

When I started researching the history of pastry I wasn't quite sure what I would find and so I was surprised to learn that the ancient Egyptians were amongst the first to enjoy a form of pastry as far back as 5,000 BC. Their cooks created small fruit-filled pastries from flour, oil, dried fruits and honey. Given that oil was used as opposed to a hard fat, the pastry would not have resembled the stiff type we use today.

At around the same time the Egyptians were baking sweet pastries, European Neolithic man was baking *galettes* of cereal paste on hot stones. These *galettes* became the precursor to hearth cakes, cooked on a griddle by an open fire or in a pot covered with embers and ashes.

The ancient Greeks utilised the knowledge of the Egyptians and went on to develop Phyllo pastry sometime around the 3rd century AD but the dough could be of Turkish origin, since baklava already existed, and so the paper-thin pastry we know today, was probably an innovation of the Ottoman sultan's kitchens at the Topkapi palace in Istanbul.

It is likely that pastry as we now know it developed in Medieval northern Europe. This is probably due to the fact that the cooking fats used there, namely lard and butter, were most suited to pastry making. Whereas those countries whose primary fat source was oil were placed at a distinct disadvantage because pastry made with oil lacked the necessary degree of stiffness to hold its shape when baked. One of the first recipes for pastry appears in Gervase Markham's *The English Hus-wife* of 1615. The earliest references to puff pastry date back to 1586 but it is possible that it was being produced far earlier than this in both France and Italy.

The Middle Ages was a time of overseas exploration when luxury food items began to be imported into Britain. Sugar, spice, dried fruits and nuts became available to the nobility with the foods cooked at banquets becoming more elaborate. Much of the pastry prepared in Medieval Britain was used to cover and protect meat as it was being cooked or to form a stiff case or 'coffyn' to hold meat and other ingredients and was not intended to be eaten. Savoury pies became a form of banquet entertainment from around the 13th century. Live animals and birds were baked under a pastry crust and then released when the pie crust was cut open, much to the delight of guests.

'Sing a song of sixpence, a pocket full of rye
Four and twenty blackbirds baked in a pie
When the pie was opened the birds began to sing
Wasn't that a dainty dish to set before the king.'

Open pastry crusts containing ingredients that were to be cooked were known as 'traps'. Although recognisable as pastry, these coarse, tough crusts were often inedible. 14th century pie bakers in London were baking savoury pasties and by this time pastry was not only edible, it was becoming popular so by the end of the century the word 'pie' had become well known throughout the country. Flathons or sweet flans started to be made in the 15th century. There were two basic types: one a custard-filled flan, the other filled with an almond paste.

Elizabeth I came to the throne in 1558 and reigned until 1603, during which years sugar was more readily available, foods became much sweeter and the Elizabethans developed a taste for it, along with crystallised roses, violets, almonds, dates, figs and raisins. Almonds were the most popular flavouring in sweet dishes along with cinnamon and cloves. Fruit pies also became popular and European cookery books from this period began to give recipes for pastry. Pastry had also become much shorter and richer, partly due to increased availability of ingredients but probably also due to the fact that is was now eaten as part of the dish rather than simply being a means of protecting or containing meats and sauces.

The Renaissance period was a time of great culinary change and development, led primarily by the Italians. When Catherine de Médici married the future king of France, Henry II, she took her chefs and pastry cooks with her to the French Court where they established the foundations of *Haute Cuisine*. Italian pastry cooks led the way in pastry making at this time and Catherine de Médici's chef, Panterelli, is credited with creating choux pastry in 1540.

By the 17th century pies had become part of everyday life throughout Britain and when the first English settlers travelled to America they took their pie-baking skills with them, where they developed classics such as pumpkin, pecan and key lime pies.

The 18th century saw the continued development of pie baking with regional apple pies such as the Banbury Apple Pie, which may have been one of the earliest double-crusted pies. It was probably developed with pastry both top and bottom so that merchants and others attending the market could simply buy them and take them away as an early form of fast-food!

Yorkshire curd tart also became a favourite from the middle of the 18th century. The curds, a by-product of the Yorkshire dairy industry, were baked with eggs, sugar and rosewater in a pastry case.

Fruit pies continued to be much in demand throughout the country especially amongst farm workers in fruit-growing areas where pie was a hearty, filling end to a meal. Cheese became a common accompaniment to apple pie and even began to be baked within the pie in some parts of the country.

Although pasties had been eaten since the Middle Ages it was the Cornish miners who really made them their own. Usually made from meat, potato and vegetables

they sometimes contained two fillings separated by a piece of pastry – these pasties were a two-course meal in one! The raised crimped pastry rim allowed the miner to hold his pasty to eat while keeping his dirty hands clear of his meal!
In order to aid identification of the savoury half from the sweet, the miners' wives who baked the pasties for their husbands, would decorate the sweet end with scraps of pastry. This may go some way to explaining the reason for decorating sweet pies and not savoury ones.

Gooseberry pie became one of the most sought-after fruit pies during this time especially after the sugar tax was repealed in 1874, and treacle tart began to appear at the end of the century after golden syrup went on sale in 1880.

Meanwhile in Europe, Antonin Carême became one of the 19th century's greatest chefs by cooking for the rich, famous and royal and did much to further pastry work.

The Second World War and the rationing of food between 1940 and 1954 did much to change the face of British cookery. Cooking became much more basic and food much plainer during this period. Although we may think that the ingredients required for a simple apple pie are few in number, everyday ingredients such as eggs and butter were hard to come by.

'Crumble' was created during the period after the war before rationing came to an end. A resourceful cook found that a topping could be 'crumbled' from a small quantity of flour, fat and sugar and sprinkled over fruit before it was baked, whereas larger quantities of fat and flour were required to make the pastry for a fruit pie.

Since the 1980s the practice of home-cooking and in particular home-baking has diminished considerably with convenience foods becoming the order of the day. Far fewer people now than ever before know how to cook. In part this is due to the increase in numbers of working mothers and single parent families; mothers simply have not passed cookery skills on to the next generation. So although regional and homemade tarts and pies remain popular with the British public, they are rarely baked at home these days. More often they are bought from the local supermarket or eaten in restaurants.

Technological advancement has further aided and abetted the decline in the nation's culinary skills. Food manufacturers now produce high quality pastry items and ready-made pastry negating the need for pastry to be made in the home.

However I hope that soon the tide will turn and more people will experience the kind of pleasure and satisfaction I get from pastry making.

THE ESSENTIALS

PASTRY TYPES AND METHODS

PUFF PASTRY

Puff pastry is considered by many to be the finest of all pastry, unfortunately it is also the most difficult and time-consuming pastry to make - a real labour of love. But don't despair if you haven't got the time or the inclination to make it, just pick up some ready-made puff pastry from your local supermarket.

Puff pastry comprises hundreds of crisp, buttery wafer-thin layers. When you bite into these crisp fragile layers the pastry crumbles and melts in your mouth.

This type of pastry has probably been produced since the mid-fifteenth century although its production is not attributed to a specific individual and it is hard to say exactly where it originated but it is likely that its birthplace was France, where it is called *feuilletage*. There is some evidence to suggest that it was also being produced at around the same time in Italy where it is known as *sfoglia*. Both French and Italian names mean 'leaves'.

Puff pastry requires skill to make, and more importantly, time. It is known as a 'laminated pastry'. Lamination is the process of folding butter in between layers of dough. Others in this category include rough puff, also known as scotch, flaky and *demi-feuilletage* but these are to all intents and purposes simpler versions of puff pastry. On occasion *demi-feuilletage* or half-puff is used in professional kitchens but generally speaking puff pastry is used. *Demi-feuilletage* is akin to rough puff where a higher percentage of fat is rubbed into the flour. The remainder is incorporated, as for full-butter puff, in one piece.

For best effect puff pastry should be made using unsalted butter, strong plain flour, cold, acidulated water and a little salt. Flour with a protein content of 12% is fine. The quantity of butter used should be equal to that of the flour. This is commonly known as full-butter puff. In addition to being difficult to make, it is also expensive because of the amount of butter needed, so to make it easier and cheaper to produce, pastry chefs sometimes reduce the amount of fat to flour. It is best not to reduce the quantity of butter to less than 3/4 of the weight of the flour though, as this will give a noticeably poor result. However as little as 1/2 fat to flour can be used successfully but the pastry will be far less rich in flavour and have less lift.

There are two methods for making puff pastry: the French and English methods. The methods differ in respect to the way the fat is incorporated into the dough or *detrempe*. I favour the French method because I find the fat is less likely to break out from the edges of the pastry and this is the method I use in my recipes. In both cases a small quantity of fat, not more than $\frac{1}{8}$ of the total weight of fat, is rubbed into the strong flour and salt before cold acidulated water is added to form a smooth firm dough, which is rested for 15-20 minutes before the remaining fat is incorporated.

Butter is my choice of fat simply because it gives the best flavour. A fat often employed in the production of commercial puff pastry is pastry fat or margarine. This fat, composed of hydrogenated fats and oils, is specially formulated to have a high melting point and high degree of plasticity. These properties enable the pastry to withstand rough handling and be worked in higher temperature environments but despite these plus points these pastry fats lack the flavour of butter.

In both the French and English methods the fat is placed in one piece onto the dough and enveloped in it. It is essential that the dough and the fat are the same consistency, so if using butter it should be 'plasticized' before adding to the dough. To 'plasticize' the butter bash it with a rolling pin several times to make it malleable and check its consistency against that of your dough.

If you are making a quantity of puff pastry greater than 1 kilo it is often easier to mix a proportion of the flour with the butter to give a butter paste and then incorporate this paste into the dough. This technique is often used in professional kitchens where larger quantities of puff pastry are produced but when making a small quantity it's unnecessary.

For the French method the dough is rolled into a ball, two cuts are made across the top with the second at right angles to the first. Give the ball a $1/2$ turn so the cut appears as a diagonal cross on the dough. Open out each quarter of the dough and roll each piece into a rectangle attached to the centre that should remain at least three times the thickness of the rolled rectangles.

Place the plasticized fat on the thicker central piece of dough and envelop the fat with the rectangles of dough.

Alternatively there is the English method. The dough is rolled out to give a rectangle about 41cm (16 in) x 30.5cm (12 in) and the fat is spread over $2/3$ of the length. The third without the fat is then folded up over the fat and the top third folded down. The paste is then ready to roll. At this stage one of two methods can be used to make the turns in the dough that are responsible for laminating or layering the fat within the flour. These are called single or double book turns. Gently roll out the dough to give a rectangle about 41cm (16 in) x 30.5cm (12 in). The single turn is straightforward; the dough is folded into three by folding the bottom third over the middle third and then the top third folded down. The double or book turn is folded in half then each half is folded in on itself so it resembles a book. If using the single turn it is necessary to put six turns into the dough, if using the double turn it is only necessary to make four turns. The dough should be rested for 15-20 minutes between each turn.

Puff pastry is best made the day before use because it is time consuming and should not be rushed. It can be wrapped in greaseproof and cling film and kept refrigerated for three days or frozen for up to three months. If frozen, it should be allowed to defrost slowly either in a cool room or a refrigerator.

With flaky pastry the dough is made in the same way as for puff pastry but the fat is incorporated in a fashion similar to the English method but instead of it being used in one piece it is dotted over ⅔ of the rolled out pastry. The turns are made in the same way.

The use of a strong plain flour in puff pastry making provides the dough with greater elasticity than in other pastry types where a softer flour is used. This is due to the higher protein content of the flour. The proteins, gliadin and glutenin, when mixed with water and worked, give rise to the gluten structure that provides a degree of toughness, enabling the lamination of the dough to be achieved.
The addition of a little acid, usually in the form of lemon juice but sometimes vinegar, helps prevent the dough from becoming too tough. The resting of the dough allows the gluten to relax and lengthen giving it more elasticity so it is important not to over roll the dough. It is best to keep it 1cm (³/4 in) thick so that the layering of the fat in the flour is maintained, as the turns are put into the dough. It is also important not to use excess flour when rolling out the pastry and to brush excess flour off the surface of the dough when making the turns. If flour remains on the surface of the pastry, it will when baked, detract from the overall texture of the crisp, buttery, layers and all your hard work, time and effort will have been in vain.

When baked at a high temperature air expands, lifting the layers of dough, water in the dough evaporates, creating steam, the fat melts and as the layers of dough rise they separate and bake, to give crisp wafer thin sheets.

Puff pastry needs to be baked at a very high temperature 240°C, 220°C fan oven, gas 8 for savoury recipes and at the slightly lower temperature of 220°C, 200°C fan oven, gas 7 for sweet recipes.

Puff pastry is used in two forms in professional kitchens; first as virgin pastry which, as the name suggests, is untouched and secondly as trimmings. Trimmings need to be layered rather than rolled up into a ball, to preserve as much of the lamination as possible. A small percentage of trimmings can be rolled into virgin paste when the turns are being put into the dough or it can simply be kept for use as trimmings. You will find a number of recipes where you can use trimmings.

SWEET PASTRY

Sweet pastry, as the name suggests, is pastry that has been sweetened by the addition of sugar. There are several types, but unlike puff pastry the flour used is termed soft flour, but is in actual fact of medium protein content. The plain flour sold in supermarkets is perfectly suitable.

I would choose unsalted butter over any other fat but if you like 'shorter' styles of pastry then you might like to use a proportion of 'shortening' with butter, as in the American Short Pastry recipe I have given (page 33).

The continental styles of sweet pastry: *pâte sucrée*, *pâte frolle* and *pâte sablée*, are finer and richer than sweetened shortcrust or *brisée*. Ratios of fat to flour vary somewhat in sweet pastry recipes but generally the ratio is slightly more than half fat to flour. The quantity of sugar, egg, and in the case of *pâte frolle* ground almonds, also serve to enrich them further.

There are 2 methods used for making sweet pastry - rubbing in and creaming. *Pâte sucrée*, and *pâte frolle* are made using the creaming method, whereas short crust or *brisée* and *pâte sablée* are usually made by rubbing the fat into the dry ingredients. The French method of mixing the fat and liquid simultaneously into the dry ingredients can be used in the preparation of *pâte sucrée* which is made with either icing sugar or caster sugar, whereas *pâte sablée* is usually made with icing sugar. In France *brisée* or shortcrust is unsweetened but here shortcrust is often sweetened, producing a more robust pastry than the continental-style sweet pastries. This makes it suitable for use as a pie crust or base, whereas *pâte sucrée*, *pâte frolle* and *pâte sablée* are not really suitable for use as a pie-top crust.

Pâte sablée is my preferred choice of the sweet pastries since it is shortbread-like in texture and can be used to make biscuits if you wish.

Due to their rich nature *pâte sucrée*, *pâte frolle* and *pâte sablée* should not be baked at as high a temperature as less rich pastries, typically they are best baked at 180°-190°C, 160°C-170°C fan oven, gas 4-5.

Tatin pastry, American short pastry, and shortcrust pastry are all types of *brisée* but their textures vary according to the type of fat, the level of enrichment by sugar and egg, and the quantity of water used. I personally do not like overly short pastry so I tend not to use hydrogenated, white shortenings, although the American Short Pastry in the recipe section does contain shortening. As hydrogenated fats contain trans-fatty acids, that are notoriously bad for you, I prefer to stick to butter, which despite its saturated fat content, is a more natural, less refined product, with a vastly superior flavour. I also prefer to use egg rather than water to aid the formation of a smooth dough. Not only does egg enrich, it also produces a pastry that is less likely to shrink.

Although I recommend resting sweet pastry in the fridge before use, this is simply to ensure it becomes slightly firmer and is easier to roll. If you have made pastry without the use of water, it can generally be used straight away. The addition of water aids the formation of gluten, even in a pastry using flour of a lower protein content; it is the gluten that needs to be relaxed before the pastry can be used.

Some people are happy making pastry in a food processor, but I don't like this method. It is all too easy to overwork the dough and produce a pastry that is far too short, but if you use this method and are happy with the results then stick to it.

I enjoy making sweet pastry by hand, whether by rubbing in or creaming; it is easier to control the result, though it is true that you need a certain lightness of touch to make and use pastry successfully. There are many pitfalls that can be avoided and I discuss these in the section on Hints and Tips (page 25).

CHOUX PASTRY

Choux pastry or *pâte à choux* is distinctly different to other pastry in appearance, texture and also in the way it is made. It is first cooked in a pan before being baked in the oven. The fat is melted in boiling water, the flour added and then it is cooked briefly to ensure all the starch grains have burst. It is left to cool for a few minutes before eggs are beaten into the mixture to give a smooth paste and it bakes to give a crisp hollow crust. It is very versatile, despite not being the type of pastry you can use to line a tart tin, as it can be piped to make a host of different shaped pastries and gateaux e.g. profiteroles, éclairs, *petits choux*, cream buns (*choux à la crème*), salambos, Gateau Religuese, Gateau St-Honoré, *beignets*, *pommes Dauphin* and gnocchi Parisienne.

STRUDEL PASTRY

This is a very fine thin pastry made from strong plain flour. It is mixed to a dough with oil, egg and water. Strudel pastry is widely used throughout Central Europe and in the Middle East where it is known by its Greek name, filo pastry. Although I enjoy making strudel pastry I do like to use commercially produced filo for some recipes where a very fine pastry is needed. The pastry itself doesn't contain added fat so it is necessary to brush it liberally with melted butter when using it. It also dries very quickly so it is best to work with only a small quantity at a time and keep the rest covered with a damp cloth.

LINING THE TART TIN

You should always lightly grease your tart or pie tin. Although pastry should not stick I find it is better to err on the side of caution. It is hard to run a knife around a fluted tin and on occasion a filling may spill over the edge and seal the pastry to the tin. Loose bottom tins are useful.

After you've rested your pastry in the fridge it should be firm enough to roll. Lightly flour the work surface and roll out the pastry making sure to turn it several times, 90˚ each time during rolling, to ensure it is evenly rolled and doesn't stick to the work surface. It is best to use as little flour as possible as excess flour will just make the pastry drier. Brush any excess flour from the pastry and lift the pastry on to the top of the greased tin, using the rolling pin. When lining a tart tin, ease the pastry into position and lift the overhanging edges up so the weight of the pastry helps it fall into the base of the tin. Push the pastry gently into place. Using the forefinger and thumb of one hand and the side of your thumb on the other hand press and lift the pastry slightly above the height of the tin to give a raised edge. This is known as thumbing up. Should your pastry fall slightly during the baking blind stage this will ensure that the tart edge has sufficient height to hold its filling.

DOCKING THE PASTRY

This term refers to the action of making small holes in the base layer of pastry, of all types, with a spiked tool. Dockers come in two forms: as rollers, for use on sheet pastry, and as small fixed pieces of equipment, for lined pastry cases, though you can of course use a fork. Docking the pastry ensures that any air trapped beneath the pastry can escape when the pastry is baked, rather than remaining trapped and causing the pastry to rise and distort.

BAKING BLIND

Baking blind is the term used to describe the first bake of a raw, unfilled pastry case. Its purpose is to fully or partially bake the pastry case prior to it being filled.

Your lined tart should have been allowed to rest for at least 20 minutes in the fridge or 10 minutes in the freezer. I like to get my pastry really cold in the freezer before baking it blind. This gives the pastry time to firm up after the warmth of being rolled and worked into the tin. Line the pastry case with a piece of greaseproof paper that is at least 7.5cm (3 in) larger than the diameter of the tin so that when pushed into the base of the case, the paper sits proud of the tin's edge. Fill the greaseproof liner with baking beans. You don't need expensive ceramic ones, a 500g bag of dried beans such as haricot will do the trick. Avoid red lentils and rice as these are harder to remove from half-baked pastry should you inadvertently spill some when removing the greaseproof. Keep your newly baked beans for use again the next time. You can also re-use the greaseproof two or three times but after this it becomes too brittle and won't hold the weight of the beans when you try to remove them.

Bake your pastry in a preheated oven at 190°C-200°C, 170°C-180°C fan oven, gas 5-6 for 10-15 minutes according to the recipe you're using, remove the beans and bake for a further 5 minutes, until the pastry is pale to golden in colour. Then brush the surface of the tart with a little egg yolk, this creates a barrier between pastry and filling, keeping your pastry base crisp. You can, at this stage, trim the pastry to even out any rough edges. In order to do this you need to use a small sharp knife and literally shave the pastry crust. Brush any pastry crumbs from your pastry case before continuing with your recipe.

INGREDIENTS

FLOUR

Although flour can be produced from many grains, as well as chestnuts and potato, wheat flour is the one most often used for pastry making. Generally speaking flour is classified as being either strong or soft. Although at one time it was classified as being strong, medium or weak, these terms are rarely used now and medium and weak have been grouped together. The harder the wheat, the higher the protein content, and the stronger the flour. The protein content of the flour determines the extent to which gluten will be produced when the flour is mixed with liquid. Strong flour will result in the formation of more gluten and soft will result in less. Gluten provides elasticity and strength and is required in order to produce good quality puff and choux pastry.

Bread flour is strong flour and cake flour is soft. Both types of flour are used for making pastry. In commercial kitchens self-raising flour is rarely used although it is commonplace in domestic kitchens. The protein content of the flour dictates the strength of the flour. Protein contents in flour range from 10-14%. Not readily available in the UK, there are soft flours with protein contents between 8-10% used exclusively for cake making. In America this type of flour is marketed as 'cake flour' and plain flour is known as all-purpose flour.

Although supermarkets sell strong flour for bread making, most flour is packaged as either self-raising or plain so for the purposes of this book I have used this terminology. Both plain and self-raising flours are soft flours. Self-raising has just had a raising agent added and so is more often used for cake rather than pastry making.

Cornflour is the other main flour type used in patisserie and confectionery. Although not used for making the pastry it is used as a thickening agent for pastry cream or crème pâtissiere. It is a very soft flour and can be added in a small quantity to a flour with a higher protein content to give a softer flour.

SUGAR

White caster cane sugar is the most refined sugar and it gives the best results in pastry making.

Granulated sugar has a coarser grain and is useful for sprinkling on top of home-style pies to give a sugar crust but it doesn't dissolve easily and is best not used in pastry or cake making. In pastry it can result in a pitted grainy looking pastry and in cakes it can give the crust a white, speckled appearance.

Unrefined sugars such as muscovado are fabulously flavoured sugars and are useful for creating rich flavoured fillings.

Icing sugar is ground from high quality granulated sugar to a fine powder and hence dissolves more easily. It is used for cooking and for decorative finishes. In professional kitchens it is possible to obtain an indelible form of icing sugar that does not dissolve on contact with a wet surface, that makes it extremely useful for dusting glazed tarts and pies. It is known as *neige décor*.

Black treacle and golden syrup are both by-products of refined sugar. They are also invert sugars which means the refining process has altered their chemical structure and so they are less likely to crystallize than ordinary sugar solutions.

Glucose is also an invert sugar often commercially made from potato. Available in liquid or powder form, it is used in liquid form to prevent sugar syrups crystallizing and to stabilise chocolate mixtures.

FAT

Unsalted butter will give the best flavour and quality end-result where a hard fat is required. The purer the butter the whiter it is; often the yellow colour is a result of added colour, albeit a natural one.

I would avoid margarine at all costs when making pastry, primarily because of its inferior flavour. Although many of the margarines manufactured for spreading, have an acceptable taste, I have yet to find a hard margarine that does.

Pastry fats and margarines specifically manufactured for pastry making are available for the professional kitchen but not the domestic market. These fats have been toughened to produce a fat with a high melting point and good degree of plasticity but lack the flavour of butter.

Hydrogenated shortening, as the name implies, is used to make the texture of the pastry shorter. The plus point is that it has very little flavour, and when mixed with butter in a recipe, gives an acceptable taste. Lard can also be used to shorten pastry but personally, I do not like the taste of pastry made using it.

EGGS

The temperature, freshness and quantity of egg you add to a recipe are the most important factors. If you keep them in the fridge always bring your eggs to room temperature before using them. Most eggs available in supermarkets are produced from chickens inoculated against salmonella and are stamped with the Lion mark. If when you crack your eggs, you notice an odd or sulphur-like smell, don't use them. Eggs fulfil many important functions in pastry making and baking; as a liquid to aid the formation of the pastry dough, as an enriching agent in the pastry, as a key ingredient in custard fillings and also to seal and glaze pastry.

MILK, CREAM AND CRÈME FRAÎCHE

I tend to use semi-skimmed or full fat milk when I'm cooking, whatever is to hand. When it comes to cream, both double and whipping are suitable for most purposes although whipping cream is often a better choice when making a mousse-like filling. It is very easy to over-whip double cream so err on the side of caution and half-whip, as it is always easier to whip it a little bit more, than try to rescue over-whipped cream. If you have ever so slightly over-whipped double cream, it is possible to rescue the situation, but if you are well on the way to making butter then you will need to throw it away and start again. If your cream is just a little over-whipped then pour in some more cold cream or milk and fold this through with a spoon, adding a little more cream or milk as needed until the cream is less stiff. I prefer the taste and texture of crème fraîche to soured cream but they are pretty interchangeable. If you replace sour cream in a recipe with crème fraîche I'd recommend cooking with the full fat rather than the reduced fat version.

GELATINE

Gelatine is made from collagen or the connective tissue in animal bones. It is extracted commercially and refined to give a transparent, almost colourless, substance that is sold in its dehydrated form. It is available in both powder and sheet form. The sheets, or leaves as they are known in professional kitchens, are a better quality product and much easier to use than the powdered gelatine. Leaf gelatine is available in three different grades: bronze, silver and gold. The grades relate to the degree of clarity achieved in the set, gold being the clearest set. Bronze gelatine is the most widely used and unless you require a totally clear aspic for a culinary competition, bronze gelatine will be more than adequate for the purpose. As leaf gelatine is readily available in supermarkets I recommend its use over powdered. Agar agar is a suitable substitute for vegetarians because it is made from a seaweed called carragheen.

FRESH AND DRIED FRUIT

Always choose the freshest fruit available and where possible buy British. Most fruits are available year round but it makes sense to buy locally produced, seasonal fruit when possible.

Dried fruits are mostly imported, as many varieties of commonly used dried fruits are simply not grown, or not grown in sufficient volume, in this country e.g. grapes for raisins and sultanas, lemons for candied peel and apricots. Try to choose plump dried fruits.

A general rule of thumb when using chocolate in desserts, is to buy a good quality variety of dark chocolate, such as Green & Blacks or one of the supermarket's own label brands of continental chocolate. Many people believe that in order for a dark chocolate to be good it must have a cocoa solid content of 70%. This isn't strictly true. One of my favourite dark chocolates, produced by Valrhona, has a cocoa solid content of 64%. There are a number of variables, including the blend and roast of the beans, as well as the style and recipe of the chocolate, that impact on its quality. The reason for using dark chocolate over milk, is that once the chocolate has been melted and combined with other ingredients, its flavour will be greatly diminished, so you need to start with a chocolate that has more chocolate flavour and that is always dark chocolate. If you would like to know more about chocolate I thoroughly recommend the book *Chocolate the definitive guide* by Sara Jayne Stanes also published by Grub Street.

Chocolate can be a tricky ingredient to work with. Although the recipes in this book don't require any specialist chocolate knowledge or skills, the following points will come in handy.

- When melting chocolate always chop or break the chocolate into regular sized pieces to speed up the process.

- Always buy as good a quality chocolate as you can find, you cannot hope to create a great tasting dessert with inferior tasting chocolate.

- When using chocolate, ensure chopping boards, mixing bowls and any other equipment the chocolate comes into contact with are clean and dry. This is not just good hygienic practice, chocolate and water simply do not mix. Most recipes require chocolate to be melted before being used and if any water finds its way into the melting chocolate, the structure of the chocolate will be altered and it will become thick and stodgy, making it difficult to incorporate into other ingredients. This can sometimes happen when you are melting chocolate over hot water. If the water is boiling, as opposed to simmering very gently, steam may condense on the inside of the bowl and mix with the chocolate or the boiling water may even boil up into the bowl containing the melting chocolate. You can also melt your chocolate in the microwave but this too has its dangers. Chocolate burns very easily so you need to take care and keep a close eye on your chocolate. If you choose to use a high setting to melt your chocolate then set the timer for 30 seconds at a time. When I have large quantities of chocolate to melt I often use the defrost setting, this takes longer but the risk of burning the chocolate is greatly reduced.

- Allow melted chocolate to cool slightly before adding eggs or egg yolks otherwise the heat will cause the eggs to over thicken the chocolate.

Allow melted chocolate to cool slightly before adding it to creamed butter and sugar, or to whipped cream, otherwise the chocolate will melt the butter or cream.

- Do not stir melted chocolate in an attempt to cool it more quickly as this has the effect of aerating the chocolate and it will become thick and stodgy, making it harder to use.

- Always wrap and store chocolate in an airtight container, away from strong odours and extremes of heat.

SPICES

ALLSPICE is produced from the dried berry of a tropical American tree grown mainly in Jamaica. Allspice is its English name, so named because its flavour resembles a mixture of other spices. It is also known as Jamaica Pepper, where it is widely used in savoury dishes, such as the famous jerk chicken.

Christopher Columbus supposedly discovered allspice in the late 15th century. He took it back to Spain with him where it was given the name 'pimiento' or pepper in Spanish.

CARDAMOM is the third most expensive spice after saffron and vanilla. The fruit of the cardamom plant is a small 3-sided pod. They are picked before they are ripe and then dried. Green cardamom is considered true cardamom and when fully ripe the seeds are black. The larger brown pods are of another species and are not considered true cardamom.

Cardamom is used extensively in Indian cuisine to flavour both savoury and sweet dishes, whereas in Europe its use is primarily confined to Germany and Sweden where it appears in cakes, breads and pickles. Much of the world's supply of cardamom is used by the Arab world to make Arabic coffee.

CINNAMON is the dried bark of *Cinnamomum verum*, known as true cinnamon in England. Cassia is a spice very similar to cinnamon but it is produced from a different species of tree and is sometimes referred to as false cinnamon, although in America and France the term cinnamon can be applied to both cinnamon and cassia.

The use of cinnamon can be traced back thousands of years. The Arabs traded cinnamon to both the ancient Greeks and Romans and it became a popular spice to use with meats. It was being used by the Anglo Saxons in wine but became more popular after the Crusaders returned from the Holy Land and spread the spice further afield.

In European cookery it is used predominantly in baking cakes, breads and pastry.

CLOVES like nutmeg are indigenous to Moluccas in Indonesia although they are now grown in other countries including Ceylon, Penang, Zanzibar and Madagascar.

Cloves probably arrived in Europe sometime around the 8th century and take their name from the French, *clou,* meaning nail. They may have arrived in England before the first Crusaders returned from the Holy Land but the Crusaders did much to introduce spices, including cloves, to a wider audience. In English cooking they are used to spice festive foods such as Christmas pudding and mulled wine and also other baked goods such as cakes, biscuits and apple pies.

GINGER is thought to have originated in South East Asia and has been cultivated since ancient times. It was prized by the Roman Empire for medicinal purposes, such as an aid to digestion. Ginger continued to be exported to Europe after the fall of the Roman Empire and it was in use in England from Anglo-Saxon times. It was used in both sweet and savoury dishes during medieval times but by the 18th century its use had become limited to sweet baked goods.

NUTMEG In the late 18th century the British planted nutmeg in countries which they thought would be suitable, but it wasn't until the 1860's, when they planted them in Grenada, that they found somewhere the plants thrived.

Nutmeg and mace are two spices obtained from the same tree, which is native to the Indonesian island of Moluccas. Mace appears as a thin sheath covering the nutmeg or seed and is less widely used than nutmeg. In England nutmeg is largely used in sweet dishes especially milk puddings and custards.

SAFFRON is the world's most expensive spice, produced from the stigmas of the crocus flower. In the 14th century the plant was introduced to England and began to be cultivated in and around the town of Walden in Essex, renamed Saffron Walden, where it was grown until the end of the 18th century.

Saffron features heavily in cuisine from India but is also used in dishes from the Mediterranean and other parts of Europe. It is used in both sweet and savoury dishes but features predominantly in sweet dishes in English cookery such as custards, creams and Cornish buns and cakes.

VANILLA is the most expensive spice after saffron. In 2001 the vanilla crop failed and the price sky-rocketed. The main variety is Bourbon, and Madagascar grows the best Bourbon vanilla in the world. It produces around 85% of the world's supply, Uganda produces around 10% and Kenya and Tahiti the remainder. Vanilla, the fruit of a celadon coloured orchid, was first cultivated in Mexico many centuries ago and it left Mexico in the early 16th century on ships bound for Spain, where it was prized for its scent before the Spanish discovered it also had a wonderful aromatic flavour.

Vanilla is the most widely used spice in dessert making. America is the world's largest consumer followed by France. It is used both on its own and with other flavours such as chocolate, which it complements, to give a more rounded flavour profile.

Vanilla is available in supermarkets in several different forms. I love vanilla pods but I usually have a bottle of vanilla extract in my cupboard as well. Just recently I purchased some vanilla paste because I couldn't get hold of any extract. I liked the fact that it was as easy to use as the extract with the added bonus of delivering hundreds of vanilla seeds to my mixture. I'd recommend trying it but make sure you buy Nielsen-Massey vanilla products, as these are the best on the domestic market.

EQUIPMENT

You really don't need too much equipment in order to make and bake pastry at home although it's essential that you know whether the temperature settings on your oven are accurate, and if they aren't, what adjustments need to be made.

Some of the following equipment is essential, whereas other pieces are only required for certain recipes, so don't rush and buy things if you don't need them.

I am fortunate to have a fantastic Aladdin's cave of a kitchen shop near to where I live which has always stocked everything I have ever needed in the way of small kitchen equipment. I realise most people won't be quite so lucky so I recommend trying John Lewis kitchen departments, if you have one nearby, or Nisbets, who offer a next day mail order service, (tel 0845 140 5555, www.nisbets.co.uk).

ESSENTIAL EQUIPMENT

SET OF ACCURATE SCALES

MIXING BOWLS

FINE MESH SIEVE, PREFERABLY STAINLESS STEEL

ROLLING PIN There are numerous styles and weights of rolling pin available. I prefer wooden to marble or plastic. If you buy a wooden rolling pin make sure that you clean it with a damp cloth and do not immerse it in water otherwise it is likely to warp, and will no longer be of any use when it comes to rolling pastry.

SMALL PASTRY BRUSH 2.5cm (1 in) is a good size.

MEASURING SPOONS

MEASURING JUG

TWO KNIVES, 20cm (8 in) cooks knife and 10cm (4 in) vegetable or paring knife are useful sizes.

TART TINS, 23cm (9 in) and 25.5 (10 in) are useful sizes.

PIE DISH, the old-fashioned, rectangular enamelled ones are best. I have found a 19cm ($7^{1}/_{3}$ in) wide x 26cm ($10^{1}/_{4}$ in) long pie dish to be a good standard size.

DEEP PIE DISH, the typical American-style pie dish with sloping sides, 23cm (9 in) diameter x 4cm ($1^{1}/_{2}$ in) deep.

PIE PLATE is another old-fashioned piece of bakeware. They are often enamelled but metal ones are available. They are simply wide rimmed plates. They were much used in the northern counties in the last century, probably because pies could be made more cheaply in them on account of the fact that the dishes are shallow and require less filling in relation to weight of pastry.

BAKING TRAY, there are some recipes in this book where you simply require a baking tray rather than a tin so if you haven't got a baking tray, I'd suggest investing in one.

RECIPE SPECIFIC EQUIPMENT

ELECTRIC HAND WHISK, whisking double cream by hand isn't too arduous but egg whites are another thing entirely.

LARGE PASTRY BRUSH, will come in handy for brushing off excess flour as you make the turns in your pastry.

PALETTE KNIFE, if you plan to buy one look for a step palette knife as these are much easier to use. Of all my small equipment my step palette knife is my most treasured item.

HAND WHISK

SPEED PEELER

PIPING BAG, 40cm (15¾ in) is a decent size.

PLAIN NOZZLES, ideally a 6mm (¼ in) and a 1.5cm (¾ in) will come in useful.

BUN OR MUFFIN TINS

SAUCEPANS, preferably stainless steel.

LATTICE ROLLER/ CUTTER, a small plastic cutter that can be used to cut strips of puff pastry is available from Nisbets.

SUGAR THERMOMETER, these can be purchased from cook shops and are also available from Nisbets.

HINTS AND TIPS

Some of the following hints and tips are common sense whilst others have come through years of experience.

TEMPERATURE TIPS

- Try to make pastry, especially puff pastry, in a cool kitchen. If you have a granite or marble work surface this is ideal. If you are making pastry in the heat of summer make the pastry first thing in the morning.

- Always preheat your oven and make sure the oven has reached the correct temperature before baking your pastry. If the oven is too cold the fat will melt but not be absorbed by the flour.

- Wrap and rest the pastry in the refrigerator until it is firm enough to roll.

- Ensure pastry is firm before it is baked. If the weather is warm, refrigerate the pastry for a little longer before baking it.

- If the pastry recipe requires water make sure the water is cold. Some puff pastry recipes even recommend using ice-cold water.

BUTTER TIPS

- Butter should not be too hard, so unless your kitchen is very warm bring it to room temperature before using it.

- If rubbing in butter and/or other fat, remember that the aim is to take the mixture to the point where it resembles fine breadcrumbs. Beyond this and it may start to clump together. This can cause the pastry to become overly short and difficult to roll.

- Check that your butter is unsalted or at the very least only slightly salted. Using slightly salted butter is fine but other recipes such as pastry cream or crème pâtissière and caramel sauce really do require that you use unsalted butter.

SUGAR TIPS

- Make sure you use caster sugar not granulated sugar for pastry making as granulated, with its larger crystals, can remain undissolved and give pastry a gritty, grainy appearance and texture.

- Use refined sugar for making pastry.

- Always use cane sugar for making caramel and Italian, or cooked, meringue as it has fewer impurities than beet sugar. Tate & Lyle sugar is produced from sugar cane whereas Silver Spoon is produced from sugar beet.

FLOUR TIPS

- Use the correct type of flour.

- I would recommend sifting all flour before use. This serves not only to remove any flour clumps but also to aerate the flour.

- Many people make the mistake of using too much flour when rolling out pastry, this can make it overly dry. So brush any excess flour from rolled pastry before baking.

EGG TIPS

- If your past experiences of making shortcrust pastry have been less than successful try using egg instead of water as the liquid content. I find shortcrust pastry shrinks far less when this is done.

- If eggs are stored in the fridge bring them to room temperature before you use them.

- Buy free range eggs.

GENERAL TIPS

- Check that your ingredients are in date, and that they are the ones specified in the recipe.

- Weigh out your ingredients. Stick to either metric or imperial measurements and do not mix them.

- Pastry requires a light hand. Overworking will give a tough and or greasy pastry so work lightly and firmly to the point where it forms a smooth dough and stop at that point.

- When rolling pastry, roll it in one direction only. Lift the pastry using the rolling pin and turn it 90˚ to allow you to roll it in another direction. This helps prevent uneven rolling and overstretching of the pastry, keeping it an even thickness. Try not to overstretch and stress pastry when rolling it, as this can lead to excessive shrinkage.

- Once pastry has been rolled always allow it to rest before baking.

- I prefer to grease my tins because the majority of tins are fluted, and it is almost impossible to effectively release pastry by running a knife around a fluted tin.

Also, occasionally, the filling will run over the pastry edge between the tin and the pastry, and bake the pastry to the tin.

- Always bake tarts and pies with a bottom crust in metal tins, as bottom-crusted pies don't always cook through in ceramic ones. However, it's perfectly acceptable to bake a top-crusted pie in a ceramic pie dish.

- Always put tart tins, pie dishes and pie plates on baking trays before putting them in the oven, making it easier to clean up any spillages. It also makes it easier to remove the tart or pie from the oven when it is cooked.

- Keep any puff pastry trimmings and lay them out on top of each other, to keep the layers in the same direction. Pastry can be kept wrapped in the fridge for two to three days or frozen for up to three months. Use other leftover pastry for a lattice or as decorative trimmings on pie tops.

CONVERSION CHART

WEIGHTS		VOLUME		LENGTH		OVEN TEMP	
15g	1/2oz	25ml	1fl oz	3mm	1/8 in	150˚C	gas 2
25g	1oz	50ml	2fl oz	6mm	1/4 in	170˚C	gas 3
50g	2oz	75ml	3fl oz	1cm	1/2in	180˚C	gas 4
75g	3oz	100ml	3$\frac{1}{2}$fl oz	2cm	3/4 in	190˚C	gas 5
100g	3$\frac{1}{2}$oz	125ml	4$\frac{1}{2}$fl oz	2.5cm	1 in	200˚C	gas 6
115g	4oz	150ml	1/4pt	5cm	2 in	220˚C	gas 7
125g	4$\frac{1}{2}$oz	175ml	6fl oz	6.5cm	2$\frac{1}{2}$ in	240˚C	gas 8
150g	5oz	200ml	7fl oz	7cm	2$\frac{3}{4}$ in		
175g	6oz	250ml	9fl oz	7.5cm	3 in		
200g	7oz	300ml	1/2pt	8.5cm	3$\frac{1}{4}$ in	If using a fan oven	
225g	8oz	350ml	12fl oz	9cm	3$\frac{1}{2}$ in	you will need to drop	
250g	9oz	400ml	14fl oz	10cm	4 in	the oven	
300g	10oz	450ml	3/4pt	12.5cm	5 in	temperature,	
325g	11oz	500ml	18fl oz	15cm	6 in	somewhere between	
350g	12oz	600ml	1pt	18cm	7 in	10-20˚C, as they run	
375g	13oz			20cm	8 in	hotter than non-fan	
400g	14oz	tsp = teaspoon		23cm	9 in	ovens.	
425g	15oz	tbsp= tablespoon		25.5cm	10 in		
450g	1lb	1.25ml	1/4tsp	28cm	11 in		
500g	1lb 2oz	2.5ml	1/2tsp	30.5cm	12 in		
600g	1lb 5oz	5ml	1tsp	35.5cm	14 in		
650g	1lb 7oz	15ml	1tbsp	40cm	15$\frac{3}{4}$ in		
750g	1lb 10oz			41cm	16 in		
900g	2lb						
1kg	2lb 4oz						

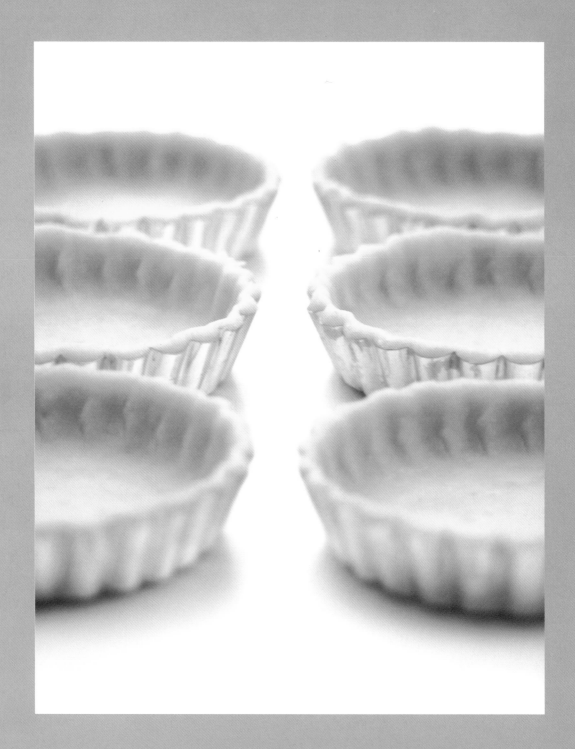

BASIC PASTRY, SAUCE & ICE-CREAM RECIPES

PUFF PASTRY
Pâte feuilletage

There is no getting away from the fact that puff pastry is time consuming to make but it's well worth attempting once in a while to appreciate how good it is when homemade but rather than not making a recipe, because it uses puff pastry, buy a block of ready-made pastry from the supermarket.

Makes 500g (1lb 2oz)
125g (4¹/₂oz) strong plain flour, sifted
125g (4¹/₂oz) plain flour, sifted, plus extra for rolling
Pinch of salt
250g (9oz) unsalted butter, room temperature but not soft
1 tsp lemon juice
125ml (4¹/₂fl oz) ice-cold water

Mix the flours and salt together, then rub in 25g (1oz) of the butter. Add the lemon juice to the water and gradually add the acidulated water to the flour to form a smooth firm dough. If mixing the dough in a food mixer use the dough hook and mix the dough for 5 minutes. If making the pastry by hand knead the dough on a work surface for 5 minutes, in the same way as for bread. Mould the dough into a smooth ball, wrap in greaseproof paper then cling film and refrigerate for 20 minutes to relax the dough.

Plasticize the butter by bashing it with a rolling pin so it is about 1.5cm (3/4 in) thick and malleable. Wrap it in greaseproof paper. If very soft, refrigerate until needed, but preferably just put it somewhere cool. The butter needs to be the same texture as the dough. If too soft the fat is likely to break out when the pastry is rolled and the pastry will not rise well when baked.

Place the dough on a lightly floured board. Make 2 cuts into the ball of dough. The second cut at right angles to the first. The dough ball is given a ¹/₄ turn so the cut appears as a diagonal cross on the dough. Each quarter of the dough is rolled out to give a thin rectangle or flange attached to the central piece of dough, which should remain at least 3 times the thickness of the rolled rectangles or flanges. The plasticized fat is placed on the thicker central piece of dough and the rectangles or flanges are bought up and wrapped over it. This method of making puff pastry is known as the French method.

Gently roll out the dough to give a rectangle about 40cm (15³/4 in) x 30.5cm (12 in). Fold in half along its widest length to find the midpoint of the dough. Open up the dough and fold each half in on itself so it resembles an open book then fold the 2 halves together so the dough is now 4 folds thick. This is the book turn or double turn. Roll the dough gently to level out the surface. Wrap in cling film and refrigerate for 20 minutes before repeating this rolling out process.

The dough needs to be rolled out a further 3 times to put 3 more turns into the dough. Each turn needs to be made in the same direction as the last so if you are right handed keep the open fold on your right and make each turn of the dough to the right. After each turn is made, rest the dough in the fridge for 20 minutes. The puff pastry is then ready to use.

Bake at 240°C, 220°C fan oven, gas 8 for savoury recipes and 220°C, 200°C fan oven, gas 7, for sweet recipes.

TIP If you want to make the pastry ahead of time and freeze it is best to make 3 turns in the dough and then after the dough is defrosted make the fourth and final turn. Rest the pastry for 20 minutes before using.

SWEET SHORT PASTRY 1
Pâte sucrée

A crisp sweet pastry, useful for most sweet tarts and pies.

Makes three 23cm (9 in) tarts or two 25.5cm (10 in) tarts
200g (7oz) softened unsalted butter
200g (7oz) caster sugar
2 eggs
400g (14oz) plain flour, sifted

Cream the butter and sugar together taking care not to over beat. Mix in the eggs and then mix in the flour to form a smooth paste.

Roll the pastry out to about 2.5cm (1 in) thick, then wrap in greaseproof paper and then cling film and refrigerate until needed. As this recipe makes enough to line 3 x 23cm (9 in) tart tins you may want to divide into three and freeze the two remaining portions.

Bake at 180°C-190°C, 170°C-180°C fan oven, gas 4-5.

SWEET SHORT PASTRY 2
Pâte frolle

A crisp sweet pastry enriched with ground almonds. This recipe was given to me by Duncan Campbell when he was the pastry chef at Claridges Hotel, London.

Makes three 23cm (9 in) or two 25.5cm (10 in) tarts
225g (8oz) softened unsalted butter
150g (5oz) icing sugar, sifted
1 egg, plus 1 yolk
400g (14oz) plain flour, sifted
75g (3oz) ground almonds

Cream the butter and sugar together taking care not to over beat. Mix in the egg and egg yolk and then the flour and ground almonds, to form a smooth paste.

Roll the pastry out to about 2.5cm (1 in) thick, wrap in greaseproof paper and then cling film and refrigerate until needed. If you want to freeze some of the pastry simply divide and wrap individually.

Bake at 180°C-190°C, 170°C-180°C fan oven, gas 4-5.

SWEET SHORT PASTRY 3
Pâte sablée

This is my all time favourite sweet pastry. It's a delicate shortbread-like pastry that is surprisingly easy to use. This recipe came from an old Polish pastry chef called Carol who worked at The Berkeley Hotel, Knightsbridge many years ago.

Makes two 23cm (9 in) or two 25.5cm (10 in) tarts
375g (13oz) plain flour, sifted
125g (4¹/₂oz) icing sugar, sifted
200g (7oz) unsalted butter, diced
Grated zest ¹/₂ lemon
5 egg yolks

Mix together the flour, icing sugar and butter until the mixture resembles fine breadcrumbs. Add the lemon zest and the yolks and mix to form a smooth paste.

Roll the pastry out to about 2.5cm (1 in) thick, wrap in greaseproof paper and then cling film and refrigerate until needed. If you want to freeze some of the pastry simply divide and wrap individually.

Bake at 180°C-190°C, 170°C-180°C fan oven, gas 4-5.

STRUDEL PASTRY

Makes one strudel
225g (8oz) strong plain flour, sifted
Pinch salt
25ml (1fl oz) vegetable oil
100ml (3^1/2fl oz) warm water
1 egg

Put the flour into a mixing bowl with the salt. Combine the remaining ingredients in a jug. Pour the liquid ingredients into the flour and mix to a smooth paste. If using a machine use the dough hook on a low speed setting. Remove the dough from the bowl and knead the dough on a lightly floured surface for 5 minutes then wrap the dough in cling film and allow to rest for 15 minutes in a warm place. The dough is then ready to use.

Roll the dough out to a rectangle on a lightly floured work surface until it is about 30.5cm (12 in) long and 20cm (8 in) wide. Then using the rolling pin lift the dough onto a clean, lightly floured, kitchen cloth or tea towel. Using the backs of your hands stretch the dough out further, taking the rectangle to the edges of the tea towel or until the dough becomes paper-thin. The rectangle will be about 40cm (15^1/2 in) long and 30.5cm (12 in) wide. The dough is now ready to fill and roll.

Bake at 200˚C-220˚C, 190˚C- 200˚C fan oven, gas 6-7.

AMERICAN SHORT PASTRY

Makes one 23cm (9 in) diameter x 4cm (1^1/2 in) deep pie
450g (1lb) plain flour, sifted
1/2 tsp baking powder
175g (6oz) unsalted butter, diced
100g (3^1/2oz) white vegetable fat or shortening
100g (3^1/2oz) caster sugar
2 egg yolks
75ml (3fl oz) water

Mix the flour and baking powder and rub-in 2/3 of the butter and then cut the remaining butter and shortening into the flour. Cutting a proportion of the fat into the flour produces pastry with a flakier texture. Add the sugar and then mix in the egg yolks and water.

Mix to form a smooth paste. Wrap in greaseproof paper and then cling film and refrigerate until needed.

Bake at 190˚C-200˚C, 170˚C-180˚C fan oven, gas 5-6.

TATIN PASTRY

Although I don't often make Tarte Tatin I much prefer to use this pastry rather than puff pastry.

Makes one 20cm (8 in) Tarte Tatin
250g (9oz) plain flour, sifted
125g (4^1/2oz) soft unsalted butter
1 tbsp caster sugar
Pinch salt
1 egg, plus 1 yolk

Rub the flour and butter together until the mixture resembles fine breadcrumbs, then add the sugar and salt. Add the egg and yolk and mix until the dough is smooth. Do not over work. Wrap in greaseproof paper and cling film and refrigerate until needed.

Bake at 190°C-200°C, 170°C-180°C fan oven, gas 5-6.

SHORT CRUST PASTRY

Makes one 23cm (9 in) diameter x 4cm (1^1/2 in) bottom-crust, deep pie
450g (1lb) plain flour, sifted
225g (8oz) unsalted butter
Pinch salt
1 egg , plus 1 yolk
50ml (2fl oz) water

Rub the flour, butter and salt together until the mixture resembles fine breadcrumbs.

Add the egg and yolk and mix to form a smooth paste. Wrap in greaseproof paper and cling film and refrigerate until needed.

Bake at 190°C to 200°C, 170°C-180°C fan oven, gas 5-6.

RICH SHORT CRUST PASTRY

Makes one 19cm (7^1/$_2$ in) wide x 26cm (10^1/$_4$ in) long pie dish
250g (9oz) plain flour
150g (5oz) unsalted butter, diced
Pinch salt
75g (3oz) caster sugar
1 egg, plus 1 yolk

Rub the flour, butter and salt together until the mixture resembles fine breadcrumbs. Stir the sugar through. Add the egg and egg yolk and mix to form a smooth paste. Wrap in greaseproof paper and cling film and refrigerate until needed.

Bake at 190˚C-200˚C, 170˚C-180˚C fan oven, gas 5-6.

SCONE PASTRY

This recipe is essentially a richer version of scone dough and is used for topping American-style cobblers, grunts and slumps.

Makes one 19cm (7^1/$_2$ in) wide x 26cm (10^1/$_4$ in) long pie dish
75g (3oz) unsalted butter, diced
250g (9oz) self-raising flour
75g (3oz) caster sugar
1 egg
6-8 tbsp milk

Rub the butter into the flour and stir the sugar through. Beat the egg with the milk, pour into the dry ingredients and mix lightly to a smooth paste. Use the scone pastry immediately. Roll out on a lightly floured work surface to 1cm (^{1}/$_2$ in) thick and use to top a fruit pie. Bake at 190˚C, 170˚C fan oven, gas 5.

NUT PASTRY

Makes one 25.5cm (10 in) tart or 23cm (9 in) deep pie
200g (7oz) plain flour, sifted
100g (3¹/₂oz) icing sugar, sifted
150g (5oz) unsalted butter, cut into small pieces
100g (3¹/₂oz) ground almonds or ground hazelnuts
Grated zest 1 lemon
3 egg yolks

Mix the flour and icing sugar together and then rub in the butter until the mixture resembles fine breadcrumbs. Stir in the ground nuts. Add the lemon zest and the yolks and mix to form a smooth paste.

Roll the pastry out to about 2.5cm (1 in) thick, then wrap in greaseproof paper and then cling film and refrigerate until needed. If you want to freeze some of the pastry simply divide and wrap individually.

Bake at 180°C-190°C, 170°C-180°C fan oven, gas 4-5.

CHOUX PASTRY
Pâte à choux

Makes about 30 profiteroles
250ml (9fl oz) water
125g (4¹/₂oz) unsalted butter, diced
75g (3oz) strong plain flour, sifted
75g (3oz) plain flour, sifted

3-4 eggs, beaten
Pinch salt
Pinch sugar
1 egg yolk
1 tbsp milk

Pour the water into a large pan and add the butter. Bring to the boil and when boiling vigorously remove from the heat and add the sifted flours. Beat in the flour and return the pan to the heat for 1-2 minutes stirring until the paste comes away from the sides of the pan and no flour is visible.

Remove the paste from the pan and allow it to cool slightly. Put the paste into a mixing bowl and gradually add the beaten eggs. The pastry should be pipeable but also hold its own shape. Mix together the egg yolk and milk and brush the choux buns with egg wash.

Bake at 220°C, 200°C fan oven, gas 7.

TIPS Chill your greased (not oiled) baking trays in the freezer to make piping the choux pastry that much easier.

You can spoon the mixture into small mounds rather than use a piping bag and nozzle, although the shapes will be less uniform.

RASPBERRY SAUCE

A very simple and fresh tasting sauce that can be served with fruit desserts, tarts and ice cream.

500g (1lb 2oz) defrosted, frozen raspberries
50-75g (2-3oz) icing sugar, sifted
Juice of 1/2 lemon

Whiz the raspberries in a food processor or blender for 30 seconds to 1 minute. Sieve the raspberry juice into a bowl. Ideally use a stainless steel or plastic sieve as the acidity of the fruit will react with other metals and discolour the purée. Add the icing sugar and lemon juice to taste. This sauce can be refrigerated for 24 hours.

HOT FUDGE SAUCE

I always remember my surprise when I found out this American-style sauce was actually a hot chocolate sauce rather than a toffee caramel sauce. It is simple to make and can be used to accompany ice cream, chocolate, coffee and vanilla based desserts.

200g (7oz) dark chocolate, chopped
142ml carton double cream

Put the chocolate into a mixing bowl over a pan of simmering water or melt in the microwave on a low setting.

Bring the cream to the boil in a small pan. Stir the cream slowly into the melted chocolate. Serve the sauce warm. This sauce is best made and used on the same day.

TIP If I am melting a small quantity of chocolate in the microwave I use the high temperature setting but stir the chocolate gently every 30 seconds until it is melted. When melting large quantities I use a lower heat setting and check the chocolate every 3-4 minutes.

If you want to make a dark chocolate ganache to make chocolate truffles, use 1/2 the quantity of cream to chocolate and prepare using the same method. When the ganache has cooled and thickened, the mixture can be spooned or piped into shape, before being dipped in tempered chocolate or rolled in cocoa powder.

CARAMEL SAUCE

Rich and full flavoured, this sauce is great served with apple and pear desserts or simply with vanilla ice cream.

115g (4oz) caster sugar
142ml carton double cream
50g (2oz) cold unsalted butter, diced

Heat the sugar in a small pan over a medium heat. Resist the temptation to stir, if you need to move the sugar around because it is cooking quicker in one area, move the sugar gently with a wooden spoon. When the sugar has caramelised reduce the heat and carefully whisk in the cream. The cream will splutter when you pour it into the pan. Remove the pan from the heat and whisk in the butter a little at a time. This sauce can be refrigerated for 3-4 days and gently reheated.

CHOCOLATE SAUCE

A simple quick sauce for profiteroles and other puddings.

200g (7oz) dark chocolate
300ml (1/2pt) double cream
1 tbsp brandy (optional)

Melt the chocolate in a bowl over a pan of simmering water or on a low heat in the microwave. Heat the cream in a small pan bringing it almost to the boil. Slowly pour the cream into the melted chocolate stirring continuously. Add the brandy if using.

VANILLA ICE CREAM

This is rich and creamy and tastes wonderful.

6 egg yolks
175g (6oz) caster sugar
300ml (1/2pt) full fat milk
284ml carton double cream
1 vanilla pod, split lengthways and 1 tsp vanilla extract or 2 tsp vanilla paste

Mix the egg yolks and sugar together in a mixing bowl. Pour the milk and cream into a medium pan with the split vanilla pod, if using and bring to the boil. Whisk half the liquid onto the egg yolks and sugar and return the egg yolk mixture to the remaining liquid in the pan. Reduce the heat and cook the custard gently, stirring continuously, for 6-7 minutes until the mixture thickens and coats the back of a wooden spoon.

Sieve the custard (Sauce Anglaise) into a large clean bowl and allow to cool. Scrape the vanilla seeds from the pod into the sauce and add the vanilla extract or paste, if using. I like to make the custard the day before making my ice cream and refrigerate it over night so the mixture is completely cold before churning it in the ice-cream machine.

Churn the chilled custard in an ice-cream machine.

TIP Homemade ice cream is best eaten within 24 hours of making.

CALVADOS ICE CREAM

An alternative to Vanilla Ice Cream, Calvados Ice Cream works well with apple and pear desserts. Simply prepare the basic Vanilla Ice Cream recipe omitting the vanilla and add 2-3 tablespoons of Calvados to the cooked custard.

APPLES & PEARS

The use of apples and pears in dessert making has declined in recent years, ousted by increased availability of more exotic fruits. This is such a shame because both apples and pears are wonderfully versatile fruits. Admittedly many of the varieties of dessert apple now available, are sweeter than the old English-style apples and are less well suited to baking, but this can often be remedied by using a little less sugar and by adding some Bramley apple. I always choose as sharp a tasting dessert apple as I can find and add a proportion of Bramley, if the recipe allows, though unfortunately because Bramley apples disintegrate during cooking it isn't always desirable to use them. If you are lucky enough to have a farm shop or farmers' market in your area look out for locally produced apples that may be sharper tasting than many of the dessert varieties on sale in the supermarkets.

The Romans introduced new apple varieties to Britain and grafted them onto the wild British crab apple, establishing orchards and when the Normans invaded in the 11th century, they bought a knowledge of apple growing and cider making, and did much to improve apple growing in Britain.

During the Middle Ages there was a decline in apple production as the Black Death, the Wars of the Roses and droughts wracked the country but Henry VIII reversed this trend by importing apple trees from France, to create an expansion of apple orchards.

The popularity of the apple then grew throughout Britain, whereas pears remained the fruit of choice in France and Italy. The French and Italians felt the pear was a more refined fruit, whereas the British preferred the apple with its greater acidity.

In the 16th and 17th centuries orchards were planted in Kent, although they were already well established in Herefordshire, Gloucestershire and Worcestershire. By the end of the 18th century the quality of the fruits had begun to decline due to poor orchard management and it wasn't until after the Napoleonic Wars, with the introduction of tariffs on imported fruit, that fruit production began again in earnest. When the tariffs were lowered, the apple market collapsed and only recovered after 1870, when industrialisation increased incomes and fruit production became profitable.

Although Britain still produces a large number of apples, production has declined over the past 20 years. The two main reasons for rising imports appear to be: firstly during the spring when stored British apples are available, people are opting for fresher imported apples, and even when fresh British apples are available, customers are buying sweeter apples from warmer countries, rather than traditional British varieties. Secondly imported apples are sourced during April to August when British apples aren't available, but fewer apples tend to be eaten during this time, due to the increased availability of soft British fruits.

The majority of apples sold today are dessert apples but many are suitable for use in cooking, such as Braeburns, Granny Smiths and Cox's. Supermarkets sell 70% of apples bought, but they only sell about 8 different varieties. Whereas the Brogdale Horticultural Trust in Faversham, has a staggering collection of over 2,000 different varieties of apple.

The Bramley apple is the only British apple grown solely for the purpose of cooking. Although there are several dual-purpose varieties, such as the Blenheim Orange, the Golden Noble and Ribstons Pippin, that make useful cooking apples, unfortunately they are not widely sold. Bramley apples have a low sugar to acid ratio which is the reason they retain their flavour, to a greater extent than sweeter apples, when cooked. However, some sharp-tasting dessert apples, such as Cox's Orange Pippins, Granny Smiths and Braeburns, are better suited than Bramleys for use in desserts because they retain their shape when cooked, and do not breakdown to a pulp.

It is thought that the original English apple pie was made with a crust only on the top. The American apple pie was made with pastry both underneath **and** on top, and French tarts with the pastry underneath. Nowadays it is acceptable for a pie to have either a top crust only, or both a top and bottom layer of pastry, but a tart should only have a pastry base.

One of the earliest records of pear cultivation was by Feng Li, a Chinese diplomat, who in 5,000 BC gave up his job to cultivate his own orchards.

It is thought that the wild pear trees grown in Britain in the Middle Ages came from Northern Europe although there is no record of cultivation until the 13th century, when Henry III imported pear trees from La Rochelle, in France. Towards the end of the 14th century Cistercian Monks at Wardon, in Bedfordshire, introduced the Wardon pear and it became so popular for cooking, it became a fruit in its own right.

During the Middle Ages pear cultivation became important in France and Belgium, with the French popularising the pear and the Belgians introducing new and improved varieties. Towards the end of the Middle Ages Henry VIII's fruiterer, Harris, introduced pears from France, and this was followed by a pear revival in the 16th century.

The Williams Bon Chretian, bred in Berkshire, was taken to America at the end of the 18th century and planted on an estate in Massachussetts. The estate was later purchased by Enoch Bartlett who sold the pears under his own name. The Bartlett pear became one of the leading varieties in America.

From the hundreds of varieties of pears grown during the Middle Ages there are now only four varieties widely grown in Britain, they are the Conference, Doyenne du Comice, Williams and Beurré Hardy. Today China is by far the world's largest supplier of pears, followed by Italy, America and Spain.

I happen to love the Comice pear or to give it its full name the Doyenne du Comice - it is a beautiful pear for both eating and cooking but I sometimes think it would be good if the choice of British pears were a little wider. When you consider that the Brogdale Horticultural Trust has a collection of 550 different varieties, it does seem a little sad that our choice is so limited. It is possible to find locally produced pears on sale at farm shops and farmers' markets when in season, so keep a look out for some more interesting varieties.

APPLE STRUDEL

The Viennese are responsible for making apple strudel famous, with strudel pastry taking its name from 'whirlpool or eddy' and when you cut into a slice you can see why. One of my all-time favourite apple desserts, apple strudel is hard to beat, but the pastry must be thin and flaky and the apple filling must have a hint of lemon, a good level of spice and not be too sweet. On the continent they serve slices of strudel in the coffee shops but you could always choose to have it as a dessert, served warm with crème fraîche or vanilla ice cream.

Makes 1 strudel
Serves 8-10
Strudel Pastry (page 33)
8 sharp tasting eating apples, such as Granny Smiths
1 tsp grated lemon zest
1/2 tsp ground cinnamon
25g (1oz) caster sugar
75g (3oz) unsalted butter, melted

Preheat the oven to 200°C, 180°C fan oven, gas 6.

Prepare the strudel pastry, wrap it in cling film and rest it in a warm place. The dough is easier to use when it is warm.

Peel, quarter, core and thinly slice the apples, about 3mm (1/8 in) thick. Mix the sliced apple in a large bowl with the lemon zest, cinnamon and sugar.

Roll the dough out to a rectangle on a lightly floured work surface until it is about 30.5cm (12 in) long and 20cm (8 in) wide. Then, using the rolling pin, lift the dough onto a clean, lightly floured tea towel. Using the backs of your hands stretch the dough out further, taking the rectangle to the edges of the tea towel, or until the dough becomes paper-thin. The rectangle should be about 41cm (16 in) long and 30.5cm (12 in) wide.

Brush the dough with half the melted butter. Spread the apple slices evenly over the dough, leaving about 2.5cm (1 in) around the edge, then using the tea towel roll the strudel up along one of its longer sides. It is easier to do this by rolling it away from you. Use the tea towel to help transfer the strudel to a greased baking tray. Shape the strudel into a horseshoe shape and brush with more of the melted butter. Bake for 25 minutes until golden brown. Half way through cooking, brush with the remaining butter.

NORMANDY APPLE TART

Packed full of fruit, this French tart uses produce local to the Normandy area, namely apples, creamy unsalted butter and Calvados. The French tend to use eating apples but I suggest using Bramleys for the cooked apple filling; it gives a sharp flavour that counters the sweetness of the glaze.

Makes one 23cm (9 in) tart
Serves 6-8
Sweet Short Pastry recipe 1 (page 31)
Use 1/3 of the quantity of pastry, about 250g (9oz), to line a 23cm (9 in) tart tin, wrap and freeze the remaining pastry
750g (1lb 10oz) sharp tasting apples, such as Bramleys

25g (1oz) unsalted butter
2 tbsp Calvados
15-25g (1/2-1oz) caster sugar
1 egg yolk
2 dessert apples
3 tbsp apricot jam

Preheat the oven to 190°C, 170°C fan oven, gas 5.

Prepare the pastry and rest it for 15 minutes in the fridge. Lightly flour a clean work surface and roll out the pastry to 3mm (1/8 in) thick. Line a 23cm (9 in) tart tin with the pastry. Lightly prick the base and then rest it for 20 minutes in the fridge or 10 minutes in the freezer.

Peel, core and roughly chop the apples. Melt half the butter in a small pan, add the apples, reduce the heat to low and place a piece of greaseproof paper on top of the apples, or cover the pan with a lid, and cook gently for 10-15 minutes, stirring occasionally. Remove the paper, add the Calvados and cook for a further 2-3 minutes, stirring continually to evaporate any excess water. Sweeten the apples to taste.

Blind bake the pastry case for 10-15 minutes, remove baking beans, and bake for a further 5 minutes. The pastry should be pale to golden in colour. Brush the pastry case with the egg yolk and bake for a further minute. Remove the pastry case from the oven.

Peel, core and thinly slice the dessert apples, about 2mm (less than 1/8 in) thick. Fill the pastry case with the cooked Bramley apples and arrange the apple slices in overlapping concentric circles, starting from the outer edge of the tart. Melt the remaining butter and brush over the apple slices.

Return the tart to the oven and bake for 10 minutes, until the buttered slices start to colour a little.

Heat the apricot jam with a tablespoon of water, boil for a minute and brush the glaze liberally over the surface of the tart. Serve the tart warm with cream.

TIP Covering the apples keeps in the steam and helps prevent the apples from burning on the bottom of the pan, it also speeds up the cooking process.

AMERICAN APPLE PIE

The pie found its way to American shores with the English settlers in the late 15th and early 16th centuries, and although apple pie is now perceived to be an all-American dessert, as the saying 'as American as apple pie' demonstrates, this is a common misconception. Fruit pies such as apple and gooseberry were being made in England in the time of Chaucer, predating the discovery of America by over a century. The settlers did plant apple seeds from which orchards grew, but it would have been some years before a supply of apples was available.

This apple pie is made in the fashion of apple pies to be found in Britain; a double-crusted, deep-dish affair of short, slightly sweetened pastry, lightly spiced with cinnamon. The addition of shortening to the American-style pastry increases the shortness of the crust, and the use of self-raising flour, has the effect of thickening the crust, to give a more cake-like texture. The end result is very different to our traditional style of pie but nevertheless very enjoyable.

Makes one 23cm (9 in) deep pie
Serves 6-8
American Short Pastry (page 33)
900g (2lb) dessert apples
1½ tsp ground cinnamon
Grated zest ½ lemon
15g-25g (½-1oz) unrefined light brown sugar
15g-25g (½-1oz) granulated sugar

Preheat the oven to 190°C, 170°C fan oven, gas 5.

Prepare the pastry and rest it for 15 minutes in the fridge. Lightly grease a 23cm (9 in) diameter 4cm (1½ in) deep pie dish. Roll out just over half of the pastry on a lightly floured surface, and line the base of the pie dish. Do not trim the excess pastry at this stage. Lightly prick the base of the case. Rest the lined case and remaining pastry in the fridge for 20 minutes.

Peel, core and slice the apples 3mm (⅛ in) thick. Place in a bowl and add the cinnamon, lemon zest and brown sugar, to taste. Mix thoroughly and then pile into the pie dish.

Roll out the remaining pastry. Dampen the rim of the lined pie dish with a little water and using the rolling pin, lift the pastry on to the apples. Press down lightly to seal the edges. Trim any excess pastry. Make a small slit in the pastry lid to allow steam to escape. Brush the pastry with a little water and sprinkle liberally with the granulated sugar.

Bake the pie for 25 minutes and then lower the temperature to 180°C, 160°C fan oven, gas 4 and bake for a further 30-35 minutes, until golden brown. If the pastry starts to colour too much, cover with foil. The pie needs to be cooked for this length of time to ensure the apple is cooked through. Serve hot or cold.

N'AWLINS APPLE PIE

Founded by the French in 1718, New Orleans was governed by the French, Spanish and British before returning to North American rule. It became home to French Canadian (Acadians), Irish and German immigrants as well as African slaves in the early 18th century. This array of cultures left its mark on the cuisine of Louisiana as two distinct styles developed; Cajun and Creole. Cajun was the more refined, with its roots in French cuisine, whilst Creole was more rustic home-style cooking. Over time as chefs shared the foods of their homelands with others, the food of Louisiana evolved. This apple pie recipe is based on one I enjoyed during a visit to this city.

Makes one 23cm (9 in) deep pie
Serves 6-8
American Short Pastry (page 33)
75g (3oz) raisins
75ml (3fl oz) bourbon
900g (2lb) dessert apples

1 tsp ground cinnamon
Grated zest 1/2 lemon
75g (3oz) pecans, chopped
15g-25g (1/2-1oz) unrefined light brown sugar
15g-25g (1/2-1oz) granulated sugar

Preheat the oven to 190°C, 170°C fan oven, gas 5.

Prepare the pastry and rest it in the fridge for 15 minutes. Lightly grease a 23cm (9 in) diameter, 4cm (1 1/2 in) deep, pie dish. Roll out just over half of the pastry on a lightly floured surface and line the base of the pie dish. Do not trim the excess pastry at this stage. Lightly prick the base of the case. Rest the lined case and remaining pastry in the fridge for 20 minutes.

Put the raisins in a small pan, add the bourbon and heat gently for 1 minute.

Peel, core and slice the apples 3mm (1/8 in) thick - if you cut the apple slices too thickly they will not cook through. Place in a bowl and add the cinnamon, lemon zest, pecans, bourbon soaked raisins and brown sugar to taste. Mix thoroughly and then pile mixture into the pie dish.

Roll out the remaining pastry. Dampen the rim of the lined pie dish with a little water and using the rolling pin, lift the pastry lid on top of the apples. Press down lightly to seal the edges. Trim any excess pastry. Make a small slit in the pastry lid to allow steam to escape. Brush the pastry with a little water and sprinkle liberally with the granulated sugar.

Bake the pie for 25 minutes, and then lower the temperature to 180°C, 160°C fan oven, gas 4 and bake for a further 30-35 minutes, until golden brown – if the pastry starts to colour too much cover with foil. The pie needs to be cooked for this length of time to ensure the apple is cooked through. Serve hot or cold.

APPLE SLICE

This puff pastry slice is based on the popular French classic, *Bande aux fruits*.
A strip of puff pastry is topped with either a little pastry cream or frangipane and
then fruits are placed on top, to cover the filling before being baked. The pastry
is then sliced and can be served as a dessert or eaten mid-morning, with a cup
of coffee.

Makes one 30.5cm (12 in) x 12.5cm
   (5 in) slice
Serves 4
Puff Pastry (page 30)
Use 1/2 the amount in the recipe,
   wrap and freeze the remaining pastry
150ml (1/4pt) milk (1 tbsp reserved
   for the egg wash)
3 egg yolks

2 tbsp caster sugar
2 tbsp cornflour
Small knob unsalted butter
2 tsp vanilla extract
1 1/2 dessert apples
1 tbsp unsalted butter, melted
3 tbsp apricot jam
1 tsp lemon juice

Make the puff pastry the day before or have some ready in the freezer to defrost.
   Preheat the oven to 220°C, 200°C fan oven, gas 7.
   Bring the milk (less the reserved 1 tablespoon) to the boil in a small pan. Mix
together 2 of the 3 egg yolks with the sugar and then add the cornflour. Whisk a
little of the hot milk onto the egg mixture and then return the egg mixture to the
milk in the pan.
   Cook the mixture over a medium heat stirring all the time until it has thickened,
remove from the heat and pour the pastry cream into a clean bowl. Whisk in the
knob of butter and vanilla extract and cover with a piece of buttered greaseproof.
Allow to cool. The buttered greaseproof paper prevents a thick skin from forming.
   Roll out the pastry on a lightly floured work surface to 30.5cm (12 in) x 12.5cm
(5 in). Lightly prick the centre of the puff pastry strip leaving a 2.5cm (1 in) border
along each edge. Mix together the remaining egg yolk and milk, to make an
egg wash. Brush the pastry with egg wash and rest the pastry for 15 minutes in
the fridge.
   Peel, core and halve the apples. Slice each apple thinly, 2mm (less than 1/8 in).
Spread or pipe the pastry cream down the centre of the pastry, leaving the 2.5cm
(1 in) border. Lay the sliced apple on top of the pastry cream, brush the apple with
the melted butter and bake the slice for 20 minutes, until golden.
   Heat the apricot jam with the lemon juice and 1 tablespoon of water in a small
pan, boil for 1 minute. Brush the hot slice with the apricot glaze. Serve hot or cold.

TIP By keeping some of the boiled milk in the pan it helps prevent the milk solids
on the pan's base from overcooking. So when the mix is returned it is less likely to
catch and burn.

CARAMELISED APPLE TART

Caramel in its simplest form is over-cooked sugar and has an affinity with most fruits, so several years ago I simply took the idea one step further and caramelised sugar to flavour a custard, as the base for an apple tart. By cooking the apples with spice and butter before setting them in the tart, I enhanced the fruit so that when you eat a slice you experience an array of texture and flavours.

Makes one 23cm (9 in) tart
Serves 6
Sweet Short Pastry 2 (page 32)
Use 1/3 of the quantity of pastry, about 250g (9oz), wrap and freeze the remaining pastry
50g (2oz) unsalted butter
4 dessert apples, peeled, cored and cut into eight

1/2 tsp ground cinnamon
2 egg yolks
75g (3oz) caster sugar
150ml (1/4pt) milk
1 egg
1 tsp vanilla extract
1/2 tsp grated lemon zest
Icing sugar to serve

Preheat the oven to 190°C, 170°C fan oven, gas 5.

Prepare the pastry and rest it in the fridge for 15 minutes.

Roll out the pastry to 3mm (1/8 in) thick and use it to line a 23cm (9 in) tart tin, lightly prick the base and rest it for 20 minutes in the fridge or 10 minutes in the freezer.

Whilst the pastry is resting, heat the butter in a frying pan over a gentle heat, add the apple slices and cinnamon and cook for 4-5 minutes until they start to turn golden. Remove them from the pan and put to one side.

Blind bake the pastry case for 10-15 minutes, remove baking beans and bake for a further 5 minutes. The pastry should be pale to golden in colour. Brush the pastry case with a little of the egg yolk and bake for a further minute. Remove from the oven and reduce the oven temperature to 160°C, 140°C fan oven, gas 3.

Whilst the pastry case is cooking, heat 50g (2oz) of the sugar in a pan, resist the temptation to stir, if you need to move the sugar because it is cooking quicker in one area than another, move the sugar gently with a wooden spoon. When the sugar has caramelised, after about 3-4 minutes, slowly and carefully pour in the milk, take care as it will splutter. Stir the milk to dissolve the caramel. In a small bowl whisk together the egg, the remaining yolk and the remaining sugar and stir in the caramel milk.

Arrange the apple slices in the baked pastry case, placing them closely together, starting from the outside and working in. Sieve the caramel custard, add the vanilla extract and grated lemon zest, and pour the custard into the tart case. Bake for 15-20 minutes until set. Serve dusted with icing sugar.

TARTE ALSACIENNE

Alsace has an interesting history. Although now part of France it was once a part of Germany and as a result has a gastronomy very different to any other region in France. Between the Vosges and the Rhine there is a fertile plain where many fruits are grown and these find their way into the regional dishes, both sweet and savoury. Alsatian tart is one - an open, fruit, custard-based tart.

In this recipe the apple pieces are cleverly used to hold the pastry in place, whilst the pastry is baked blind, before adding a rich creamy custard.

Makes one 25.5cm (10 in) tart
Serves 8
Sweet Short Pastry 1 (page 31)
Use 1/2 of the quantity of pastry, about
   350g (12oz), wrap and freeze the
   remaining pastry
1 tbsp semolina
5 dessert apples
1 egg

2 egg yolks
50g (2oz) caster sugar
142ml carton double cream
150ml (1/4pt) milk
Grated zest 1/2 lemon
1/2 tsp ground cinnamon
3 tbsp apricot jam
1 tsp lemon juice
Icing sugar to serve

Preheat the oven to 190°C, 170°C fan oven, gas 5.

Prepare the pastry and rest it in the fridge for 15 minutes.

Roll out the pastry to 3mm (1/8 in) thick and line a 25.5cm (10 in) tart tin with it. Lightly prick the base and then rest it for 20 minutes in the fridge or 10 minutes in the freezer.

Sprinkle the base of the tart with the semolina. This absorbs moisture from the apples as they cook, helping to keep the pastry crisp. Peel, core and cut each apple into 8 thick pieces. Pack the apples tightly, in concentric circles, in the base of the pastry case. Bake for 15 minutes until golden and the apples are starting to colour. Remove from the oven and reduce the oven temperature to 160°C, 140°C fan oven, gas 3.

Mix together the egg, egg yolks, sugar, cream and milk and sieve the mixture into a jug. Add the lemon zest and cinnamon to taste. Pour the custard into the pastry case and bake the tart for 15 minutes, until the custard is just set. Remove from the oven.

Heat the apricot jam with the lemon juice and 1 tablespoon of water, in a small pan and boil for 1 minute. Brush the glaze lightly over the surface of the apple tart. When brushing the custard mixture with apricot glaze, dab rather than drag the pastry brush. Dust the pastry with icing sugar and serve.

APPLE AND PRUNE TARTE TATIN

The original Tarte Tatin was made using a short crust style pastry but it has become fashionable to use puff pastry. After Marco Pierre White's Pear Tatin won Egon Ronay's dessert of the year in 1992, Tatins became an essential item on a London restaurant's dessert menu, and they remain popular today. This recipe is based on one I used to make at Blakes Hotel for Lady Weinberg.

Makes one 20cm (8 in) tart
Serves 2-4
Puff Pastry (page 30)
Use 1/2 the amount in the recipe, wrap and freeze the remaining pastry
25g (1oz) unsalted butter
75g (3oz) caster sugar
3 sharp tasting dessert apples
6-8 no-soak pitted prunes

Make the puff pastry the day before or have some ready in the freezer to defrost.

Preheat the oven to 220°C, 200°C fan oven, gas 7.

Melt the butter gently in a 20cm (8 in) frying pan with an ovenproof handle and then sprinkle over the sugar. When the butter and sugar start to caramelise, stir occasionally a few times to mix. When the sugar and butter start to emulsify and take on a smooth consistency, remove from the heat so the caramel doesn't darken further. If the caramel becomes too dark it will be bitter.

Peel, core and halve the apples. Place the apples cut side up in the caramel and drop the prunes between the apple halves.

Roll out the pastry to the size of the pan. Lift the pastry on top of the apples and tuck the edge inside the pan. Bake in the oven for 25 minutes until the pastry is golden and the apples are cooked through. Check the apples by inserting a sharp knife. The apples are cooked when they are tender offering up little resistance to the knife.

Remove the pan from the oven, allow to stand for 5 minutes, then place a plate on top of the pan and invert, the tart should fall freely onto the plate. Dust with icing sugar and serve immediately with Vanilla or Calvados Ice Cream (page 39).

TIP You can use puff pastry trimmings but I love the way virgin pastry puffs up around the edge of the fruit.

NORMANDY PEAR TART

Although more famous for its apples than its pears, this simple tart is combined with other local produce, namely butter, cream and walnuts, to good effect. The creamy, custard filling, with a hint of lemon, complements the delicate flavour of the pear, and the walnut pastry adds a contrasting crunch to the custard's smooth texture. I prefer to use Comice pears but you can use any ripe dessert pear.

Makes one 25.5cm (10 in) tart
Serves 8
Nut Pastry (page 36)
Use 1/2 the quantity made in the recipe, wrap and freeze remaining pastry
5 ripe Comice pears
15g (1/2oz) unsalted butter
1 egg

2 egg yolks
50g (2oz) caster sugar
284ml carton double cream
1 tbsp Poire William liqueur or brandy
Grated zest 1/2 lemon
3 tbsp apricot jam
1 tsp lemon juice
Icing sugar to serve

Preheat the oven to 190˚C, 170˚C fan oven, gas 5.

Prepare the pastry. Use 1/2 the quantity made in the Nut Pastry recipe and substitute ground walnuts for the ground almonds. Simply put walnut halves or pieces in a blender and process for 2-3 minutes until finely ground. Rest pastry in the fridge for 15 minutes.

Roll out the pastry to 3mm (1/8 in) thick and line a 25.5cm (10 in) tart tin with it. Lightly prick the base and then rest it for 20 minutes in the fridge or 10 minutes in the freezer.

Blind bake the pastry for 10 minutes, remove the baking beans and bake for a further 5 minutes. Reduce the oven temperature to 160˚C, 140˚C fan oven, gas 3.

Peel, core and thickly slice the pears lengthways. Melt the butter in a pan, add the pears and cook them gently for 4-5 minutes. Arrange the pears in the pastry case.

Mix together the egg, egg yolks, sugar, cream and pear liqueur or brandy and sieve the mixture into a jug. Add the lemon zest and pour the custard into the pastry case. Bake the tart for 15-20 minutes, until the custard is lightly set. Remove from the oven.

Heat the apricot jam with the lemon juice and 1 tablespoon of water in a small pan and boil for 1 minute. Dab lightly over the surface of the tart. Dust the pastry with icing sugar and serve.

PEAR AND CHOCOLATE TART

The most famous pairing of chocolate and pear is Auguste Escoffier's *Poires Belle Hélène*, a dish of cold poached pear with vanilla ice cream, candied violets and hot chocolate sauce, created to celebrate Offenbach's Operetta about Helen of Troy. It is no longer as popular as it once was but it is a wonderful dessert. I have never seen it served with candied violets; more often it is served with toasted flaked almonds. One of the best *Poires Belle Hélène* I have eaten was served at La Coupole, the famous Parisienne brasserie. Care needs to be taken with its component parts in order to do it justice. The pear must be freshly poached – I prefer mine left at room temperature, so that the flavour of the pear is not deadened by refrigeration. The ice cream must be good quality dairy vanilla, preferably with visible vanilla seeds, and the chocolate sauce must be made from dark, bitter chocolate and cream.

This tart combines the elements of that famous dish - the delicate flavour of pear with a rich chocolate almond filling. Although a simple dessert to make, it looks very impressive, especially if the edges of the pears are caramelised with a blowtorch, before being glazed.

In this recipe fresh pears are first poached in cinnamon syrup but if you are short of time simply use tinned pears.

Makes one 25.5cm (10 in) tart
Serves 8
Sweet Short Pastry 1 (page 31)
Use 1/2 of the quantity of pastry, about 350g (12oz), wrap and freeze the remaining pastry
200g (7oz) caster sugar
1 cinnamon stick
4-5 pears, peeled, halved and cored, or 2 x 400g tins of pear halves

1 egg yolk
75g (3oz) dark chocolate
125g (4^1/2oz) unsalted butter
125g (4^1/2oz) light muscovado sugar
2 eggs
125g (4^1/2oz) ground almonds
3 tbsp apricot jam
1 tsp lemon juice
Icing sugar and Vanilla Ice Cream (page 39) to serve

If using tinned pear halves, drain and dry the contents on kitchen paper.

Preheat the oven to 190°C, 170°C fan oven, gas 5.

Prepare the pastry and rest it in the fridge for 15 minutes. Roll out the pastry to 3mm (1/8 in) and line a 25.5cm (10 in) tart tin with it. Lightly prick the base and then rest it in the fridge for 20 minutes or 10 minutes in the freezer.

Pour the caster sugar into a medium pan with 450ml (3/4pt) water. Bring to the boil, stirring to dissolve the sugar. Add the cinnamon stick and the pears. Cover with a piece of greaseproof paper and a small plate or saucer, so the pears are held below the surface of the syrup. Reduce the heat and simmer the pears for about

10 minutes until they are soft and slightly translucent. This will take less time if the pears are ripe. Do not poach if using tinned pears.

Turn off the heat and drain the pears. The syrup can be kept for a couple of weeks in the fridge - use it again to poach other fruits.

Blind bake the pastry for 10 minutes, remove baking beans and bake for a further 5 minutes. Brush the pastry case with a little of the egg yolk and bake for a further minute. Remove and put to one side. Reduce the oven temperature to 180°C, 160°C fan oven, gas 4.

Chop the chocolate and place in a heatproof bowl, over a pan of simmering water, or microwave on a low heat setting, until melted. Cream the butter and sugar together, beat in the eggs and remaining yolk then stir in the ground almonds. Lastly stir through the melted chocolate.

Dry the poached pears on kitchen paper. Slice the pear halves thinly, widthways. Quickly spoon the chocolate almond mix over the baked pastry case. Slide a pear half onto a palette knife and push each pear half gently so the pear fans out slightly. Lay the fanned pear on top of the chocolate mix. Repeat using the remaining pears.

Bake the tart for 30-35 minutes until the chocolate almond sponge is firm to the touch, and remove from the oven.

If you have a blowtorch brown the cut edges of the pear. Heat the apricot jam with the lemon juice and 1 tablespoon of water, in a small pan and boil for 1 minute. Brush the surface of the tart with the hot apricot glaze. Dust with icing sugar and serve with vanilla ice cream.

APPLE TARTE TATIN

Two French sisters Carolina and Stephine Tatin from the small town of Lamotte-Beuvron in the Loire valley created this tart in the latter part of the 19th century. One day the elder of the two sisters, Stephine, placed her tart in the oven the wrong way around so that the apples and pastry were upside-down. She served this dessert without allowing it to cool and the *tarte des demoiselles Tatin* (tart of the two unmarried women) was born. Word of this dessert reached Paris and the owner of Maxim's restaurant decided he must have the recipe. Supposedly he travelled to Lamotte-Beuvron and disguised as a gardener, he successfully managed to discover how the tart was made. The Tatin has been on Maxim's menu ever since.

A French pastry chef gave me this version of the recipe. It is a tricky recipe to master, as the apples require cooking on a very low heat, to the point where they caramelise, but do not become too dark. It is, however, worth the effort. I would only recommend trying this recipe if you have a gas hob that can be set to a low setting or a heat diffuser.

Makes one 20cm (8 in) tart
Serves 6-8
Tatin Pastry (page 34)
50g (2oz) unsalted butter
125g (4¹/₂oz) caster sugar
7 sharp tasting dessert apples such as Granny Smiths or Cox's Orange Pippin

Prepare the pastry and rest it for 15 minutes in the fridge.

Melt the butter gently in a heavy based 20cm (8 in) sauté or low sided pan and then sprinkle over the sugar. Remove the pan from the heat whilst you prepare the apples.

Peel, core and halve the apples and pack them tightly into the pan so that the cut halves are upright, starting from the outside and working in. Return the pan to the lowest heat setting on your hob and let the apples cook gently for 1-1¹/₄ hours. The apple juice, butter and sugar will caramelise very slowly but the heat must be very gentle or the apples will cook to a pulp.

After 1 hour preheat the oven to 190˚C, 170˚C fan oven, gas 5. Roll out the Tatin pastry 6mm (¹/₄ in) thick and slightly larger than the top of the pan. Using a rolling pin, lift the pastry on top of the cooked apples and tuck it inside the pan. Bake the Tatin for 25-30 minutes until the pastry is golden. Remove from the oven.

To remove the Tatin from the pan place a plate on top of the pan and then invert the pan and plate. Serve the Tatin hot or cold with crème fraîche.

PEAR AND GINGER TART

Ginger had been used in British dishes since Anglo-Saxon times but it wasn't until the 17th century, when London became the spice market of the world, that a steady supply was available throughout the country. That London held this mantle for some 200 hundred years, is directly attributable to the British East India Company, which monopolized trade with India during this time. In addition to ginger, nutmeg, cinnamon and pepper were all popular spices, used in both sweet and savoury dishes.

I developed a taste for ginger whilst working at Blakes Hotel in the early 90s, where it was used extensively throughout the eclectic menu. Ever since then Pear and Ginger Tart has been part of my repertoire.

Makes one 25.5cm (10 in) tart
Serves 8
Sweet Short Pastry 1 (page 31)
Use 1/2 of the quantity of pastry,
    about 350g (12oz), wrap and freeze
    the remaining pastry
200g (7oz) caster sugar
1 cinnamon stick
4-5 Comice pears, peeled, halved and
    cored or 2 x 400g tins pear halves
1 egg yolk

125g (4¹/₂oz) unsalted butter
125g (4¹/₂oz) caster sugar
2 eggs
1 tsp ground ginger
2 tbsp chopped crystallised stem ginger
125g (4¹/₂oz) ground almonds
3 tbsp apricot glaze
1 tsp lemon juice
Icing sugar and Vanilla Ice Cream
    (page 39), to serve

If using tinned pear halves, drain and dry the contents on kitchen paper.

Preheat the oven to 190˚C, 170˚C fan oven, gas 5.

Prepare the pastry and rest it in the fridge for 15 minutes. Roll out the pastry to 3mm (¹/₈ in) thick and line a 25.5cm (10 in) tart tin with it. Lightly prick the pastry and then rest it for 20 minutes in the fridge or 10 minutes in the freezer.

Pour the caster sugar into a medium pan with 450ml (³/₄pt) water. Bring to the boil, stirring to dissolve the sugar. Add the cinnamon stick and the pears. Cover with a piece of greaseproof paper and a small plate or saucer, so the pears are held below the surface of the syrup. Reduce the heat and simmer the pears for about 10 minutes until they are soft and slightly translucent. This may take less time if the pears are ripe. Do not poach if using tinned pears.

Turn off the heat and drain the pears. The syrup can be kept for a couple of weeks in the fridge - use it again to poach other fruits.

Blind bake the pastry for 10 minutes, remove the beans and bake for a further 5 minutes. Brush the pastry case with a little egg yolk and bake for a further minute. Remove and put to one side. Reduce the oven temperature to 180˚C, 160˚C fan oven, gas 4.

Cream the butter and sugar together, beat in the eggs and then stir in the ground almonds and the ground and crystallised ginger and put to one side.

Dry the poached pears on kitchen paper. Slice the pear halves thinly, widthways. Quickly spoon the almond mix over the baked pastry case. Slide a pear half onto a palette knife, gently pressing the pear slice forward, so the slices fan out. Lay the fanned pear on top of the almond mix. Repeat using the remaining pears. Bake the tart for 30-35 minutes until the sponge is firm to the touch.

If you have a blowtorch brown the cut edges of the pear. Heat the apricot jam with the lemon juice and 1 tablespoon of water and boil for 1 minute. Brush the surface of the tart with the hot apricot glaze. Dust with icing sugar and serve with Vanilla Ice Cream (page 39).

APPLE FLORENTINE

This recipe is adapted from Bedfordshire Apple Florentine, where spiced ale was poured into the pie, just before it was served. Instead of ale I've used cider and have added it to the pie before it is cooked, so that the flavour of the cider permeates through the apples, during cooking.

Makes one 19cm (7^1/2 in) wide x 26cm (10^1/4 in) long, pie
Serves 4-6
Rich Short Crust Pastry (page 35)
50g (2oz) unsalted butter
750g (1lb 10oz) dessert apples, peeled, cored and cut into 8
250ml (9fl oz) dry cider
1 tbsp cornflour
1 tbsp granulated sugar

Preheat the oven to 190˚C, 170˚C fan oven, gas 5.

Prepare the pastry and rest it in the fridge for 15 minutes.

Heat the butter gently in a frying pan and add the sliced apples. Cook gently for 3-4 minutes and then spoon into a 19cm (7^1/2 in) wide x 26cm (10^1/4 in) long pie dish. Add the cider to the pan and reduce the heat. Mix the cornflour with 2 tablespoons of water and stir into the cider. Stir until the cider thickens. Pour onto the apples and stir through.

Brush the lip of the pie dish with water. Roll out the pastry a little larger than the pie dish. Cut a strip from the edge of the rolled pastry to fit the width of the pie lip and press lightly onto the lip, dampen the pastry on the lip. Place the remaining pastry on top of the apples and press to seal the edge, using the back of a knife to trim any excess pastry. Make a small slit in the centre of the pie. Brush with water and sprinkle with the granulated sugar. Bake for 25-30 minutes until the pastry is golden.

TIP When pressing to seal you can crimp or fork to decorate the edge.

BRAMLEY APPLE PIE

In 1850, nurseryman Henry Merryweather discovered a previously unknown variety of apple in the garden of Matthew Bramley, in Nottinghamshire. Mary-Ann Brailsford, who had owned the house before Matthew Bramley, had planted the apple tree from seed some 50 years earlier. Merryweather was allowed to take graftings from the tree to grow and sell the apples, on condition that he called it the Bramley seedling. This he did and today the Bramley is the most widely used cooking apple in Britain. The famous cooking apple has a higher acidity and lower sugar content than dessert apples, so retains a more appley flavour when cooked. It does, however, breakdown to a greater extent than dessert apples, so sometimes I add a few dessert apples to give a chunkier apple filling. The following recipe is based solely on Bramleys.

Makes one 19cm (7¹/₂ in) wide x 26cm (10¹/₄ in) long, pie
Serves 4-6
Rich Short Crust Pastry (page 35)
750g (1lb 10oz) Bramley apples
50g (2oz) unsalted butter
1 tbsp granulated sugar

Preheat the oven to 190˚C, 170˚C fan oven, gas 5.

Prepare the pastry and rest it in the fridge for 15 minutes.

Peel, core and slice the apples thickly. If cut too thinly, they will break down too much when cooked.

Heat the butter gently in a frying pan and add the sliced apples. Cook gently for 3-4 minutes and then spoon into a 19cm (7¹/₂ in) wide x 26cm (10¹/₄ in) long pie dish.

Brush the lip of the pie dish with water. Roll out the pastry a little larger than the dish. Cut a strip from the edge of the rolled pastry, to fit the width of the pie lip, and press lightly onto the lip, dampen the pastry on the lip. Place the remaining pastry on top of the apples and press to seal the edge, using the back of a knife to trim any excess pastry. Make a small slit in the centre of the pie. Brush with water and sprinkle with the granulated sugar. Bake for 25-30 minutes until the pastry is golden.

SPICED APPLE MERINGUE PIE

I devised this tart as an alternative to lemon meringue pie. It is similar to a recipe I came across for a Scottish Butterscotch Apple Pie, although the Scottish version uses brown sugar to give the apples a butterscotch flavour, where I have chosen to add a little mixed spice. This recipe uses French, or uncooked, meringue but if you prefer you can use Italian, cooked, meringue (page 122).

Makes one 23cm (9 in) wide, deep pie
Serves 6-8
Rich Short Crust Pastry (page 35)
1 egg yolk
50g (2oz) unsalted butter
5 dessert apples, peeled, cored and cut into 8
1/2 tsp mixed spice
4 egg whites
Pinch of cream of tartar
Pinch of egg white powder
150g (5oz) caster sugar

Preheat the oven to 190°C, 170°C fan oven, gas 5.

Prepare the pastry and rest it in the fridge for 15 minutes.

Lightly grease a 23cm (9 in) diameter, 4cm (1½ in) deep pie dish. Roll out the pastry on a lightly floured surface and line the base of the pie dish. Lightly dock the base of the case and trim the excess pastry. Rest it in the fridge for 20 minutes or 10 minutes in the freezer.

Bake the pastry blind for 10-15 minutes, remove the baking beans and bake for a further 5 minutes, it should be pale to golden in colour. Brush the pastry case with a little egg yolk and bake for a further minute. Remove from the oven.

Heat the butter gently in a frying pan and add the sliced apples and mixed spice. Cook gently for 5-6 minutes, until the apples are cooked through and then spoon them into the pie dish.

Whisk the egg whites with the cream of tartar and egg white powder, until soft peaks form and add 1/3 of the sugar, whisk for 2-3 minutes, then add another 1/3 of the sugar, whisk for a further 1-2 minutes and add the remaining sugar, whisk for a further minute – the meringue should by now be thick and glossy. Spoon the meringue over the apples and bake for 4-5 minutes until the meringue starts to brown, remove from the oven and serve immediately.

SPICED PEAR PIE

Pears were a popular fruit in Britain from the Middle Ages but even more so in France and Italy. Most pears grown in Britain were of French stock, with the exception of Wardons, a type of cooking pear first grown in Wardon, Bedfordshire by Cistercian monks in the 14th century – it was so important it became a fruit in its own right. As there is little demand these days for 'cooking pears', those grown are first and foremost dessert pears, and so today's commercially grown pears are much softer and sweeter than those grown centuries ago.

Conference pears are the leading British variety, with smaller quantities of Comice, William and Hardy also grown, but due to declining pear production, imports make up a significant proportion of the pears sold in our shops.

Makes one 19cm (7$\frac{1}{2}$ in) wide x 26cm (10$\frac{1}{4}$ in) long, pie
Serves 4-6
Rich Short Crust Pastry (page 35)
900g (2lb) firm pears
25g (1oz) unsalted butter
$\frac{1}{2}$ tsp ground ginger
$\frac{1}{2}$ tsp ground nutmeg
2 tbsp raisins
Grated zest $\frac{1}{2}$ orange
Juice 1 orange
1 tbsp granulated sugar

Preheat the oven to 190˚C, 170˚C fan oven, gas 5.

Prepare the pastry and rest it in the fridge for 15 minutes. Peel, core and cut the pears into 8.

Heat the butter gently in a frying pan and add the pears and spices. Cook gently for 4-5 minutes until tender and then spoon into a 19cm (7$\frac{1}{2}$ in) wide x 26cm (10$\frac{1}{4}$ in) long pie dish. Stir through the raisins, grated orange zest and pour over the juice.

Brush the lip of the pie dish with water. Roll out the pastry a little larger than the pie dish. Cut a strip from the edge of the rolled pastry to fit the width of the pie lip and press lightly onto the lip, dampen the pastry on the lip. Place the remaining pastry on top of the pears and press to seal the edge, using the back of a knife to trim any excess pastry and use it to decorate the pie top. Make a small slit in the centre of the pie. Brush with water and sprinkle with the granulated sugar. Bake for 25-30 minutes until the pastry is golden.

TIP When pressing to seal, crimp or fork the edges to decorate.

MULLED PEAR TURNOVERS

In Medieval times mulled wine was typically drunk around Christmas and New Year. Its earliest name, from Anglo-Saxon times, was Wassail derived from 'Wes hail', meaning good health, as it was thought to have medicinal properties. To this day it remains a popular festive drink throughout Central Europe. Essentially it is hot red wine, often of dubious quality, spiced with cinnamon and clove, sweetened with sugar or honey, and flavoured with orange.

As pears are often poached in red wine, I thought poaching them in mulled wine and then making them into turnovers, would make a delicious festive alternative to mince pies and Christmas pudding.

Serves 4
Puff Pastry (page 30)
450ml (14fl oz) red wine
250g (9oz) caster sugar
1/2 cinnamon stick
3 cloves
Strip pared orange zest

1 bay leaf
4 pears, peeled, cored and thickly sliced
50g (2oz) unsalted butter
1 egg
100g (3½ oz) ground almonds
1 egg white
1 tbsp granulated sugar

Make the puff pastry the day before or have some ready in the freezer to defrost.

Pour the wine into a small pan and add 200g (7oz) of the caster sugar, bring the wine to the boil and stir to dissolve the sugar. Add the cinnamon stick, cloves, orange zest, bay leaf and pears. Cover the pears with a piece of greaseproof paper and a small plate or saucer, so the pears are kept below the surface of the syrup. Reduce the heat and simmer the pears for about 10 minutes until they are soft and slightly translucent. This will take less time if the pears are ripe.

Drain and allow the pears to cool. You may like to keep the syrup to poach other fruit or alternatively simmer and reduce the syrup until it thickens slightly and use as a sauce to serve with the turnovers.

Preheat the oven to 220°C, 200°C fan oven, gas 7.

Cream the butter and remaining caster sugar, beat in the egg and stir in the ground almonds. Put to one side.

Roll out the pastry on a lightly floured work surface to a 30.5cm (12 in) square and approximately 3mm (1/8 in) thick. Cut this large square into 4 smaller squares and trim the edges. Rest the pastry for 20 minutes in the fridge.

Brush the edges of the squares with water and spoon a little of the almond cream into the centre of each pastry square. Lay the poached pear slices on top of the almond cream and fold half the pastry square over on itself to form a triangle. Seal the edges of the turnovers and knock up the edges with a small sharp knife. Brush the pastry with egg white and sprinkle with granulated sugar. Bake for 20-25 minutes until golden and cooked through. Serve hot or cold.

RUSTIC APPLE AND ALMOND PIE

This simple free-form pie is probably similar in style to those made centuries ago by farm workers, before metal or ceramic pie dishes were widely available. It's easy to make and also adapt for use with other fruits. It's definitely a home-style family dish, not one that I ever made in hotels or restaurants. However it looks impressive and tastes great!

Makes one 23cm (9 in) pie
Serves 6-8
Rich Short Crust Pastry (page 35)
4 dessert apples
150g (5oz) caster sugar
350g (12oz) marzipan
2 tbsp granulated sugar
142ml carton double cream
25g (1oz) cold unsalted butter, cut into small pieces

Preheat the oven to 190°C, 170°C fan oven, gas 5.

Prepare the pastry and rest it for 15 minutes in the fridge.

Roll out the pastry to 30.5cm (12 in) round and place on a lightly greased baking tray.

Lightly prick the pastry base with a fork and refrigerate whilst you roll out the marzipan and prepare the apples.

Peel, core and slice the apples 6mm (1/4 in) thick and mix them in a bowl with 2 tablespoons of caster sugar. Roll out the marzipan to a 23cm (9 in) round and place in the centre of the pastry. Pile the apple slices on top of the marzipan and fold up the outer edges of the pastry, to make the pie edge. Brush the edge with water and sprinkle with the granulated sugar.

Bake for 35-40 minutes until golden. Whilst the pie is cooking make the caramel sauce.

Heat the remaining sugar in a pan, over a medium heat but resist the temptation to stir, if you need to move the sugar because it is cooking quicker in one area than another, move it gently with a wooden spoon. When the sugar has caramelised reduce the heat and whisk in the cream. Remove from the heat and then whisk in the butter. Serve the pie with the caramel sauce.

TARTE AUX POMMES FINE

Fine French apple tart is the literal translation of this recipe but it doesn't do justice to this delicate confection. The pastry needs to be thinly rolled and the apples thinly sliced, to create the perfect apple tart. The most memorable one I ate was in Nico Ladenis's restaurant at 90 Park Lane, some years ago. The tart was served with vanilla and caramel sauces, a sprinkling of crushed praline and vanilla ice cream, giving a full complement of flavours and textures.

Serves 6

500g (1lb 2oz) puff pastry trimmings (see page 27) or virgin Puff Pastry (page 30)
6 sharp tasting dessert apples, such as Granny Smiths
50g (2oz) unsalted butter, melted
3 tbsp apricot jam
1 tsp lemon juice
Icing sugar to serve
Vanilla Ice Cream (page 39) and Caramel Sauce (page 38), to serve

---

Make the puff pastry the day before or have some ready in the freezer to defrost. If you haven't got any trimmings to hand simply roll out some virgin Puff Pastry to 3mm (1/8 in) thick, fold in half and in half again. Refrigerate for 30 minutes then use as trimmings.

Preheat the oven to 220°C, 200°C fan oven, gas 7.

Roll out the pastry to 3mm (1/8 in) thick to give a 30.5cm (12 in) square. Cut 4 x 12.5cm (5 in) rounds from the pastry, re-roll any trimmings, and rest the re-rolled pastry for 10 minutes, before cutting 2 more rounds. Prick the pastry heavily with a fork, then rest it in the fridge for 15 minutes.

Peel, core and quarter the apples. Slice the apples thinly so they are almost transparent. Lay the pastry rounds on a baking tray and arrange the apple slices in neat circles, starting from the outside and working in. Brush each layer of apple slices with melted butter. The apple slices will be piled high. Bake the tarts for 15-18 minutes until the pastry is golden and the apple cooked through.

Heat the apricot jam with the lemon juice and 1 tablespoon of water in a small pan and boil for 1 minute. Brush the apple with the apricot glaze and dust the pastry edge with icing sugar. Serve with vanilla ice cream and caramel sauce.

TIP Keep any puff pastry trimmings. Lay them out on top of each other to keep the layers in the same direction.

DUTCH APPLE PIE

The American apple pie is usually attributed to the Pennsylvania Dutch who were of German descent; 'Dutch' coming from the word *Deustch*. They were primarily farmers and their cooking reflects that way of life. This dessert is made in the style of the Dutch Apple Pie - a deep pie with a lattice top. Some recipes for it contain cream, which is mixed with the apple filling, but this version is richly flavoured with rum-soaked fruits.

Makes one 18cm (7 in) deep pie
Serves 8
American Short Pastry (page 33)
with grated zest of 1 lemon and 1/2 tsp
   ground cinnamon
100g (31/2oz) sultanas
50g (2oz) raisins
100ml (31/2 fl oz) dark rum
450g (1lb) Granny Smith apples
450g (1lb) Bramley apples
25g (1oz) unsalted butter

6 tbsp apricot jam
grated zest 1/2 lemon
1/2 tsp ground cinnamon
100g (31/2oz) caster sugar
25g (1oz) finely chopped candied
   orange peel
2 tbsp granulated sugar
1 tsp lemon juice

Preheat the oven to 190˚C, 170˚C fan oven, gas 5.

Add the sultanas and raisins to the rum and heat gently in a small pan for 1-2 minutes. Remove from the heat and put to one side.

Prepare the pastry with the addition of the grated zest of 1 lemon and 1/2 tsp ground cinnamon, to the flour, and rest it in the fridge for 15 minutes. Lightly grease an 18cm (7 in) springform tin. Roll out 2/3 of the pastry on a lightly floured surface to 6mm (1/4 in) thick and line the base and sides of the tin but do not trim the excess pastry at this stage. Lightly prick the base of the case and rest the lined case and remaining pastry in the fridge for 20 minutes.

Peel, core and thickly slice the apples 1cm (1/2 in) thick, keeping the two types of apple separate. Melt the butter, add the Granny Smith apples and cook for 5 minutes then add the Bramleys and cook for a further 2-3 minutes. Stir through the sultanas and raisins, half the apricot jam, lemon, cinnamon, sugar and peel. Pour the mix into a shallow dish and allow to cool.

When cool, fill the pastry case with the apples. Roll out the remaining pastry and cut into strips 2.5cm (1 in) wide. Lay 4 strips of pastry across the apple filling and 4 at right angles to the first strips. Seal the strips at the edge of the tin and trim any excess pastry. Brush the surface with water and sprinkle with granulated sugar. Bake for 50–55 minutes. If the pastry starts to colour too much, turn the temperature down slightly and cover the pie with a piece of foil. Remove from the oven and allow to cool for 20 minutes or so before unmoulding. Heat the remaining apricot jam with the lemon juice and 1 tablespoon of water and boil for 1 minute. Brush the glaze over the pie. Serve the pie warm with cream.

PEAR AND CARAMEL LATTICE

This recipe is adapted from the Orchard Lattice recipe that appears in the Stone Fruits chapter. For me a good lattice is piled high with fruit and uses thinly rolled puff pastry, that when baked, just holds the fruit in place, rather than forming the bulk of the dish. As I love pear desserts, preferably where the pear features as the main ingredient, the idea of a pear lattice makes this irresistible.

Makes one 30.5cm (12 in) x 12.5cm
   (5 in) slice
Serves 6
Puff Pastry (page 30)
Use 1/2 of the quantity of pastry, wrap and
   freeze the remaining pastry
5 tbsp caster sugar
150ml (1/4pt) milk (1 tbsp reserved for the
   egg wash)

3 egg yolks
2 tbsp cornflour
Small knob unsalted butter
2 tsp vanilla extract
6-8 poached pears or 2 x 400g tins
   of pear halves
2 tbsp apricot jam
1 tsp lemon juice

Make the puff pastry the day before or have some ready in the freezer to defrost.

Preheat the oven to 220˚C, 200˚C fan oven, gas 7.

Heat 3 of the 5 tablespoons of sugar gently in a pan. Resist the temptation to stir; if you need to move the sugar because it is cooking quicker in one area than another, move the sugar gently with a wooden spoon. When the sugar caramelises add the milk (less the reserved 1 tablespoon) carefully because it will splutter. Bring the milk to the boil, so the caramel starts to dissolve into the milk. Don't worry if it doesn't dissolve completely.

Mix 2 of the egg yolks with the remaining 2 tablespoons of sugar and then add the cornflour. Whisk a little of the hot caramel milk onto the egg mixture and then return the egg mixture to the milk in the pan. Cook the mixture over a medium heat, stirring all the time until the mixture has thickened, cook for 2-3 minutes then remove from the heat and pour the pastry cream into a clean bowl. Whisk in the butter and vanilla extract and cover with a piece of buttered greaseproof. Allow to cool. If your pastry cream isn't completely smooth at this stage sieve it to remove any lumps.

Roll out 1/2 the pastry on a lightly floured work surface to 30.5cm (12 in) x 12.5cm (5 in). Lightly prick the puff pastry strip. Place the pastry on a baking tray and roll out the other half of the pastry to the same size. Use a lattice roller to cut this strip of pastry. Rest both strips of pastry in the fridge for 15 minutes.

Pipe the pastry cream down the centre of the pastry on the baking tray. Dry the pears on kitchen paper and lay the pears, overlapping, down the centre, so they cover the pastry cream. Mix together the remaining egg yolk and the reserved milk. Brush the edges of the pastry with the egg wash and trim the pastry leaving a 1cm (1/2 in) pastry edge on either side of the fruit. Knock up the edges with a small sharp knife.

Lay the lattice cut piece of pastry on top of the pears and open the pastry onto it, so it covers the pears. Seal the edges of the pastry close to the pears. Brush the pastry with the egg wash and trim the pastry leaving a 1cm (1/2 in) edge on either side of the fruit. Knock up the edges with a small sharp knife. Rest the pastry for 10-15 minutes in the fridge.

Bake the lattice for 15-20 minutes until golden. Remove from the oven. Heat the apricot jam with the lemon juice and 1 tablespoon of water and boil for 1 minute. Brush the pastry with the apricot glaze. Cut the lattice into slices and serve.

DORSET APPLE PIE

Although not renowned for its fruit growing today, Dorset was home to hundreds of fruit orchards in the 18th and 19th centuries, as well as having a prosperous dairy industry. Just as people from the northern counties began eating apples with cheese, to counteract the sharpness of the fruit, it seems that the people of Dorset also adopted this practice. These days the Dorset Drum Cheddar is the most suitable cheese available but in its absence, any full flavoured cheddar would make a worthy substitute.

Makes one 25.5cm (10 in) pie
Serves 8-10
Rich Short Crust Pastry (page 35)
Make 2 x recipe
450g (1lb) dessert apples
450g (1lb) Bramley apples

50g (2oz) light brown sugar
1 tsp mixed spice
75g (3oz) sultanas
115g (4oz) mature Cheddar,
   crumbled into 1cm (1/2 in) pieces

Preheat the oven to 190°C, 170°C fan oven, gas 5.

Prepare the pastry, wrap it and rest it in the fridge for 15 minutes. Roll out just over half of the pastry on a lightly floured surface, to a thickness of 3mm (1/8 in) and line the base of the pie dish. Lightly prick the pastry case. Do not trim the excess pastry at this stage. Rest the lined case and remaining pastry in the fridge for 20 minutes.

Peel, core and slice the apples. Slice the Bramleys a little thicker than the dessert apples. Mix them in a bowl with the sugar, spice, sultanas and cheese, and spoon the fruit mixture into the lined tart tin.

Roll out the remaining pastry a little thicker than before. Dampen the pie edge with water. Using the rolling pin, lift the rolled pastry on top of the fruit and press the edges together to seal. Crimp or fork, to decorate the edge. Trim any excess pastry and use it to decorate the pie top. Bake the pie for 25 minutes and then lower the temperature to 180°C, 160°C fan oven, gas 4 and bake for a further 20-25 minutes until golden brown, if the pastry starts to colour too much cover with foil.

PEAR STREUSEL TART

Streusel is the name given to the sweet, crumbly topping used on cakes, tarts and breads throughout Austria and Central Europe. Streusel comes from the German word *streusen* meaning to scatter. Streusel usually contains ground cinnamon, and has a higher ratio of sugar to flour than the British crumble, which is similar in texture, but is less crisp and sweet. It is very likely that streusel topping gave rise to the American-style coffee cakes, which are baked with a crisp crumbly topping.

This recipe is adapted from one given to me by Yolande Stanley, ex-chef pâtissier at the Ritz, London, and now Senior Pastry Chef Lecturer at Thames Valley University.

Makes one 25.5cm (10 in) tart
Serves 8
Sweet Short Pastry 1 (page 31)
Use 1/2 of the quantity of pastry,
    about 350g (12oz), wrap and freeze
    the remaining pastry
50g (2oz) raisins
2 tbsp Poire William liqueur or rum
300ml (1/2 pt) milk (1 tbsp reserved for the
    egg wash)

4 egg yolks
125g (4^1/2oz) caster sugar
4 tbsp cornflour
2 tsp vanilla extract
5 pears
50g (2oz) unsalted butter
75g (3oz) flour
50g (2oz) flaked almonds
1/2 tsp ground cinnamon

Preheat the oven to 190°C, 170°C fan oven, gas 5.

Prepare the pastry and rest it in the fridge for 15 minutes. Roll out the pastry to 3mm (1/8 in) thick and use it to line a 25.5cm (10 in) tart tin. Lightly prick the base and then rest it for 20 minutes in the fridge or 10 minutes in the freezer.

Add the raisins to the liqueur and heat gently in a small pan for 1-2 minutes. Remove from the heat and put to one side.

Bring the milk to the boil in a small pan. Mix together 3 of the 4 egg yolks with half the sugar, then add the cornflour. Whisk a little of the hot milk onto the egg mixture and then return the egg mixture to the milk in the pan. Cook the mixture over a medium heat, stirring all the time, for 3-4 minutes until the mixture has thickened. Remove from the heat and pour the pastry cream into a clean bowl. Stir in the vanilla extract and cover with a piece of buttered greaseproof; this helps prevent a thick skin from forming. Allow to cool.

Peel, core and thinly slice the pears, 6mm (1/4 in) thick. Melt 25g (1oz) of the butter in a frying pan and gently cook the pears for 4-5 minutes or until tender - this will depend upon the ripeness of the pears.

Bake the pastry blind for 10-15 minutes, remove the baking beans and bake for a further 5 minutes. Brush the pastry case with a little egg yolk and bake for a further minute.

Remove and put to one side. Reduce the oven temperature to 180°C, 160°C fan oven, gas 4.

Rub the remaining butter and flour together, then stir in the remaining sugar, the flaked almonds and ground cinnamon. Mix the pears and raisins with the pastry cream and spoon the mixture into the tart case. Sprinkle over the streusel mixture and bake for 15-20 minutes until the streusel is golden. Allow to cool before serving.

BUTTERSCOTCH APPLE PIE

I came across a recipe for butterscotch apple pie, where brown sugar was added to the apples, to give a butterscotch flavour but I was disappointed with the result so I took the idea and developed this recipe. I made a butterscotch sauce and added this to the apples before cooking the pie to give a much richer and fuller flavour. It is very sweet, but if you enjoy butterscotch or sticky toffee-style desserts you'll definitely like this recipe.

Makes one 19cm (7^1/$_2$ in) wide x 26cm (10^1/$_4$ in) long pie
Serves 4-6
Rich Short Crust Pastry (page 35)
115g (4oz) unsalted butter, cut into small pieces
125g (4^1/$_2$oz) caster sugar
100ml (3^1/$_2$fl oz) double cream
6 dessert apples, peeled, cored and cut into 8

Preheat the oven to 190°C, 170°C fan oven, gas 5.

Prepare the pastry and rest it in the fridge. Melt 50g (2oz) of the butter gently and sprinkle the sugar evenly over the melted butter. Allow the butter and sugar to caramelise without stirring. If the sugar is cooking quicker in one area than another move the sugar gently with a wooden spoon. When the butter and sugar are a pale caramel colour, carefully add the cream, taking care as it will splutter. Remove from the heat and then whisk in 25g (1oz) of the butter, a little at a time. Put to one side.

Melt the remaining butter in a frying pan or large pan and cook the apples for 4-5 minutes, until just tender. Pour over the butterscotch sauce and spoon the apples and sauce into a 19cm (7^1/$_2$ in) wide x 26cm (10^1/$_4$ in) long pie dish.

Brush the lip of the pie dish with water. Roll out the pastry a little larger than the pie dish. Cut a strip from the edge of the rolled pastry to fit the width of the pie lip and press lightly onto the lip, dampen the pastry on the lip. Place the remaining pastry on top of the apples, seal the edges and make a small slit in the centre of the pie. Brush with water and bake for 25-30 minutes until the pastry is golden. Serve hot with custard.

TIP When sealing the pie crust, crimp or fork to decorate.

SCONE-TOPPED PEAR PIE

This pie is adapted from fruit cobbler, an American deep-dish fruit dessert. The recipe is thought to have originated in Germany and been taken by German migrants to America in the 18th century. Fruit cobblers topped with scone rounds, which in America are known as biscuits, were likened to 'cobblestones' hence the name. In New England on the East Coast of America cobblers are also known as grunts or slumps.

Instead of cutting out rounds of scone dough, in this recipe, I've covered the fruit with a layer of the dough to give a scone crust. It gives a soft-topped pie, with a cake-like crust. The addition of crushed amaretti biscuits adds a bit of crunch to the soft dough.

As scone pastry is made with self-raising flour or with plain flour and the addition of baking powder, it should not be made in advance, but made and used straight away, so prepare the fruit for this pie before making the scone pastry.

Makes one 19cm (7^1/$_2$ in) wide x 26cm (10^1/$_4$ in) long pie
Serves 4-6
Scone Pastry (page 35)
Use the recipe with the addition of 100g (3^1/$_2$oz) crushed amaretti biscuits
50g (2oz) unsalted butter
900g (2lb) pears
1 tsp ground ginger
1 tbsp granulated sugar
Clotted cream to serve

Preheat the oven to 190˚C, 170˚C fan oven, gas 5.

Peel, core and roughly chop the pears. Heat the butter gently in a frying pan and add the pears and ground ginger. Cook gently for 4-5 minutes until the pears are tender - this will depend on the ripeness of the pears. Spoon them into a 19cm (7^1/$_2$ in) wide x 26cm (10^1/$_4$ in) long pie dish.

Prepare the scone pastry, adding the crushed amaretti biscuits just before you add the milk.

Brush the lip of the pie dish with water. Roll out the pastry on a lightly floured work surface, to fit the pie dish. Using a rolling pin, lift the pastry on top of the pears. Gently push down the edges onto the rim of the dish. Trim any excess scone pastry and use to make a few small scones. Brush the surface with water and sprinkle with the granulated sugar. Bake for 20-25 minutes until golden. Serve warm with clotted cream.

PEAR, MASCARPONE AND CHOCOLATE TART

I developed this tart a few years ago when mascarpone first became popular as an alternative 'cream cheese'. The filling resembles that of a cheesecake so it will appeal to cheesecake lovers and chocolate fans alike, and if pears are not your fruit of choice, cherries make an excellent substitute. It is very rich so a little goes a long way but it will keep for several days if stored in an airtight container in the fridge. If time is short use tinned pear halves, simply drain and dry on kitchen paper.

Makes one 25.5cm (10 in) tart
Serves 8
Sweet Short Pastry 1 (page 31)
Use 1/2 of the quantity of pastry, about 350g (12oz), wrap and freeze the remaining pastry
300g (10oz) caster sugar
5 pears, peeled, halved and cored or 2 x 400g tins of pear halves

500g (1lb 2oz) mascarpone
1 egg
3 egg yolks
150g (5oz) dark chocolate
3 tbsp apricot jam
1 tsp lemon juice

Preheat the oven to 190°C, 170°C fan oven, gas 5.

Prepare the pastry and rest it in the fridge for 15 minutes. Roll out the pastry to 3mm (1/8 in) thick and use it to line a 25.5cm (10 in) tart tin. Lightly prick the case and then rest it for 20 minutes in the fridge or 10 minutes in the freezer.

Pour 200g (7oz) of the caster sugar into a medium pan with 450ml (3/4pt) water. Bring to the boil, stirring to dissolve the sugar. Add the pears, cover with a piece of greaseproof paper and a small plate or saucer, so the pears are held below the surface of the syrup. Reduce the heat and simmer the pears for about 10 minutes until they are soft and slightly translucent. This may take less time if the pears are ripe. (Do not poach tinned pears.) Turn off the heat and drain the pears. The syrup can be kept for a couple of weeks in the fridge, use it again to poach other fruits.

Bake the pastry blind for 10 minutes, remove the baking beans and bake for a further 5 minutes. Brush the pastry case with a little egg yolk and bake for a further minute. Remove and put to one side. Reduce the oven temperature to 180°C, 160°C fan oven, gas 4.

Chop the chocolate and melt it in a heatproof bowl, over a pan of simmering water or in the microwave on a low setting. Mix together the mascarpone, remaining sugar, egg and egg yolks. Then stir in the melted chocolate. Slice the pear halves thinly widthways. Spoon the chocolate mixture into the pastry case. Slide a pear half onto a palette knife, gently press the pear slice forward, so the slices fan out. Lay the fanned pear on top of the chocolate mix. Repeat using the remaining pears. Bake the tart for 20-25 minutes until lightly set.

If you have a blowtorch, brown the cut edges of the pear. Heat the apricot jam with the lemon juice and 1 tablespoon of water in a small pan and boil for 1 minute. Brush the apricot glaze lightly over the surface of the tart. Allow the tart to cool slightly before serving.

LANCASHIRE APPLE SLICE

Cheese was often eaten with apple pie in the north of England; it was found that the creaminess of the cheese counteracted the tartness of the apple and Lancashire apple slice was probably created in response to this tradition.

Serves 6
Puff Pastry (page 30)
2 Granny Smith apples
1 egg yolk
1 tbsp milk
1 tbsp caster sugar
75g (3oz) Lancashire cheese, grated
50g (2oz) sultanas

Make the puff pastry the day before or have some ready in the freezer to defrost.

Preheat the oven to 220˚C, 200˚C fan oven, gas 7.

Peel, core and thinly slice the apples, 3mm (1/8 in) thick. Roll out the pastry on a lightly floured work surface, to give a 25.5cm (10 in) square. Cut the square into 2 strips: one 15cm (6 in) wide and one 10cm (4 in) wide. Place the 10cm (4 in) wide strip on a baking tray and lightly prick the surface. Rest the pastry for 20 minutes in the fridge.

Mix the egg yolk with the milk and brush the edge of the pastry strip on the baking tray. Lay the apple slices over the pastry, leaving a 1cm (1/2 in) border around the edge.

Sprinkle with the sugar, the cheese and the sultanas.

Fold the remaining piece of pastry in half, lengthways, and cut slits 2.5cm (1 in) in from the edge of the pastry and 1cm (1/2 in) apart along its length. Lay the pastry on top of apples and cheese then crimp and seal the edges. Brush with egg wash and bake for 25-30 minutes or until golden and the pastry is cooked through.

TIP Keep any puff pastry trimmings. Lay them out on top of each other to keep the layers in the same direction.

BANBURY APPLE PIE

Banbury was a prosperous market town by the 16th century. Although wool was its main trade, it had started to develop other specialist markets, including a baker's market at Bread Cross. This verse from the mid 16th century suggests that apple pies were being made and sold from around the same time as Banbury cakes. Unlike other pies of this period, which were either flathons (open flans) or made with a top pastry crust in a pie dish, Banbury Apple Pie was made with both a top and bottom pastry crust, this may have been so that they could be sold and taken away without the need for a pie dish.

'Ride a cock horse to Banbury Cross
To see what Tommy can buy
A penny white loaf, a penny white cake
And a tuppenny apple pie'

Makes one 23cm (9 in) deep pie
Serves 6-8
Rich Short Crust Pastry (page 35)
2 x recipe
750g (1lb 10oz) dessert apples
100g (3^1/$_2$ oz) sultanas

1/4 tsp ground cinnamon
1/4 tsp ground nutmeg
25g (1oz) light muscovado sugar
grated zest and juice 1 orange
1 tbsp milk
1 tbsp granulated sugar

Preheat the oven to 190˚C, 170˚C fan oven, gas 5.

Prepare the pastry, wrap it and rest it in the fridge. Lightly grease a 23cm (9 in) diameter x 4cm (1^1/$_2$ in) deep pie dish. Roll out half the pastry to a thickness of 6mm (1/4 in) and line the pie dish. Lightly prick the pastry case. Do not trim the excess pastry. Rest the pastry in the fridge whilst preparing the apples.

Peel, core and thinly slice the apples 3mm (1/8 in) and put into a mixing bowl. Add the sultanas, spice, sugar and orange zest and juice, and toss together. Put the apple mix into the lined pie dish.

Roll out the remaining pastry and dampen the pie edge with water. Lift the rolled pastry on top of the apples and seal the edges. Make a small slit in the centre of the pie. Brush with milk and sprinkle with granulated sugar. Bake the pie for 25 minutes and then lower the temperature to 180˚C, 160˚C fan oven, gas 4 and bake for a further 25-30 minutes until golden brown, if the pastry starts to colour too much cover with foil. Serve hot or cold.

PECAN CRUSTED PEAR PIE

This is an American inspired pear pie, with a thick pastry crust studded with sweet, crunchy pecans. I like to serve it *à la mode* 'American style' with a large scoop of vanilla ice cream but it tastes just as good served with cream or custard.

Neither apples nor pears are native to America - both were planted by settlers in the 16th and 17th centuries - and it wasn't until the late 18th century that the William pear, renamed the Bartlett, first arrived in America from Britain.

Makes one 23cm (9 in) deep pie
Serves 6-8
Rich Short Crust Pastry (page 35)
Make 2 x pastry recipe
8 large ripe pears
2 tbsp muscovado sugar
$1/4$ tsp ground nutmeg
125g ($4^1/2$oz) pecans, chopped
1 tbsp milk
1 tbsp granulated sugar

Preheat the oven to 190°C, 170°C fan oven, gas 5.

Prepare the pastry, wrap it and rest it in the fridge. Lightly grease a 23cm (9 in) diameter x 4cm ($1^1/2$ in) deep pie dish. Roll out half the pastry to a thickness of 6mm ($1/4$ in) and line the pie dish. Lightly prick the pastry case. Do not trim the excess pastry. Rest the pastry in the fridge whilst preparing the pears.

Peel, core and thickly slice the pears. Place the pears into the lined pastry case and sprinkle with the sugar and nutmeg.

Scatter half the nuts onto the work surface and place the remaining pastry on top of the nuts. Scatter the rest of the nuts on top of the pastry, and roll out the pastry, to roll the nuts into the pastry. Dampen the pie edge with water. Using a rolling pin, lift the rolled pastry on top of the pears and seal the edges. Make a small slit in the centre of the pie. Brush with milk and sprinkle with granulated sugar. Bake the pie for 20 minutes and then lower the temperature to 180°C, 160°C fan oven, gas 4 and bake for a further 30-35 minutes until golden brown, if the pastry starts to colour too much, cover with foil. Serve warm with vanilla ice cream.

STONE FRUITS

Peaches, apricots, plums, and cherries are all stone fruits, and as they are cultivated in the warm temperate regions throughout the world, there are only short gaps in year-round availability.

Peaches were one of the earliest crops to be domesticated - records date back to their cultivation in China, in 551 BC. Closely related to almonds, they are a member of the rose family and were called 'Persian apples' by the Romans. From China they travelled to Persia along the Silk Route and then on through Europe and Britain between 300-400BC, with the Greeks and Romans. They went to the New World with the Spanish in the 16th and 17th centuries and America is now one of the world's top producers. China, Italy, Spain, Greece and France also produce large crops.

To be at their best peaches should be fully ripened on the tree but they are picked early for long-distance export, which is why fresh ones eaten during the summer months in peach growing countries, taste so much better than those purchased in Britain. They are wonderful eaten raw but cooked gently, they retain their perfume and flavour. Peaches survive the canning process better than most fruits and although their flavour and texture are altered, they still taste good.

Nectarines are a type of peach but they are more susceptible to disease than the peaches due to their smooth skin, however they do lack the delicate flavour of the peach.

Apricots are also thought to have originated in China. Seeds were bought to Central Asia and then taken by Alexander the Great to the Middle East and on to Greece and Italy, where the name means 'precious' in Latin.

They are a versatile fruit but do not ripen after picking, nor do they travel well, hence they are often disappointing when purchased fresh from supermarkets.

For this reason apricots are often canned or dried; some of the most flavoursome dried are Turkish, they are darker in colour and have a more honeyed taste. Hunza apricots from Kashmir are also highly regarded.

Plums vary in colour from intense dark blue, almost black, to pale yellow and green, and are thought to have originated in Western Asia. There are more than 1,000 varieties grown worldwide and over 300 varieties are grown in Britain. The Brogdale Horticultural Trust in Kent holds the national collection of 350 varieties. The most commonly grown are the Victoria plum and the greengage.

In France the greengage is known as *Reine Claude,* named after the wife of François I. Sir William Gage is credited with having bought it to Britain in 1724. The seedlings having lost their labels in transit, were named after their patron. However, records show that greengages may have arrived in Britain directly from Italy at an earlier date and were known by their Italian name *verdocchia.*

The Victoria plum was discovered in Alderton, Sussex in 1940. Its value as a commercial variety was recognised and it has been grown extensively throughout Southern England ever since, despite the fact they are not considered to be the most flavoursome of plums.

Damsons, or Damask plums, were introduced to Britain in the 12th century by Crusaders returning from Syria, and were grown during the middle ages but it wasn't until the 19th century that they were planted in any great number. They became popular in the North West of the country and were used in the woollen industry to dye cloth. In 1996 the Westmorland Damson Association was set up to restore the local orchards and in April each year they organise a Damson Day, where local people come to buy and sell damson produce, including jams, cheese, jellies, pies and cakes.

Prunes are produced from certain varieties of sweet dried plums, one of the most famous being the *Prune d'Agen* from the South West of France. The monks of Clairac crossed a damson with a local plum to produce what they called the Ente plum and they found that when dried, it could be preserved for a whole year. By the 16th century orchards were flourishing throughout the region and the plum had taken the name of the port of Agen to become the famous D'Agen prune.

Cherries remain one of the few fruits that are not available all year round, despite being grown worldwide. They are available from May through to November. Wild cherries have been eaten since prehistoric times but it was the Romans who did much to advance the growth of wild cherry trees across Britain. In the 16th century, Kent was a large producer of cherries but these days Germany and America dominate production. There are two types: the sweet or dessert cherry and the sour cherry. It is the sour cherry which is better suited for culinary use and processing. Sour cherries are classified into two types: the light coloured amarelle and the dark griotte.

In France the griotte is famously used to produce liqueur-dipped, chocolate-covered cherries and in Germany the morello, a type of griotte, is used to make Black Forest gateau, cherry strudel and Kirsch.

As fresh cherries are expensive and have a very short season you can replace them with canned or bottled fruit. At Christmas time especially, you can often find fruits, bottled in syrups, flavoured with brandy and liqueur, and these can be used to make great-tasting desserts.

PEACH TATIN

I worked briefly in a London brasserie with a Master French pastry chef who introduced me to peach Tatin. It's not common place and the result is gorgeous – a real change from apples or pears. In this recipe the peaches are only partially cooked before the pastry top is added, unlike the Apple Tart Tatin (page 56) where the apples are cooked completely, very slowly over a low heat, until the sugars within the fruits themselves, have caramelised.

Makes one 20cm (8 in) tart
Serves 6-8
Tatin Pastry (page 34)
25g (1oz) unsalted butter
75g (3oz) caster sugar
12 firm peaches

Preheat the oven to 190˚C, 170˚C fan oven, gas 5.

Prepare the pastry and rest it for 15 minutes in the fridge. Melt the butter gently in a 23cm (9 in) frying pan with ovenproof handle and then sprinkle over the sugar. When the butter and sugar start to caramelise, stir occasionally a few times, to mix. When the sugar and butter start to form a smooth consistency and look a bit like melted fudge turn off the heat; if the caramel becomes too dark it will be bitter.

Peel, stone and halve the peaches. If the peaches do not peel easily plunge them into a pan of boiling water of 5-10 seconds and this will make them easier to peel. Pack the peach halves tightly into the pan cut side up. Work from the outside in.

Roll out the pastry on a lightly floured work surface, a little larger than the size of the pan. Lift the pastry on top of the peaches and tuck the edge inside the pan.

Bake for 25-30 minutes until the pastry is golden and the peaches are cooked through. Check the peaches by inserting a sharp knife. They are cooked when they are tender. Remove the pan from the oven, allow to stand for 5 minutes, then place a plate on top of the pan and invert, the tart should fall freely onto the plate. Serve warm with ice cream.

APRICOT BOURDALOUE

Sometime during the Belle Epoque or 'Gilded Era' of 1901-1914, a Parisian pastry chef, working in the Bourdaloue area, created a tart based on a frangipane cream, covered with crushed macaroons. The original tart contained poached pears but I prefer the following version with apricots.

Makes one 25.5cm (10 in) tart
Serves 8
Sweet Short Pastry 1 (page 31)
Use 1/2 of the quantity of pastry, about
    350g (12oz), wrap and freeze the
    remaining pastry
125g (4^1/2oz) unsalted butter
125g (4^1/2oz) caster sugar

2 eggs
125g (4^1/2oz) ground almonds
40g (1^1/2oz) ratafia biscuits, crushed
5-6 ripe medium apricots,
    halved and stoned or 2 x 400g tins
    of apricot halves
5 tbsp apricot jam
2 tsp lemon juice

If time is short or fresh apricots unavailable you can use tinned apricot halves, simply drain and dry on kitchen paper.

Preheat the oven to 190˚C, 170˚C fan oven, gas 5.

Prepare the pastry and rest it for 15 minutes in the fridge. Lightly flour a clean work surface and roll out the pastry to 3mm (1/8 in) thick. Use it to line a 25.5cm (10 in) tart tin. Lightly prick the base then chill it in the fridge for 20 minutes or 10 minutes in the freezer.

Cream the butter and sugar together, beat in the eggs and then stir in the ground almonds and the crushed ratafia. Spread the almond mix over the pastry case and place the apricots, cut side up, over the surface of the tart. Bake the tart for 20 minutes, then reduce the oven temperature to 180˚C, 160˚C fan oven, gas 4. Bake for a further 25-30 minutes, until the almond sponge is firm to the touch.

Heat the apricot jam with the lemon juice and 3-4 tablespoons of water and boil for 1 minute. Sieve the jam and then pour a little of the hot sauce over slices of the warm tart.

RUSTIC PLUM TART

I love fruit tarts and this is one of my favourites. My friend Liz, a fellow pastry chef, first showed me how to make it and I used to cook it for the members of the Athenaeum Club in London's Pall Mall. This has a real farmhouse feel to it and by using dark red plums, such as Brignole or Santa Rosa, you achieve a dramatic colour contrast between fruit and pastry.

Makes one 25.5cm (10 in) tart
Serves 8
Sweet Short Pastry 1 (page 31)
Use 1/2 of the quantity of pastry, about 350g (12oz) to line a 25.5cm (10 in) tart tin, wrap and freeze the remaining pastry
125g (41/2oz) unsalted butter

125g (41/2oz) light muscovado sugar
2 eggs
125g (41/2oz) ground almonds
5-6 ripe dark plums, halved and stoned
2 tbsp plain flour
3 tbsp apricot jam
1 tsp lemon juice
Icing sugar and Vanilla Ice Cream, to serve

Preheat the oven to 190˚C, 170˚C fan oven, gas 5.

Prepare the pastry and rest it for 15 minutes in the fridge. Lightly flour a clean work surface and roll out the pastry to 3mm (1/8 in) thick. Use it to line a 25.5cm (10 in) tart tin. Lightly prick the base and rest it for 20 minutes in the fridge or 10 minutes in the freezer.

Cream the butter and sugar together, beat in the eggs and then stir in the ground almonds. Spread the almond mix over the pastry case. Make 3 cuts in each plum half, 1/2 to 2/3 of the way through. Place the plums, cut side up, in the almond mix, evenly positioned over the surface of the tart. Dust the plums with the flour - this helps absorb excess moisture from the plums, as they cook.

Bake the tart for 40-45 minutes until the almond sponge is firm to the touch. If the tart starts to colour too much reduce the oven temperature to 180˚C, 160˚C fan oven, gas 4 and cover the tart with foil. When the tart is baked, remove from the oven.

Heat the apricot jam with the lemon juice and 1 tablespoon of water and boil for 1 minute. Brush the surface of the tart with the hot apricot glaze and dust the pastry crust with icing sugar. Serve warm with Vanilla Ice Cream (page 39).

APRICOT AND VANILLA CUSTARD TART

Custard-based tarts date back to the 15th century, when they were known as flathons. Often the custard was poured over a base of candied fruits, which were extremely popular at this time.

This apricot tart is French pâtisserie-style and uses a rich creamy vanilla custard.

Makes one 25.5cm (10 in) tart
Serves 8
Sweet Short Pastry 1 (page 31)
Use 1/2 of the quantity of pastry, about
    350g (12oz) to line a 25.5cm (10 in)
    tart tin, wrap and freeze the
    remaining pastry
5-6 ripe medium apricots, halved and
    stoned
1 egg

2 egg yolks
50g (2oz) caster sugar
284ml carton double cream
125ml (41/2fl oz) milk
Grated zest 1/2 lemon
2 tsp vanilla extract
2 tbsp apricot jam
1 tsp lemon juice
Icing sugar to serve

Preheat the oven to 190˚C, 170˚C fan oven, gas 5.

Prepare the pastry and rest it for 15 minutes in the fridge. Lightly flour a clean work surface and roll out the pastry to 3mm (1/8 in) thick. Use it to line a 25.5cm (10 in) tart tin. Lightly prick the base, then rest the pastry for 20 minutes in the fridge or 10 minutes in the freezer.

Bake the pastry case blind for 10-15 minutes, remove the baking beans and bake for a further 5 minutes. The pastry should be pale to golden in colour. Brush the pastry case with a little of the egg yolk and bake for a further minute. Remove from the oven. Reduce the oven temperature to 160˚C, 140˚C fan oven, gas 3.

Place the apricots cut side down in the pastry case. Mix together the egg, egg yolks, sugar, cream and milk, and sieve the mixture into a jug. Add the lemon zest and vanilla to taste. Pour the custard into the pastry case and bake the tart for 15-20 minutes, until the custard is just set. Remove from the oven.

Heat the apricot jam with the lemon juice and 1 tablespoon of water and boil for 1 minute. Brush lightly over the surface of the tart. Dust the crust with icing sugar and serve.

TIP When glazing custard tarts use dabbing brush strokes, so as not to drag the custard.

APRICOT DANOISE

This was one of the first tarts I made when training at Westminster College. *Danoise* is the French for Danish, and the tart is so called because it is filled and finished with the ingredients used to make Danish pastries, namely fruit, frangipane (almond cream), apricot glaze and water icing.

Makes one 25.5cm (10 in) tart
Serves 8
Sweet Short Pastry 1 (page 31)
Use 1/2 of the quantity of pastry, about
    350g (12oz), wrap and freeze the
    remaining pastry
1 egg yolk
125g (4^{1}/2oz) unsalted butter

125g (4^{1}/2oz) caster sugar
2 eggs
125g (4^{1}/2oz) ground almonds
4 tbsp apricot jam
4 poached apricots, halved and stoned
15g (1/2oz) flaked almonds
Juice 1/2 lemon
50g (2oz) icing sugar, sifted

Preheat the oven to 190°C, 170°C fan oven, gas 5.

Prepare the pastry and rest it for 15 minutes in the fridge. Lightly flour a clean work surface and roll out the pastry to 3mm (1/8 in) thick. Use it to line a 25.5cm (10 in) tart case. Lightly prick the base and rest it for 20 minutes in the fridge or 10 minutes in the freezer.

Cream the butter and sugar together, beat in the eggs and then stir in the ground almonds. Spread 2 tablespoons of the apricot jam over the base of the pastry and then top with the apricot halves, cut side down. Spread the almond mix over the fruit and sprinkle over the flaked almonds. Bake the tart for 25 minutes and then lower the oven temperature to 180°C, 160°C fan oven, gas 4, and bake for a further 20-25 minutes, until the almond sponge is firm to the touch.

Heat the remaining jam with the lemon juice and 1 tablespoon of water and boil for 1 minute. Mix the icing sugar in a small bowl with 1-2 tablespoons of hot water. Remove the tart from the oven and brush, first with the hot apricot glaze, and then the water icing. Serve hot or cold.

APRICOT AND MARZIPAN PIE

I am sure that someone somewhere has probably laid claim to creating this pie but I've not come across a recipe for it. I had the idea of combining apricots with marzipan beneath a pie crust, and the combination works to great effect. Make sure the apricots are ripe because these will have the best flavour, and try to buy a good quality marzipan, one that has a high almond content, such as Lübeck, made from aromatic Mediterranean almonds.

Makes one 19cm (7$\frac{1}{2}$ in) wide x 26cm (10$\frac{1}{4}$ in) long pie
Serves 4-6
Rich Short Crust Pastry (page 35)
700g (1lb 10oz) ripe apricots, stoned and halved
150g (5oz) marzipan
1 tbsp granulated sugar

Preheat the oven to 190°C, 170°C fan oven, gas 5.

Prepare the pastry and rest it for 15 minutes in the fridge.

Stuff each apricot half with a piece of marzipan and put into a 19cm (7$\frac{1}{2}$ in) wide x 26cm (10$\frac{1}{4}$ in) long pie dish. Brush the lip of the pie dish with water. Lightly flour a clean work surface and roll out the pastry a little larger than the pie dish. Cut a strip from the edge of the rolled pastry to fit the width of the pie lip and press pastry lightly onto the lip. Place the remaining pastry on top of the apricots and make a small slit in the centre of the pie. Brush with water and sprinkle with the granulated sugar.

Bake for 35-40 minutes until the pastry is golden. Serve hot with custard.

PEACH GALETTES WITH MASCARPONE CREAM

This recipe is a simple, rustic dessert that can be made ahead of time and assembled at the last minute. So it's a good choice for when you are entertaining. If peaches are out of season you could use plums or apples.

Makes 6

Puff Pastry (page 30)
1 egg yolk
1 tbsp milk
150g (5oz) white chocolate

250g (9oz) mascarpone
75g (3oz) unsalted butter
6 large ripe peaches, halved and stoned
50g (2oz) caster sugar
100ml (3½ fl oz) double cream

Preheat the oven to 220°C, 200°C fan oven, gas 7.

Make the puff pastry the day before or have some ready in the freezer to defrost.

Roll out the pastry 3mm (⅛ in) thick to give a 25.5cm (10 in) square. Cut 4 x 12.5cm (5 in) rounds from the pastry, re-roll any trimmings, and rest the re-rolled pastry for 10 minutes, before cutting 2 more rounds. Lightly prick the rounds in the centre and then rest the pastry in the fridge for about 15 minutes.

Mix together the egg yolk and milk. Lay the rounds on a baking tray and brush lightly with the egg wash. Bake the pastry rounds for 15-18 minutes until golden and cooked through. Remove from the oven and allow to cool. You could prepare these the day before if need be.

Chop the white chocolate and place in a heatproof bowl over a pan of simmering water or heat on a low setting in the microwave, until melted.

In a small bowl beat the mascarpone to soften it and stir through the white chocolate, put to one side. This is really quick to prepare so it could be made at the last minute.

Melt half of the butter gently in a frying pan and add the peach halves, cook for 4-5 minutes or until the peaches are tender. Remove and put to one side. The fruit could also be prepared ahead of time, covered and left at room temperature until needed.

Pour the sugar into a small heavy-based pan and heat gently until the sugar caramelises and is pale in colour. (It will continue to cook and darken in colour when the butter is added.) Remove from the heat and whisk in the remaining butter a little at a time. Then stir in the cream. This caramel sauce could be made the day before and gently reheated.

Spoon the mascarpone cream on top of the cooled galettes and top with the peaches. Drizzle over the caramel and serve immediately.

TIP Keep any puff pastry trimmings. Lay them out on top of each other to keep the layers in the same direction. You can freeze them and use them for one of the recipes that require trimmings.

GREENGAGE CRUMBLE TART

Sir William Greengage is credited with introducing the greengage, a type of yellow green plum, to Britain in 1724, although plum trees of the same description had arrived from Italy sometime earlier. Whilst in transit Sir William's trees lost their identifying labels and were given the name of their patron by Sir William's gardener. Sadly they are not as popular as they once were, so if you have trouble getting hold of them substitute another variety of plum.

Recipes for 'crumble' did not begin to appear until after the Second World War and were probably created during Rationing, as crumble requires smaller quantities of fat and flour than pastry. Crumble tart is definitely a modern hybrid but nevertheless it makes a great comfort pudding especially when served with custard.

Makes one 25.5cm (10 in) tart
Serves 8
Sweet Short Pastry 2 (page 32)
Use 1/2 of the quantity of pastry, about 350g (12oz), wrap and freeze the remaining pastry
50g (2oz) unsalted butter
50g (2oz) flour

25g (1oz) oats
50g (2oz) Demerara sugar
25g (1oz) ground almonds
1/2 tsp ground cinnamon
1 tbsp semolina
750g (1lb 10oz) greengages, halved and stoned
2-3 tbsp caster sugar

Preheat the oven to 190°C, 170°C fan oven, gas 5.

Prepare the pastry and rest it for 15 minutes in the fridge. Lightly flour a clean work surface and roll out the pastry to 3mm (1/8 in) thick. Roll out the pastry and use it to line a 25.5cm (10 in) tart tin. Lightly prick the base and rest it in the fridge for 20 minutes or 10 minutes in the freezer.

In a small bowl rub the butter, flour and oats together then add the sugar, ground almonds and cinnamon. Put to one side.

Bake the pastry case blind for 10 minutes, remove the baking beans and bake for a further 2-3 minutes. The pastry should be pale to golden in colour. Sprinkle the base of the case with the semolina and then arrange the greengages, cut side down, evenly over the base of the pastry case and sprinkle with the caster sugar. Spoon the crumble mix evenly over the fruit. Bake the tart for 30-35 minutes until the crumble is golden and the fruit tender.

Serve warm with custard.

APRICOT AND ALMOND TART

This French-style tart looks fantastic with its up-turned apricot halves filled with whole toasted almonds. It is one of several that I made regularly for the dessert trolley of the River Restaurant at The Savoy Hotel. That apricots and almonds have such a great affinity for each other is apparent from the moment a forkful of tart passes your lips!

Makes one 25.5cm (10 in) tart
Serves 8
Sweet Short Pastry 2 (page 32)
Use 1/2 of the quantity of pastry, about
    350g (12oz) to line a 25.5cm (10 in) tart
    tin, wrap and freeze the remaining
    pastry
125g (4 1/2 oz) unsalted butter
125g (4 1/2 oz) light muscovado sugar

2 eggs
150g (5oz) ground almonds
5-6 ripe apricots, halved and stoned or
    2 x 400g tins of apricot halves
10-12 whole blanched almonds, toasted
3 tbsp apricot jam
1 tsp lemon juice
Icing sugar and Vanilla Ice Cream
    (page 39), to serve

If time is short or fresh apricots unavailable you can use tinned apricot halves, simply drain and dry on kitchen paper.

Preheat the oven to 190°C, 170°C fan oven, gas 5.

Prepare the pastry and rest it for 15 minutes in the fridge. Lightly flour a clean work surface and roll out the pastry to 3mm (1/8 in) thick. Line a 25.5cm (10 in) tart tin with the pastry. Lightly prick the base and rest it for 20 minutes in the fridge or 10 minutes in the freezer.

Cream the butter and sugar together, beat in the eggs and then stir in the ground almonds. Spread the almond mix over the pastry case and place the apricots cut side up over the surface of the tart. Bake the tart for 40-45 minutes until the almond sponge is firm to the touch. If the tart starts to colour too much reduce the oven temperature to 180°C, 160°C fan oven, gas 4 and cover the tart with foil.

When the tart is baked, remove from the oven and place one almond in each apricot half.

Heat the apricot jam with the lemon juice and 1 tablespoon of water and boil for 1 minute. Brush the surface of the tart with the hot apricot glaze. Dust with icing sugar and serve with vanilla ice cream.

TIP If using an apricot jam with large pieces of fruit sieve the glaze once it is made, before using it to glaze the tart.

CINNAMON CRUSTED PLUM PIE

Plums were a very popular fruit in the 17th and 18th centuries, in particular the damson and greengage. The sweeter Victoria, Brignole and Santa Rosa plums have now replaced these in popularity. Today plums are the fourth largest tree crop after apples, pears and peaches. In Blaisdon, Gloucestershire they still have a plum day where people can buy and sell produce made from the local, red Blaisdon plum.

Makes one 23cm (9 in) deep pie
Serves 6-8
Rich Short Crust Pastry (page 35)
675g (1^1/2lbs) dark plums, halved and stoned
2 tbsp flour
2 tbsp brown sugar
Grated zest ^{1}/2 orange
4 tbsp granulated sugar
2 tsp ground cinnamon

Preheat the oven to 190°C, 170°C fan oven, gas 5.

Lightly grease a 23cm (9 in) diameter, 4cm (1^1/2 in) deep, pie dish.

Prepare the pastry and rest it for 15 minutes in the fridge. Lightly flour a clean work surface and roll out just over half of the pastry on a lightly floured surface and line the base of the pie dish. Do not trim the excess pastry at this stage. Lightly prick the base of the case. Rest the lined case and remaining pastry in the fridge for 20 minutes.

In a bowl, mix the plums with the flour, brown sugar and orange zest. Put mixture into the bottom of the pie dish. Brush the edges of the pie with a little water.

Mix together the granulated sugar and the cinnamon. Sprinkle a little of the sugar on the work surface and roll out the pastry on the sugar. Sprinkle the pastry with half the remaining cinnamon sugar and lightly roll the sugar into the pastry. Lift the pastry on top of the plums. Seal and crimp the edges, then trim any excess pastry. Brush the pie top with a little water and sprinkle with the remaining cinnamon sugar.

Use any trimmings to decorate the pie top. Bake for 40-45 minutes until the plums are tender and the pie crust is golden in colour. If the pastry starts to colour too much cover with foil and reduce the oven temperature slightly.

Serve warm with Vanilla Ice Cream (page 39).

PEACH MELBA LATTICE PIE

The legendary chef Auguste Escoffier created Melba in 1893 to honour Dame Nellie Melba. The original dessert as it appeared in *Le Repertoire de la Cuisine,* comprised strawberries, nectarines, peaches and pears, on vanilla ice cream, covered with raspberry purée. These days Peach Melba, as it is now known, consists of peaches, raspberries, vanilla ice cream and maybe some raspberry sauce. I took the present day combination and devised this fruit pie.

Makes one 23cm (9 in) deep pie
Serves 6-8
Rich Short Crust Pastry (page 35)
Use 1¹/₂ x pastry recipe
250g (9oz) frozen raspberries
2 tbsp cornflour
2 tbsp raspberry liqueur (optional)
7 large peaches, stoned and thickly sliced
1 tbsp milk
Vanilla Ice Cream (page 39), to serve

Preheat the oven to 190°C, 170°C fan oven, gas 5.

Lightly grease a 23cm (9 in) diameter, 4cm (1¹/₂ in) deep, pie dish. Prepare the pastry and rest it for 15 minutes in the fridge. Lightly flour a clean work surface and roll out just over half of the pastry on a lightly floured surface and line the base of the pie dish. Trim the excess pastry. Lightly prick the base of the case. Rest the lined case and remaining pastry in the fridge for 20 minutes.

Put the raspberries in a pan with 100ml (3¹/₂fl oz) water and heat gently. Strain the fruit and put to one side. Return the liquid to the pan. Mix the cornflour with 3 tablespoons of water and stir into the liquid. Bring to the boil, reduce the heat and stir until the liquid thickens. Add the raspberries and raspberry liqueur, if using, to the pan.

Put the peach slices into the pastry case and spoon over the raspberries. Roll out the remaining pastry and cut strips 2.5cm (1 in) wide. Lay 4 strips of pastry across the tart and 4 at right angles to the first strips, seal them on the edge of the tart tin. Brush the pastry lattice with milk and bake the tart for 35-40 minutes until golden. Serve warm with ice cream.

ORCHARD LATTICE

I used to make fruit lattice bands at The Savoy. It was a popular dessert and I made several each day. They always looked so impressive served on a long silver platter that was polished daily by 'Bluey' in the silver room, so called because of his one blue blind eye.

The lattice was piled high with different orchard fruits including pears; apricots and cherries brushed with apricot glaze and dusted with icing sugar.

Makes one 30.5cm (12 in) x 10cm
    (4 in) slice
Serves 6
Puff Pastry (page 30)
150ml (1/4pt) milk (1 tbsp reserved for the
    egg wash)
3 egg yolks
50g (2oz) caster sugar

2 tbsp cornflour
Small knob unsalted butter
2 tsp vanilla extract
3 poached pears, halved
4 ripe apricots, halved and stoned
4 ripe plums, halved and stoned
3 tbsp apricot jam
1 tsp lemon juice

Preheat the oven to 220°C, 200°C fan oven, gas 7.

Make the puff pastry the day before or have some ready in the freezer to defrost.

Bring the milk (less the reserved 1 tablespoon) to the boil. Mix 2 of the egg yolks with the sugar and then add the cornflour. Whisk a little of the hot milk onto the egg mixture and then return the egg mixture to the milk in the pan. Cook the mixture over a medium heat, stirring all the time, until it has thickened, remove from the heat and pour the pastry cream into a clean bowl. Whisk in the butter and vanilla extract and cover with a piece of buttered greaseproof. Allow to cool.

Roll out half the pastry thinly on a lightly floured work surface, to form a strip 30.5cm (12 in) x 13cm (5 in). Lightly prick the pastry. Lay the pastry on a baking tray and roll out the other half of the pastry to the same size. Use a lattice roller to cut this strip of pastry. Rest both strips of pastry in the fridge for 15 minutes.

Pipe the pastry cream down the centre of the pastry on the tray. Dry the fruits on kitchen paper and lay them tightly together down the centre of the pastry, covering the pastry cream.

Mix together the remaining egg yolk and the reserved milk. Brush the edges of the pastry with the egg wash. Lay the lattice-cut pastry on top of the fruit and open out the pastry so the lattice is visible. Seal the pastry edges close to the fruit.

Brush the pastry with the egg wash and trim away excess pastry, leaving about 1cm (1/2 in) on either side of the fruit. Rest the pastry in the fridge for 10 minutes before baking for 20-25 minutes, until golden. Remove from the oven. Heat the apricot jam with the lemon juice and 1 tablespoon of water in a small pan and boil for 1 minute. Brush the pastry with the apricot glaze. Cut the lattice into slices and serve.

TIP Keep any puff pastry trimmings. Lay them out on top of each other to keep the layers in the same direction.

PRUNE TART

Prunes are the Marmite of fruits; you either love them or hate them. One year, while on holiday in south-west France, I came across plump D'Agen prunes filled with white and dark chocolate ganache, not everyone's cup of tea, but I loved them. Chocolate and prunes are a surprisingly good combination and if like me, you like both ingredients you should try them together, even simply served on top of a bowl of muesli. However if you're not fond of prunes you could make this tart with dried apricots.

Makes one 25.5cm (10 in) tart
Serves 8
Sweet Short Pastry 2 (page 32)
Use 1/2 of the quantity of pastry,
    about 350g (12oz), wrap and freeze
    the remaining pastry

150ml (1/4pt) Armagnac or brandy
250g (9oz) prunes, stoned and halved
4 egg yolks
125g (41/2oz) caster sugar
400ml (14fl oz) double cream
1 vanilla pod, split lengthways

Preheat the oven to 190°C, 170°C fan oven, gas 5.

Gently warm the Armagnac or brandy and add the prunes. Put to one side. Prepare the pastry and rest it for 15 minutes in the fridge. Lightly flour a clean work surface and roll out the pastry to 3mm (1/8 in) thick. Use it to line a 25.5cm (10 in) tart tin. Lightly prick the base and rest it for 20 minutes in the fridge or 10 minutes in the freezer.

Bake the pastry case blind for 10-15 minutes, remove the baking beans and bake for a further 5 minutes. The pastry should be pale to golden in colour. Brush the pastry case with a little egg yolk and bake for a further minute. Remove the pastry case from the oven.

Reduce the oven temperature to 160°C, 140°C fan oven, gas 3.

Lay the prunes, cut side down, in the pastry case. Pour the prune liquid into a small pan and reduce to 1-2 tablespoons. Mix this together with the egg yolks and all but 2 tablespoons of the sugar and whisk in the cream. Sieve the mixture and then scrape the seeds from the vanilla pod into the custard. Pour the custard over the prunes and bake for 20-25 minutes until lightly set.

Allow the tart to stand for 10 minutes. Heat the grill to high, sprinkle the tart with the remaining sugar and grill for 3-4 minutes until the sugar caramelises.

TIP You can rinse and dry the vanilla pod and either re-use it or store it in caster sugar, to impart a wonderful vanilla scent to your sugar. Once you have re-used it you can dry it and grind it (in a food processor) with some granulated sugar to give a powdered vanilla sugar to use to flavour cakes, cream or custard.

CHERRY GOUGÈRE

Classically speaking a gougère is a cheese choux pastry from the Burgundy region of France, so I may well be stretching the boundaries of my creative licence by calling this hot cherry pudding gougère. Generally desserts made from choux pastry are served cold so I thought it would be interesting to create a hot choux pastry dessert. Although I prefer to use fresh cherries, the canned variety are easier to use, as long as they have been pitted! As the pastry itself is fairly bland make sure you flavour the cherries and sweeten them to your taste. Serve with Vanilla Ice Cream (page 39) or lashings of cream.

Makes one 22cm (8 in) round pie
Serves 6
Choux Pastry (page 36)
2 x 400g tins of cherries, stoned
3 tbsp brandy
1 tbsp cornflour
25g (1oz) sugar
1 egg yolk
1 tbsp milk

Set the oven to 220°C, 200°C fan oven, gas 7 and lightly grease a 22cm (8 in) round pie dish.

Pour the cherries and all but 2-3 tablespoons of the juice into a small pan and heat gently. Mix the cornflour and the reserved juice together and stir into the cherries with the brandy and continue to stir until the liquid thickens. Add sugar to taste.

Prepare the choux pastry. Using a 1.5cm (3/4 in) piping tube, pipe 1/2 the pastry onto the base, around the edge of the dish. Spoon the cherries into the middle of the dish and then pipe the remaining choux pastry in lines across the top of the cherries. Mix together the egg yolk and milk and brush the choux pastry with egg wash. Bake for 20-25 minutes until the pastry is risen and golden. Remove from the oven dust with icing sugar and serve.

CHERRY CLAFOUTIS TART

Clafoutis, originally from the Limousin region of France, is also very popular in and around the Central Massif, and it was in the Auvergne region, many years ago, that I first ate and enjoyed this pudding. The original dessert was a simple batter pudding made with a dash of Kirsch, Armagnac or rum. These days it is often made with cherries but you can also use other soft fruits, such as berries and poached apricots.

This recipe is richer than most, almost custard like in texture. Try using fresh cherries when in season as they are so much nicer than canned fruit. I love the contrast in texture between the pastry and the filling but if you want a quick dessert simply bake the batter in an ovenproof dish.

Makes one 23cm (9 in) tart
Serves 6-8
Sweet Short Pastry 1 (page 31)
Use 1/3 of the quantity of pastry about
    250g (9oz), wrap and freeze the
    remaining pastry
150g (5oz) fresh or canned cherries, pitted

3 tbsp brandy
2 eggs
1 egg yolk
75g (3oz) caster sugar
1 tsp vanilla extract
142ml carton double cream
1 tbsp flour

Preheat the oven to 190˚C, 170˚C fan oven, gas 5.

Roll out the pastry to 3mm (1/8 in) thick and use it to line a 23cm (9 in) tart tin. Lightly prick the base and rest the pastry for 20 minutes in the fridge or 10 minutes in the freezer. Drain the cherries and put the syrup into a small pan. Soak the cherries in the brandy.

Bake the pastry blind for 10-15 minutes, remove the baking beans and bake for a further 5 minutes. The pastry should be pale to golden in colour. Brush the pastry case with the egg yolk and bake for a further minute. Remove the pastry case from the oven. Reduce the oven temperature to 180˚C, 160˚C fan oven, gas 4.

Drain the cherries and spoon them into the pastry case.

Mix together the eggs, the sugar and vanilla then whisk in the cream, flour and remaining brandy from the drained cherries. Pour the mixture over the cherries and bake for 20 minutes until lightly set.

Heat the cherry syrup and reduce by two-thirds. When the tart is cooked remove from the oven. Dust with icing sugar, drizzle with warm syrup and serve with Vanilla Ice Cream (page 39).

CHOCOLATE CHERRY TART

It is likely that the Romans were responsible for bringing the cherry to Britain, sometime after 43AD. Wild cherry trees grew along the routes of the old Roman roads, from cherry stones dropped by the Roman legions who ate the fruits bought with them from Italy.

Chocolate and cherry are a popular pairing and both the sweet and sour varieties work well with dark bitter chocolate. Cherries are one of the few fruits that despite worldwide cultivation are not available all year round so if you can't buy fresh cherries, canned ones give a good result.

Makes one 23cm (9 in) tart
Serves 6-8
Sweet Short Pastry 1 (page 31)
Use 1/3 of the quantity of pastry about
    250g (9oz), wrap and freeze the
    remaining pastry
150g (5oz) fresh pitted cherries or canned
    cherries, drained and pitted
50g (2 oz) caster sugar if using fresh
    cherries

2 tbsp brandy
100g (3½oz) dark chocolate
75g (3oz) unsalted butter
1 egg yolk
75g (3oz) caster sugar
2 eggs
100g (3½oz) ground almonds

Preheat the oven to 190°C, 170°C fan oven, gas 5.

Prepare the pastry and rest it for 15 minutes in the fridge. Roll out the pastry to 3mm (1/8 in) thick and use it to line a 23cm (9 in) tart tin. Lightly prick the base and then rest the pastry for 20 minutes in the fridge or 10 minutes in the freezer.

If using fresh cherries remove the stalks and stones and place the cherries in a small pan with 100ml (3½fl oz) water and 50g (2oz) sugar, simmer gently for 3-4 minutes until the cherries are tender. Drain the cherries and put them in a bowl with the brandy.

Melt the chocolate and butter in a heatproof bowl over a pan of simmering water or on a low heat in the microwave.

Bake the pastry blind for 10-15 minutes, remove the baking beans and bake for a further 5 minutes. The pastry should be pale to golden in colour. Brush the pastry case with the egg yolk and bake for a further minute. Remove the pastry case from the oven.

Remove from the oven and reduce the oven temperature to 160°C, 140°C fan oven, gas 3.

Separate the eggs and add 75g (3oz) sugar, egg yolks and ground almonds to the chocolate.

Whisk the egg whites until they are stiff. Fold the whites into the chocolate mix and then stir through the cherries. Spoon the mix into the pastry case. Bake for 20 minutes until just set. Serve warm with ice cream.

DAMSON CHEESE TART

Plum cultivation developed during the 17th and 18th centuries and Britain took a prominent role in developing improved varieties of damsons. They became very popular and were used widely in preserves, including jams and cheeses.

Fruit cheeses, so called because they are made in moulds before being turned out and sliced, are made from fruit pulp cooked with sugar. Quince cheese or *membrillo,* as it is known by the Spanish, is the best known but other fruits such as blackcurrants and apples also make good fruit cheese. It can be served as a sweetmeat but is more often served with cold meats or cheese.

Damson cheese is often served with roast lamb in Cumbria and Damson Day is celebrated each April in Westmorland, Cumbria.

Makes one 23cm (9 in) tart
Serves 4-6
Sweet Short Pastry 3 (page 32)
Use 1/2 of the quantity, wrap and freeze the remaining pastry
900g (2lb) damsons
450g (1lb) sugar

Wash the damsons and put them in a pan. Pour water half way up the fruit, bring to the boil, reduce the heat and simmer the fruit until very soft, about 20 minutes. Then sieve the fruit.

Weigh the fruit pulp and return it to the pan. There should be about 400-450g of damsons. Add the same amount of sugar and boil for 45-50 minutes stirring frequently to prevent the fruit from catching and burning on the base of the pan.

Preheat the oven to 190°C, 170°C fan oven, gas 5.

Roll out the pastry to 3mm (1/8 in) thick and use it to line a 23cm (9 in) pie plate. Lightly prick the base and then rest the pastry for 20 minutes in the fridge or 10 minutes in the freezer.

Spoon the damson cheese into the pastry case and bake for 20 minutes until the pastry is golden. Serve with clotted cream.

TIP Refrigerate any leftover damson cheese and spread thickly on hot buttered toast.

CITRUS
& TROPICAL

It is quite amazing how a little grated zest or squeeze of lemon juice can transform a dish, bringing flavours alive and so when it comes to citrus and tropical desserts, lemon-based are my first choice.

Lemons are originally from South-East Asia where they have been cultivated for over 4,000 years. Spread by the Arabs from the 7th century, when they invaded Spain and North Africa, by the mid 15th century lemons were being cultivated in Italy and other parts of the Mediterranean but it wasn't until several hundred years later, in the 19th century, that the British first began to use them to combat scurvy in the British navy.

Closely related to the lemon, **limes** are smaller and more fragrant. Cultivated in tropical and sub tropical countries, they are used in Caribbean, Mexican and West Indian cuisine. They are thought to have originated in the East Indies and been taken by the Arabs to North Africa at the end of the 10th century and then taken by the Crusaders to the Mediterranean during the 12th and 15th century.

There are hundreds of varieties of citrus fruits grown commercially throughout the world but it is the sweet **orange** that is by far the most important, its primary use, unsurprisingly being for the production of orange juice.

Sweet oranges appear to have originated in Northern India and were spread throughout Asia, North Africa and Europe from the 1st centuries BC to medieval times. The name orange is thought to be a corrupted form of the Spanish word for an orange, *naranja*.

Christopher Columbus is credited with having taken oranges, lemons and limes to the New World and they were taken by the Spanish immigrants to Florida and by the 18th century growth of citrus fruits was widespread throughout the state.

Different varieties of oranges are available at various times, making it a year-round fruit. I always think of November as orange-time, when new season Navels arrive in the shops, followed post-Christmas by bitter Spanish Sevilles, used to make marmalade. The blood orange, so called due to its dark red flesh, is available from December through April.

Pineapples are thought to have originally come from Brazil and Paraguay and been taken to the Caribbean by the Carib Indians who were accomplished maritime travellers. The fruit was named *anana* or 'excellent fruit'. Despite being discovered by Christopher Columbus on his second voyage to the Caribbean, they remained relatively rare until the mid 20th century because the fresh fruit would often spoil on the long journey, but preserved fruits were brought back during the 18th and 19th centuries.

Pineapples are most often used raw in fruit salads, platters and for decorating desserts, although in recent years it has become fashionable to roast them with vanilla and other spices, or use them as the basis of tart Tatin, which works surprisingly well.

Mango, another tropical fruit, is wonderfully luscious and sweet when ripe. Known as the 'apple of the tropics' they are thought to be one of the first fruits to have been cultivated by man. There are a number of varieties but the Indian variety, Alphonso, is the most highly prized for eating. The season for the Alphonso is short and as it is best eaten fresh, I choose varieties such as Kent or Haden for cooking.

Mangoes originated in India where they have been grown for over 4,000 years. The Mogul Emperor Akbar, who ruled Delhi in the late 16th century, is said to have had a mango orchard of 100,000 hectares. The Portuguese took them to Africa in the 16th century, by the end of the century they had reached South Africa, by the 18th century Brazil and in the 19th century they were introduced to Florida. Interestingly more mangoes are eaten worldwide than any other fruit.

Bananas are from Malaysia and were taken from there to India and then by the Arabs to Africa. In the 15th century the Portuguese then took them to the Americas and the Caribbean. When first discovered the fruits were much smaller than those of today, hence the name comes from the Arabic word 'banan' meaning finger. Although usually eaten uncooked there are a large number of both sweet and savoury dishes, where the fruit is cooked, such as bananas flambé, Maryland chicken where the chicken is garnished with fried bananas and bacon and baked bananas. Bananas are not widely used in pâtisserie because they discolour soon after peeling. Although dipping or brushing the bananas with lemon juice can delay this, they do deteriorate quickly.

In spite of this banana sales have topped apple sales, to make bananas the nation's number one fruit, with ninety-five per cent of UK households purchasing them and consuming 140 million bananas each week.

MANGO TARTE TATIN

I'm not sure when I first had the idea to make a mango tarte Tatin but I do know that it really is rather good! You need to make sure you slice the mango fairly thickly, and that the fruit is ripe but not soft, or it will breakdown when it is cooked.

Makes one 20cm (8 in) tart
Serves 4
Puff Pastry (page 30)
Use 1/2 recipe or 250g (9oz) puff pastry trimmings
2 ripe medium mangoes
40g (11/2oz) unsalted butter
100g (31/2oz) caster sugar

Preheat the oven to 220°C, 200°C fan oven, gas 7.

Make the puff pastry the day before or have some ready in the freezer to defrost.

Lightly flour a clean work surface and roll out the pastry to 3mm (1/8 in) thick and cut a round, a little larger than the base of the pan. Prick the pastry all over with a fork and then refrigerate until needed.

Peel and stone the mangoes and cut the flesh into slices 6mm (1/4 in) thick.

Put the butter and sugar into a heavy-based frying pan with ovenproof handle or shallow cast iron casserole. Melt the butter over a medium heat and caramelise the sugar, stirring occasionally. When the butter and sugar have formed a light-coloured caramel remove from the heat. Carefully arrange the mango slices over the base of the pan.

Top with the disc of puff pastry and tuck the edges of the pastry down the side of the pan. Bake the tart for 20-25 minutes until the pastry is golden.

Remove and allow to stand for 5 minutes before turning out onto a plate. Serve immediately with Vanilla Ice Cream (page 39) or crème fraîche.

TIP If you haven't got any trimmings to hand simply roll out some virgin puff pastry to 3mm (1/8 in) thick, fold in half and in half again and refrigerate for 30 minutes then use as trimmings.

BLOOD ORANGE TART

Orange tart was supposed to have been a favourite of Queen Charlotte of Mecklenburg, wife of George III, who reigned from 1760-1820. One of the earliest recorded recipes for orange tart dates back to 1780; it comprised an orange custard filling topped with meringue so it appears to have been an orange meringue pie.

Blood oranges, which are available from December through to April, give this tart a delicate flavour and pretty pink hue. Maltese blood oranges, if you can find them, are particularly well suited to this recipe as their juice is slightly sour. If you want to make the tart when blood oranges aren't in season use whatever oranges are available and reduce the sugar by 50g (2oz) and add the juice of half a lemon.

Makes one 25.5cm (10 in) tart
Serves 8
Sweet Short Pastry 2 (page 32)
Use 1/2 of the quantity of pastry about 350g (12oz), wrap and freeze the remaining pastry

1 egg yolk
3 blood oranges
350g (12oz) caster sugar
6 eggs
284ml carton double cream

Preheat the oven to 190°C, 170°C fan oven, gas 5.

Prepare the pastry and rest it for 15 minutes in the fridge. Lightly flour a clean work surface and roll out the pastry to 3mm (1/8 in) thick. Use it to line a 25.5cm (10 in) tart tin. Lightly prick the base and rest it for 20 minutes in the fridge or 10 minutes in the freezer.

Bake the pastry blind for 10-15 minutes, remove the baking beans and bake for a further 5 minutes. The pastry should be pale to golden in colour. Brush the pastry case with a little of the egg yolk and bake for a further minute. Remove the pastry case from the oven and allow to cool. Reduce the oven temperature to 170°C, 150°C fan oven, gas 3.

Thinly pare the zest from 2 of the 3 blood oranges and remove any pith. Put the pared zest into a small pan and cover with cold water. Bring to the boil, then drain and refresh under cold running water. Repeat this process once more. Julienne (thinly slice) the zest. Return the blanched zest to the pan. Add 150ml (1/4pt) cold water and 175g (6oz) of the sugar, less 2 tablespoons. Heat to dissolve the sugar, then simmer very gently for 20-25 minutes, until the orange is tender. Drain the orange and spread it on a sheet of greaseproof paper sprinkled with 1 tablespoon of caster sugar. Sprinkle with the remaining 1 tablespoon of caster sugar.

Grate the zest of the remaining blood orange and put to one side. Squeeze the juice from the 3 oranges and measure out 150ml (1/4pt) of juice. Lightly whisk together the eggs and remaining 175g (6oz) of the sugar, then stir in the orange juice. Skim any froth and remove. Then stir in the cream, skim any froth and remove.

Sieve the custard and then add the grated zest. Put the custard to one side.

Pour the orange custard mixture into the pastry case and bake the tart for 30-35 minutes until lightly set.

Allow to stand for 30 minutes before slicing. Just before serving cover with the candied orange zest.

LEMON AND ALMOND TART

This moist lemon tart is based on an almond cream or frangipane and the use of light muscovado sugar adds a caramel note to the filling. Although simple, it is the sort of tart you can dress up or down. Serve it on its own as an everyday dessert or jazz it up with a selection of fresh berries and a spoonful of lemon sorbet for a special occasion.

Makes one 25.5cm (10 in) tart
Serves 8
Sweet Short Pastry 1 (page 31)
Use 1/2 of the quantity of pastry about 350g (12oz),
  wrap and freeze the remaining pastry
1 egg yolk
125g (4 1/2oz) unsalted butter
125g (4 1/2oz) light muscovado sugar
2 eggs
125g (4 1/2oz) ground almonds
Grated zest 3 lemons
3 tbsp lemon curd
6 tbsp icing sugar

Preheat the oven to 190°C, 170°C fan oven, gas 5.

Prepare the pastry and rest it for 15 minutes in the fridge. Lightly flour a clean work surface and roll out the pastry to 3mm (1/8 in) thick. Use it to line a 25.5cm (10 in) tart tin, lightly prick the base and rest it for 20 minutes in the fridge or 10 minutes in the freezer.

Cream the butter and sugar together, beat in the eggs and then stir in the ground almonds and all but 1 teaspoon of the lemon zest. Spread the lemon curd over the pastry base and spread the lemon almond mixture on top. Bake the tart for 35-40 minutes until the almond sponge is firm to the touch. If the tart starts to colour too much, cover with foil and reduce the oven temperature to 180°C, 160°C fan oven, gas 4.

Mix the icing sugar with the remaining lemon zest and 1-2 tablespoons of boiling water and brush over the surface of the warm tart. Serve warm.

LIME AND GINGER CREAM PIE

This recipe is very similar to that for Key Lime Pie; it uses condensed milk and relies upon the acidity of the lime juice to set the milk. I first came across it when I was developing dishes for Sainsburys, the supermarket chain. Someone mentioned to me that they used this quick method as the base for a cheesecake. I thought the creamy lime filling would work well teamed with ginger and dark chocolate so I took the idea and came up with this pie.

Makes one 23cm (9 in) tart
Serves 8
Sweet Short Pastry 3 (page 32)
Use 1/2 of the quantity, wrap and freeze the remaining pastry
1 egg yolk
2 x 397g cans condensed milk
Juice and grated zest of 3 limes (125ml/4¹/2fl oz)
50g (2oz) stem ginger
25g (1oz) dark chocolate
142ml carton whipping cream

Preheat the oven to 190°C, 170°C fan oven, gas 5.

Prepare the pastry and rest it for 15 minutes in the fridge. Lightly flour a clean work surface and roll out the pastry to 3mm (1/8 in) thick. Use it to line a 23cm (9 in) tart tin, lightly prick the base and rest it for 20 minutes in the fridge or 10 minutes in the freezer.

Bake the pastry blind for 10-15 minutes, remove the baking beans and bake for a further 5 minutes. The pastry should be pale to golden in colour. Brush the pastry case with a little egg yolk and bake for a further minute. Remove the pastry case from the oven, turn off the oven and allow to cool.

Mix the condensed milk with the lime juice and zest. Finely chop half the stem ginger and stir through the mix. Finely shred the remainder and put to one side. Pour the lime mixture in the pastry case and refrigerate until set, about 2 hours.

Before serving chop the chocolate and place in a heatproof bowl over a pan of simmering water or heat on a low setting in a microwave until melted. Drizzle the melted chocolate over the top of the pie.

Lightly whip the cream and pipe swirls of cream around the edge of the pie. Sprinkle over the remaining ginger.

BANANA CREAM PIE

My mother made this pie when we were children. We lived in Canada for a year in the early 70s and I think the recipe came from a neighbour. It probably originated in the southern states of America, where homemade pies are a way of life.

Makes one 23cm (9 in) deep pie
Serves 6-8
Rich Short Crust Pastry (page 35)
4 egg yolks
500ml (18fl oz) milk
250g (9oz) caster sugar
50g (2oz) cornflour

15g (1/2oz) unsalted butter
1 tsp vanilla extract
2 medium bananas
Pinch of cream of tartar
Pinch of egg white powder

Sugar thermometer

Preheat the oven to 190˚C, 180˚C fan oven, gas 5.

Lightly grease a 23cm (9 in) diameter, 4cm (11/2 in) deep pie dish. Prepare the pastry and rest it for 15 minutes in the fridge. Lightly flour a clean work surface and roll out the pastry to 3mm (1/8 in) thick. Line the pie dish, trim the excess pastry and crimp the edge. Lightly prick the base of the case and rest it for 20 minutes in the fridge or 10 minutes in the freezer.

Blind bake the pastry for 10-15 minutes, remove the baking beans and bake for a further 5 minutes, until pale to golden in colour. Brush the pastry with a little of the egg yolk and bake for a further minute. Remove from the oven and allow to cool.

Bring the milk to the boil in a small pan. Mix together the egg yolks and 75g (3oz) of the sugar and then add the cornflour. Whisk a little of the hot milk onto the egg mixture and then return the mixture to the milk in the pan. Cook it over a medium heat, stirring all the time, for 3-4 minutes until mixture has thickened, remove from heat and pour the pastry cream into a clean bowl. Stir in the butter and vanilla extract and cover with a piece of buttered greaseproof. Allow to cool.

Spoon half the pastry cream into the pastry case and slice the bananas on top. Spoon over the remaining pastry cream.

Place the remaining sugar in a small pan with 100ml (31/2fl oz) water, heat gently to dissolve the sugar, then bring to the boil and boil without stirring until the sugar thermometer reads 121˚C, 250˚F. Whilst the sugar is boiling, whisk the egg whites in a large clean bowl with the cream of tartar and egg white powder, until they form soft peaks. When the sugar reaches 121˚C, 250˚F remove the sugar thermometer and place it into a jug of boiling water, pour the cooked sugar in a slow, steady stream into the whisked egg whites, whilst whisking on a low speed. Once the sugar has been added, increase the speed and continue to whisk for about 5 minutes until the meringue has cooled slightly.

Spoon the meringue over the filling and bake in the oven for 5-10 minutes until the meringue is golden brown.

BANOFFEE PIE

This pie was created in the Hungry Monk Restaurant in Sussex in 1972. The original recipe used short crust pastry, and coffee flavouring in the cream, but I have adapted it to use sweet pastry and prefer to flavour the cream with vanilla.

The original recipe advocated boiling the cans of condensed milk for 5 hours but I've found from experience that 3 hours is long enough. However you need to make sure you keep the cans covered with water, if not there is a risk that they might explode!

Fortunately I never experienced a condensed milk explosion but I'm sure there were a few times when I came close. Although I still use this method, the manufacturers of condensed milk do not recommend it, so I suggest cooking the milk in the microwave as described in the method below.

Makes one 23cm (9 in) pie
Serves 6-8
Sweet Short Pastry 3 (page 32)
Use 1/2 of the quantity, wrap and freeze
   the remaining pastry
1 egg yolk
115g (4oz) unsalted butter

5 tbsp golden syrup
397g can condensed milk
284ml carton whipping cream
1 tsp vanilla extract
1 tbsp caster sugar
2 bananas
2 tbsp grated dark chocolate

Preheat the oven to 190°C, 170°C fan oven, gas 5.

Prepare the pastry and rest it for 15 minutes in the fridge. Lightly flour a clean work surface and roll out the pastry to 3mm (1/8 in) thick. Line a 23cm (9 in) tart tin, lightly prick the base and rest it for 20 minutes in the fridge or 10 minutes in the freezer.

Bake the flan case blind for 10-15 minutes, remove the baking beans and bake for a further 5 minutes. The pastry should be pale to golden in colour. Brush the pastry case with a little of the egg yolk and bake for a further minute. Remove it from the oven and allow to cool. Turn off the oven.

Melt the butter in a large glass bowl in the microwave then add the golden syrup and condensed milk and return the bowl to the microwave. Cook for 8-9 minutes on high until the milk has caramelised. Stir every 1-2 minutes. Pour into the pastry case. Allow to cool slightly then refrigerate until firm.

Just before serving, lightly whip the cream and stir in the vanilla extract and sugar. Slice the bananas on top of the caramel and top with the whipped cream. Decorate with grated chocolate.

PINEAPPLE AND RUM CUSTARD GALETTES

The galette dates from Neolithic times when they took the form of thick cereal pastes, cooked on hot stones. By the Middle Ages they had evolved into hearth cakes, such as the galette of Perugia, made from yeasted pastry with lemon zest, topped with butter and sugar, and much later still became the puff pastry galette of Normandy, filled with jam and fresh cream and the traditional *galette des Rois* (Twelfth Night Cake) made with ground almonds popular all over France. The term galette is also applied to small round biscuits and crêpes in parts of Brittany.

These puff pastry galettes are the simplest of tarts, a round of pastry topped with pastry cream and fruit. This recipe is inspired by flavours of the Caribbean but you can use your choice of seasonal fruit.

Makes 6

Puff Pastry (page 30)
1 egg yolk
1 tbsp milk
50g (2oz) unsalted butter
125g (4½oz) caster sugar
75ml (3fl oz) double cream
200ml (7fl oz) milk

3 egg yolks
2 tbsp cornflour
1 tsp vanilla extract
4 tbsp dark rum
½ medium pineapple, cut into chunks
½ tsp ground allspice
Caramel Sauce (page 38) and Vanilla
    Ice Cream (page 39), to serve

Preheat the oven to 220˚C, 200˚C fan oven, gas 7.

Make the puff pastry the day before or have some ready in the freezer to defrost.

Roll out the pastry 3mm (⅛ in) thick to give a 30.5cm (12 in) square. Cut 4 x 12.5cm (5 in) rounds from the pastry. Re-roll the trimmings and rest them for 10 minutes, before cutting out a further 2 rounds. Lightly prick the rounds in the centre and then rest the pastry in the fridge for about 15 minutes. Mix together 1 egg yolk and 1 tablespoon of milk.

Gently melt half the butter in a heavy-based pan and then sprinkle over 50g (2oz) of the sugar. When the butter starts to brown and the sugar starts to caramelise, stir occasionally a few times to mix. Remove from the heat so the caramel doesn't darken much more; if the caramel becomes too dark it will be bitter. Stir in the cream, it may splutter a bit, and pour the sauce into a clean bowl.

Bring the milk to the boil in a small pan. Mix together the remaining egg yolks and remaining sugar and then add the cornflour. Whisk a little of the hot milk onto the egg mixture and then return the egg mixture to the milk in the pan. Cook the mixture over a medium heat stirring all the time until it has thickened, remove from the heat and pour the pastry cream into a bowl. Whisk in half the rum and butter and cover with a piece of buttered greaseproof paper.

Melt the remaining butter in a frying pan, add the pineapple chunks and cook

gently for 4-5 minutes until the pineapple is tender, then add the allspice and remaining rum and cook for a further minute.

Lay the pastry rounds on a baking tray and brush lightly with the egg wash. Top with spoonfuls of the pastry cream and the pineapple and bake the pastry discs for 12-15 minutes until golden and cooked through. Transfer to serving plates, drizzle with caramel sauce and serve with vanilla ice cream.

TIP Any pastry trimmings can be folded in the direction of the layers, frozen and used at a later date.

TROPICAL MINCEMEAT LATTICE

Mincemeat pies were a medieval tradition of spiced meat, usually mutton, developed after the returning Crusaders brought back spices from the Holy Land. The pies became associated with Christmas and were originally made in an oblong shape to represent Christ's cradle. Over the years the pies grew smaller and changed in shape from oblong to round. The filling also changed until it resembled the filling we now recognise as the English mince pie - a rich confection of dried fruits.

I liked the idea of adding a twist to the traditional version so I added some tropical fruit and coconut and used a lattice top to show off the filling.

Makes one 25.5cm (10 in) tart
Serves 8
Rich Short Crust Pastry (page 35)
Make 1¹/2 x pastry recipe
50g (2oz) desiccated coconut
3 tbsp dark rum

600g (1lb 5oz) mincemeat
1 mango, peeled, stoned and chopped
1/4 medium pineapple, peeled, cored and
    cut into chunks
1 tbsp milk
Icing sugar and cream to serve

Preheat the oven to 190˚C, 170˚C fan oven, gas 5.

Prepare the pastry and rest it for 15 minutes in the fridge. Roll out ³/4 of the pastry on a lightly floured surface and line the base of the 25.5cm (10 in) tart tin. Trim the excess pastry. Lightly prick the base of the case. Rest the lined case and remaining pastry in the fridge for 20 minutes.

Mix together the coconut, rum and mincemeat. Spread the mincemeat into the tart case and top with the mango and pineapple.

Roll out the remaining pastry and cut strips 2.5cm (1 in) wide. Lay 4 strips of pastry across the tart and 4 at right angles to the first strips, seal them on the edge of the tart tin. Brush the pastry lattice with milk and bake the tart for 35-40 minutes until golden. Dust with icing sugar and serve warm with cream or brandy butter.

KEY LIME PIE

The Keys region in Florida is home to both the Key lime, a very sour lime, and a custard-based pie made from the fruit, Key Lime Pie. Before the opening of the railway in 1912, the Keys' isolation meant fresh commodities were hard to come by so Borden's condensed milk, invented by Gail Borden in 1859, was a useful storecupboard ingredient. The basic recipe is simple; essentially it is a lime-flavoured custard pie, deep yellow in colour. The lime juice curdles the milk and egg yolks causing it to set, so there is no need to bake it but because people prefer not to eat raw eggs, the pies are usually baked. The original pie was made with a pastry crust but biscuit crust has now become standard.

Makes one 23cm (9 in) tart
Serves 8
Sweet Short Pastry 3 (page 32)
Use 1/2 of the quantity, wrap and
 freeze the remaining pastry
1 egg yolk
3 eggs

397g can condensed milk
Juice and grated zest of 3 limes
 (125ml/4 1/2fl oz)
175g (6oz) caster sugar
Pinch cream of tartar
Pinch of egg white powder
Sugar thermometer

Preheat the oven to 190°C, 170°C fan oven, gas 5.

Prepare the pastry and rest it for 15 minutes in the fridge. Lightly flour a clean work surface and roll out the pastry to 3mm (1/8 in) thick. Line a 23cm (9 in) tart tin, lightly prick the base and rest it for 20 minutes in the fridge or 10 minutes in the freezer.

Bake the pastry blind for 10-15 minutes, remove the baking beans and bake for a further 5 minutes. The pastry should be pale to golden in colour. Brush the pastry case with a little egg yolk and bake for a further minute. Remove the pastry case from the oven and allow to cool.

Separate the eggs and put the whites to one side. Add the condensed milk, the lime juice and the grated lime zest to the egg yolks and mix well. Pour the mixture into the pastry case and bake for 15 minutes until lightly set.

Place the sugar in a small pan with 100ml (3 1/2fl oz) water, heat gently to dissolve the sugar then bring to the boil and boil without stirring until the sugar thermometer reads 121°C, 250°F. Whilst the sugar is boiling, whisk the egg whites in a large clean bowl with the cream of tartar and egg white powder, until they form soft peaks. When the sugar reaches 121°C, 250°F remove the sugar thermometer and place it in a jug of boiling water. Pour the cooked sugar in a slow steady stream into the whisked egg whites, whilst whisking on a low speed. Once the sugar has been added, increase the speed and continue to whisk for about 5 minutes, until the meringue has cooled slightly.

Spoon the meringue on top of the pie filling and brown the meringue in the oven for about 5 minutes. Allow the pie to cool for 30 minutes then refrigerate for at least 2 hours before serving.

LEMON CHIFFON PIE

Chiffon pies are an American creation that became popular after the first recipe appeared in 1929, when they were also known as Sissy Pies. The chiffon filling is light and fluffy, consisting of whisked egg white incorporated into a light egg custard mix.

Makes one 25.5cm (10 in) tart
Serves 8
Sweet Short Pastry 2 (page 32)
Use 1/2 of the quantity of pastry about 350g (12oz), wrap and freeze the remaining pastry
1 egg yolk
3 leaves (12g powdered) gelatine
500ml (18fl oz) milk (1 tbsp reserved for the egg wash)

6 egg yolks
125g (4¹/₂oz) caster sugar
2 tsp vanilla extract
Grated zest of 4 lemons
400ml (14fl oz) whipping cream
2 egg whites
Pinch of cream of tartar
Pinch of egg white powder
1 tbsp toasted flaked almonds

Preheat the oven to 190°C, 170°C fan oven, gas 5.

Prepare the pastry and rest it for 15 minutes in the fridge. Lightly flour a clean work surface and roll out the pastry to 3mm (1/8 in) thick. Use it to line a 25.5cm (10 in) tart tin. Lightly prick the base and rest it for 20 minutes in the fridge or 10 minutes in the freezer.

Bake the pastry blind for 10-15 minutes, remove the baking beans and bake for a further 5 minutes. The pastry should be pale to golden in colour. Brush the pastry case with a little of the egg yolk and bake for a further minute. Remove it from the oven and allow to cool. Turn off the oven.

Soak the leaf gelatine in cold water or sprinkle the powdered gelatine onto hot water and stir to dissolve.

Bring the milk to the boil in a small pan. Separate the eggs and put the whites to one side. Mix together the egg yolks and sugar. Whisk a little of the hot milk onto the egg mixture and then return the egg mixture to the milk in the pan. Cook the mixture over a gentle heat stirring all the time until the mixture has thickened slightly and coats the back of a wooden spoon. Remove from the heat and pour the custard into a clean mixing bowl.

Remove the soaked gelatine from the bowl and squeeze to remove excess water then stir into the custard, or if using the powdered gelatine, heat it gently to dissolve, then use.

Sieve the custard. Cool the custard over a bowl of iced water until it starts to thicken. Then add the vanilla extract and grated lemon zest and allow to cool.

Lightly whip the cream and fold half into the custard, put the remainder in the fridge. Whisk the whites stiffly with the cream of tartar and egg white powder and

then fold them into the lemon cream. Spoon the lemon cream into the prepared pastry case level with the surface and then refrigerate until set.

Decorate with the remaining whipped cream and sprinkle with toasted flaked almonds.

TIP If you slightly overcook your custard (Sauce Anglaise) it is possible to remedy the situation if you act quickly. Pour the custard into a clean bowl and either add a splash of cold cream or a couple of ice cubes. Fill the sink with cold water and put the bowl into the water. These actions help arrest the cooking process.

If you have overcooked your custard to the point of no return, and it is beginning to resemble scrambled egg, then there is nothing to do save throw it away and start again.

LEMON TART

Tarte au citron, torta di limone or lemon tart – it's great in whichever language you say it and is one of my favourites.

It is an all-time classic which was popularised by Marco Pierre White in the early 90s and now regularly appears on dessert menus everywhere. One of the best ones I ever ate was at Marco's first restaurant Harvey's, in 1990, where the lemon tart was accompanied by a small lemon soufflé, and was divine.

I love lemon tart when it has been freshly baked and is served at room temperature on its own or with a little fresh raspberry sauce. The following recipe is based on one I used to make at The Savoy.

Makes one 25.5cm (10 in) tart
Serves 8
Sweet Short Pastry 2 (page 32)
Use 1/2 of the quantity of pastry about
    350g (12oz), wrap and freeze the
    remaining pastry

1 egg yolk
7 eggs
250g (9oz) caster sugar
5 lemons
284ml carton double cream

Preheat the oven to 190°C, 170°C fan oven, gas 5.

Prepare the pastry and rest it for 15 minutes in the fridge. Lightly flour a clean work surface and roll out the pastry to 3mm (1/8 in) thick. Use it to line a 25.5cm (10 in) tart tin. Lightly prick the base and rest it for 20 minutes in the fridge or 10 minutes in the freezer.

Bake the pastry blind for 10-15 minutes, remove the baking beans and bake for a further 5 minutes. The pastry should be pale to golden in colour. Brush the pastry case with a little of the egg yolk and bake for a further minute. Remove it from the oven and allow to cool. Reduce the oven temperature to 170°C, 150°C fan oven, gas 3.

Lightly whisk together the eggs and the sugar. Grate the zest of 2 lemons and then squeeze the juice of all 5 lemons. Add the lemon juice to the eggs and sugar. Skim and remove any froth. Then stir in the cream, skim and remove any froth. Sieve the custard and then add the grated zest. Pour the lemon custard into the pastry case and bake the tart for 30-35 minutes until lightly set. Allow to stand for 30 minutes before slicing.

LEMON MERINGUE PIE

Lemon-flavoured custards and puddings had been enjoyed since Medieval times but it wasn't until the 17th century that meringue first appeared. At this time it was called 'sugar puff'. Although its invention was credited to a Swiss pastry chef named Gasparani in 1720, as the word had already entered the English language before this date it seems unlikely to be true. The first recognisable recipes for lemon meringue pie appeared from the middle of the 19th century.

The following recipe is adapted from one given to me by my mother and was a favourite of mine when I was a child. This recipe uses Italian meringue which I prefer because it is so much smoother and mallowy than the everyday uncooked meringue, also known as French meringue. However if you don't own a sugar thermometer simply make uncooked meringue.

Makes one 23cm (9 in) deep pie
Serves 6-8
Rich Short Crust Pastry (page 35)
1 egg yolk
Juice of 8 lemons
350g (12oz) caster sugar
3 eggs

50g (2oz) cornflour
25g (1oz) unsalted butter
Grated zest of 4 lemons
3 egg whites
Pinch of cream of tartar
Pinch of egg white powder

Preheat the oven to 190°C, 170°C fan oven, gas 5.

Lightly grease a 23cm (9 in) diameter, 4cm (1½ in) deep pie dish. Prepare the pastry and rest it for 15 minutes in the fridge. Roll out the pastry on a lightly floured surface and line the pie dish, trim the excess pastry and crimp the edge. Lightly prick the base of the case. Rest the pastry for 20 minutes in the fridge or for 10 minutes in the freezer.

Bake the pastry blind for 10-15 minutes, remove the baking beans and bake for a further 5 minutes. The pastry should be pale to golden in colour. Brush the pastry case with a little egg yolk and bake for a further minute. Remove it from the oven and allow to cool. Turn off the oven.

Mix together the lemon juice, 175g (6oz) of the sugar, the eggs, any remaining egg yolk and the cornflour, in a mixing bowl, then pour into a medium pan. Slowly bring to the boil whisking all the time. Cook over a medium heat, stirring constantly, for 2-3 minutes until the mix has thickened. Remove from the heat and stir in the butter and the grated zest. Pour into a clean bowl and cover with a piece of buttered greaseproof paper. Cool to room temperature before spooning into the prepared case. Refrigerate until set, for about 1 hour.

Place the remaining sugar in a small pan with 100ml (3½fl oz) water, heat gently to dissolve the sugar, then bring to the boil and boil without stirring until the sugar thermometer reads 121°C, 250°F. Whilst the sugar is boiling, whisk the egg whites in a large clean bowl with the cream of tartar and egg white powder,

until they form soft peaks. When the sugar reaches 121˚C, 250˚F remove the sugar thermometer and place it in a jug of boiling water, pour the cooked sugar in a slow steady stream into the whisked egg whites, whilst whisking on a low speed. Once the sugar has been added increase the speed and continue to whisk for about 5 minutes until the meringue has cooled slightly.

Preheat the oven to 190˚C, 170˚C fan oven, gas 5.

Spoon the meringue on top of the pie filling and brown the meringue in the oven for about 5 minutes. Serve with cream.

ORANGE AND ELDERFLOWER CHIBOUST TART

The creamy filling used in this tart is named after its creator, a pâtissier named Chiboust. He created Gateau St-Honoré in 1846 in honour of the district in Paris where he worked, and it was filled with the deliciously light cream, now known as *crème Chiboust*. *Crème Chiboust* is based on pastry cream, lightened with meringue and set with a little gelatine. It is not as fashionable as it once was which is a shame because it is a wonderful confection.

Makes one 23cm (9 in) tart
Serves 8
Sweet Short Pastry 2 (page 32)
Use 1/2 of the quantity of pastry about 350g (12oz), wrap and freeze the remaining pastry
1 egg yolk
3 leaves (or 12g powdered) gelatine
300ml (1/2pt) milk (1 tbsp reserved for the egg wash)
4 eggs

175g (6oz) caster sugar
4 tbsp cornflour
2 tbsp elderflower cordial
Grated zest of 3 oranges
3 tbsp apricot jam
1 tsp lemon juice
Pinch of cream of tartar
Pinch of egg white powder
Orange segments and berries to decorate

Sugar thermometer

Preheat the oven to 190˚C, 170˚C fan oven, gas 5.

Prepare the pastry and rest it for 15 minutes in the fridge. Lightly flour a clean work surface and roll out the pastry to 3mm (1/8 in) thick. Use it to line a 25.5cm (10 in) tart tin. Lightly prick the base and rest it for 20 minutes in the fridge or 10 minutes in the freezer.

Bake the pastry blind for 10-15 minutes, remove the baking beans and bake for a further 5 minutes. The pastry should be pale to golden in colour. Brush the pastry case with a little egg yolk and bake for a further minute. Remove the pastry case from the oven and allow to cool. Turn off the oven.

Soften the leaf gelatine in cold water or sprinkle the powdered gelatine onto hot water and stir to dissolve.

Bring the milk to the boil in a small pan. Separate the eggs and put the whites to one side. Mix together the egg yolks and 50g (2oz) sugar and then add the cornflour. Whisk a little of the hot milk onto the egg mixture and then return the egg mixture to the milk in the pan. Cook the mixture over a medium heat, stirring all the time for 3-4 minutes, until the mixture has thickened, remove from the heat and pour the pastry cream into a clean mixing bowl. Remove the soaked gelatine from the bowl and squeeze to remove excess water, then stir into the pastry cream or if using the powdered gelatine, heat gently to dissolve, then use. Add the elderflower cordial and grated orange zest and cover with a piece of buttered greaseproof. Allow to cool.

Place the remaining sugar in a small pan with 75ml (3fl oz) water, heat gently to dissolve the sugar then bring to the boil and boil without stirring until the sugar thermometer reads 121°C, 250°F. Whilst the sugar is boiling whisk 2 of the egg whites in a large clean bowl with the cream of tartar and egg white powder, until they form soft peaks. When the sugar reaches 121°C, 250°F remove the sugar thermometer and place it in a jug of boiling water and pour the sugar in a slow steady stream into the whisked egg whites, whilst whisking on a low speed. Once the sugar has been added increase the speed and continue to whisk for about 5 minutes, until the meringue has cooled slightly.

Fold the meringue through the orange pastry cream and spoon into the pastry case.

Level the surface and refrigerate until set, about 1 hour.

Gently heat the apricot jam with the lemon juice and 2 tablespoons of water, boil for 1 minute. Sieve to remove any apricot pieces. Carefully brush the surface of the tart.

Decorate with the orange segments and berries.

ROASTED VANILLA PINEAPPLE TARTS

This recipe is designed with entertaining in mind. Its component parts can be prepared ahead of time for a quick 'assembly job' finish. The caramel sauce can be made 2-3 days in advance and refrigerated; simply warm gently in a pan over a low heat when needed. The pastry cases can be made the day before and stored in an airtight container and the pineapple can be roasted several hours ahead of time and reheated 5 minutes before serving.

Makes 6 small tarts
Sweet Short Pastry 3 (page 32)
Use 1/2 of the quantity, wrap and freeze
   the remaining pastry
1 egg yolk
1 medium pineapple

100g (3 1/2 oz) unsalted butter
2 vanilla pods
50g (2oz) caster sugar
6 tbsp double cream
1 tbsp rum
500ml tub vanilla ice cream

Preheat the oven to 190°C, 170°C fan oven, gas 5.

Prepare the pastry and rest it for 15 minutes in the fridge. Lightly flour a clean work surface and roll out the pastry to 3mm (1/8 in) thick, and line six 12.5cm (5 in) diameter tartlet tins. Lightly prick the bases and rest them in the fridge for 20 minutes or 10 minutes in the freezer.

Bake the pastry blind for 10-12 minutes, remove the baking beans and bake for a further 2-3 minutes. The pastry should be pale to golden in colour. Brush the pastry cases with a little of the egg yolk and bake for a further minute. Remove from the oven and allow to cool.

Peel, core, quarter and remove the eyes from the pineapple then cut into 1cm (1/2 in) thick slices.

Liberally butter a roasting tray and lay the pineapple in the tray. Cut half the butter into small pieces and dot over the pineapple. Cut the vanilla pods in half lengthways and scrape the seeds out over the pineapple. Roast the pineapple for 20-25 minutes until tender.

While the pineapple is cooking, melt the remaining butter in a pan with the sugar. Cook until the sugar caramelises then whisk in the cream, taking care as the hot sugar will bubble and spit when the cold cream is added. Remove from the heat and add the rum.

When the pineapple is cooked remove from the oven. Spoon the pineapple into each tartlet case top with a scoop of vanilla ice cream and then drizzle with the caramel sauce. Serve immediately.

LEMON AND RASPBERRY TARTS

I based the recipe for these tarts on one for a self-saucing lemon pudding which separates on cooking, to give a light foamy sponge atop a thick lemon curd. I have added a few fresh raspberries to give a contrast to the lemon filling. Try them served with fresh raspberry sauce.

Makes 12 small tarts
Sweet Short Pastry 3 (page 32)
Use 1/2 of the quantity, wrap and freeze
   the remaining pastry
1 egg yolk
50g (2oz) unsalted butter
75g (3oz) caster sugar

Grated zest 2 lemons
2 eggs
25g (1oz) plain flour
200ml (7fl oz) milk
Juice of 1 lemon
125g (41/2oz) raspberries
Fresh raspberry sauce (page 37), to serve

Preheat the oven to 190°C, 170°C fan oven, gas 5.

Prepare the pastry and rest it for 15 minutes in the fridge. Lightly flour a clean work surface and roll out the pastry to 3mm (1/8 in) thick. Line a 12-hole bun tin, lightly prick the bases and chill for 20 minutes in the fridge or 10 minutes in the freezer.

Bake the pastry blind for 6-8 minutes, remove the baking beans and bake for a further 2-3 minutes. The pastry should be pale to golden in colour. Brush the pastry cases with a little egg yolk and bake for a further minute. Remove from the oven and allow to cool.

Cream the butter and sugar and add the lemon zest. Separate the eggs and put the whites to one side. Mix together the egg yolks, flour, milk and lemon juice. The mixture will curdle. Beat the curdled mixture into the creamed mixture. Whisk the egg whites until they are stiff then fold into the lemon mixture and spoon into the tart cases. Drop a few raspberries into the centre of each tart and bake for 10 minutes until lightly set. Serve straight away with fresh raspberry sauce.

BERRIES

When it comes to eating fresh berries, I prefer the sweet, such as raspberry, strawberry, blueberry and blackberry over the sharp tasting ones like blackcurrants and redcurrants but when it comes to cooked fruit, the sharper tasting ones often make the better pie.

There is no doubt that berries can be pricey, less so in the summer months when the home-grown berries hit the shops, so try to make the most of them then. At other times of the year frozen berries including raspberries, blueberries and various mixed berries can often make a useful substitute. Frozen berries won't work on the tops of tarts, you need fresh ones for that, but they are fine mixed with other fruits to make fruit pies or when baked as part of a tart filling. Always choose frozen berries over canned; some canned fruits such as pears and cherries are good but canned berries are invariably too mushy and too sweet.

Berries are the most delicate of fruits and deteriorate very quickly so try to buy fruits on the day you are going to use them or at the very earliest the day before. I always find raspberries squash very easily so I empty them from their plastic containers and remove any damaged fruits before placing them on kitchen paper, I find it helps prevent further deterioration.

Strawberries are the most popular British soft fruit and it seems likely the Romans brought the plants here. There are 2 possible explanations for its name, the first is that the name straw comes from the Anglo Saxon, 'streow' meaning hay and the 'hay berry' was so called because it ripened at the same time as the hay was mown but the second and more plausible reason is that strawberry comes from the word 'strew' and refers to the plant's tendency to stray.

By the 14th century the strawberry was widely cultivated across Europe and by the 15th century Londoners were able to buy strawberries on the city's streets. The popularity of the berry continued with the creation of different varieties. In the 17th century an American variety *F. virginiana,* was introduced to Britain and it became the forerunner to the modern strawberry. In the 19th century Thomas Andrew Knight produced 2 varieties, the Downton and the Elton, and Michael Keens produced the Keens Seedling.

By the beginning of the 20th century huge swathes of farmland in the south of the country had been turned over to growing strawberries. One area was Hamble Valley in the southern corner of Hampshire. During the six-week strawberry season trains would takes thousands of pounds of strawberries on a daily basis, to London, Glasgow, Cardiff and Manchester. By the 1920's the industry there was thriving and continues to be a large strawberry producing area.

Now the growing season has been extended from six weeks to six months by the use of polytunnels and the use of firmer fruits with a longer shelf life, such as Elsanta, have helped reduce losses during transportation. Unfortunately the virtual monoculture of the Elsanta comes at a cost. It not only strips the strawberry season of diversity, it is also not eco-friendly. Methyl bromide, a chemical detrimental to the ozone layer is widely used to sanitise the soil because of this variety's susceptibility to soil-borne disease.

As with strawberries it is thought the Romans also introduced **raspberry** plants to Britain. Greek legend has it that raspberries were white until one day when the nymph Ida wishing to appease the young god Jupiter, scratched her breast on the thorns of the bush, staining the fruits a bright red.

The British **blackcurrant** crop is under serious threat from global warming as the plants require sustained periods of cold to flower and fruit. It isn't just the blackcurrant that is under threat, other soft fruits, as well as apples and pears, are also being affected by increasingly warm weather.

Blackcurrant growers have been told that the currant varieties will not be able to produce fruit within the next 15-20 years because of climate change and as it takes 15-20 years to develop new varieties, the future of the British blackcurrant growers is looking less than bright. Glaxo SmithKline who purchase 90% of the British blackcurrant crop for the production of Ribena are, however, looking to fund research into the development of new varieties.

Redcurrants, **white currants** and **gooseberries** are all related to the blackcurrant. Redcurrants were popular from the 15th century in Northern Europe and were used to make redcurrant juice and preserves. Redcurrants are no longer as popular as they once were but they are still used to produce redcurrant jelly, which is served with roast meat and game. At one time redcurrants and blackcurrants would have been used to make the traditional British summer pudding but with the increasing availability of softer sweeter berries they have fallen out of fashion. The main use for redcurrants tends to be as a decorative fruit on top of mousse-type desserts and gateaux. White currants are rarely seen and like redcurrants are generally just used to decorate desserts.

Early pagan cultures believed fairies sheltered from danger in prickly gooseberry bushes, hence they became known as 'fayberries'. From the 15th century they were cultivated in home gardens and gooseberry juice became popular in the 16th century for medicinal purposes. The name gooseberry seems to have come from its culinary use as it was used to make a sauce served with goose. In the 18th century gooseberries became very popular and clubs or societies were set up, devoted to the growing and showing of gooseberries. After the sugar tax of 1874 was repealed the demand for gooseberries became even greater but sadly since the mid 20th century the gooseberry's popularity has declined, with the introduction of more exotic sweeter fruits.

Blackberries are one of my favourite berries. They have grown wild in Asia, Europe and America for thousands of years and were first cultivated in the 1850's. Their season spans the end of summer and the beginning of autumn when the apple season begins and this probably accounts for their famed partnership with apples.

Interestingly, in World War I, children were given time off school to collect blackberries for the production of blackberry juice for the soldiers because it was thought to be a health-giving berry.

There are several less commonly seen berries, which include the **Tay berry**, **loganberry** and **boysenberry**. They tend not to be grown on the same commercial scale as other berries but are sometimes found in farm shops and farmers' markets.

The Tay berry, named after the river Tay in Scotland, was introduced by the Scottish Horticultural Research Institute and developed from a raspberry-blackberry cross. The loganberry, developed in California, was also produced from crossing the blackberry and raspberry, as was the boysenberry. However, it is the two native berries, the blueberry and the cranberry that are of most commercial value to North America.

Native American Indians had been gathering **blueberries** for years before the first settlers arrived, they called the berry the 'star berry' on account of its five-pointed star-shaped calyx. When the English settlers arrived in the 17th century they struggled to feed their families until the Native American Indians showed them how to plant corn and gather and dry blueberries, for storage through the winter months.

In recent years blueberries have become popular in Britain, not simply because they are a fabulous tasting little berry, but also because they are known as a health-giving superfood, rich in antioxidants.

The **cranberry** was also widely used by the Native American Indians before the pilgrims arrived. It was the pilgrims who named it 'craneberry' because its small pink blossom hung downward resembling the neck, head and beak of the crane. Cranberries are most notably used to produce cranberry juice but they are also sold in fresh, frozen and dried form and used in the manufacture of baked goods and confectionery.

CRANBERRY APPLE AND ORANGE PIE

This fruity pie is really flavourful. Perhaps not the most popular of berries, cranberries are however a versatile fruit. They combine particularly well with apple and orange and can be used in both sweet and savoury dishes. Fresh cranberries are also known affectionately as 'bog berries', in the regions where they are grown, on America's East Coast, as although some are now dry-harvested, many are still wet-harvested from the marshy bogs. They are available fresh in supermarkets from November through December, although frozen and dried cranberries are available year round.

Makes one 23cm (9 in) deep pie
Serves 6-8
Rich Short Crust Pastry (page 35)
200g (7oz) cranberries, fresh or frozen
75g (3oz) light muscovado sugar
6 large dessert apples
25g (1oz) unsalted butter
1/4 tsp ground cinnamon
Grated zest and juice 1 orange
1 tbsp milk
1 tbsp granulated sugar

Preheat the oven to 190°C, 170°C fan oven, gas 5.

Prepare the pastry and rest it for 15 minutes in the fridge.

Put the cranberries in a pan with 100ml (3 1/2fl oz) water, add the sugar and simmer for 15-20 minutes until tender.

Peel, core and slice the apples 6mm (1/4 in) thick. Melt the butter in a medium pan and add the apples. Cook the apples gently for 4-5 minutes, stirring occasionally. Add the cinnamon, orange zest and juice and then stir in the cooked cranberries. Spoon the mix onto a plate and allow to cool.

Lightly grease a 23cm (9 in) diameter 4cm (1 1/2 in) deep pie dish. Roll out just over half of the pastry on a lightly floured surface and line the base of the pie dish. Lightly prick the base. Do not trim the excess pastry. Rest the pastry in the fridge whilst the fruit is cooling. Spoon the cooled mix into the lined pie dish.

Roll out the remaining pastry and dampen the pie edge with water. Using the rolling pin, lift the rolled pastry on top of the apples and seal the edges. Make a small slit in the centre of the pie. Brush with milk and sprinkle with granulated sugar.

Bake the pie for 40-45 minutes until golden brown, if the pastry starts to colour too much cover with foil. Serve hot or cold.

BLUEBERRY AND LEMON RICOTTA TART

This recipe is based on *Crostata di Ricotta*, the classic, ricotta tart, popular throughout Italy. Ricotta is a versatile cheese and in this recipe it gives a gloriously light filling. I thought the combination of light, creamy lemon-flavoured ricotta and soft plump blueberries would work really well together, and I was right. The tart looks and tastes gorgeous. It's best served at room temperature within a few hours of baking.

Makes one 23cm (9 in) tart
Serves 6-8
Sweet Short Pastry 2 (page 32)
   Use 1/3 of the quantity of pastry, about 250g (9oz), wrap and freeze the remaining pastry
500g (1lb 2oz) ricotta cheese

200g (7oz) caster sugar
1 egg
2 egg yolks
Grated zest 1 unwaxed lemon
125g (4¹/₂oz) fresh blueberries
Pared zest 1 unwaxed lemon

Preheat the oven to 190°C, 170°C fan oven, gas 5.

Prepare the pastry and rest it for 15 minutes in the fridge. Roll out the pastry on a lightly floured work surface to 3mm (1/8 in) thick. Use it to line a 23cm (9 in) tart tin. Lightly prick the base and then rest the pastry for 20 minutes in the fridge or 10 minutes in the freezer.

Bake the pastry blind for 10-15 minutes, remove the baking beans and bake for a further 5 minutes. The pastry should be pale to golden in colour. Brush the pastry case with a little of the egg yolk and bake for a further minute. Remove the pastry case from the oven. Reduce the oven temperature to 180°C, 160°C fan oven, gas 4.

Mix together the ricotta, half the caster sugar, the egg, egg yolks and the grated lemon zest. Fold through 2/3 of the blueberries. Spoon the mixture into the pastry case, level the surface with the back of the spoon and sprinkle over the remaining blueberries. Bake the tart for 20 minutes or until lightly set.

Put the pared zest into a small pan and cover with cold water. Bring to the boil, then drain and refresh under cold running water. Repeat this process. Julienne (thinly slice) the blanched zest and return it to the pan. Add 100ml (3¹/₂fl oz) water and the remaining sugar less 2 tablespoons. Cook the zest until the sugar syrup becomes thick and syrupy. Drain the lemon zest and spread on a sheet of greaseproof paper sprinkled with 1 tablespoon of caster sugar. Sprinkle the lemon zest with the remaining caster sugar.

Remove the tart from the oven and allow to cool for at least 30 minutes before serving. Decorate with the candied lemon zest and serve. Refrigerate any leftover tart.

STRAWBERRY AND RHUBARB PIE

Rhubarb's origin can be traced back almost 5,000 years to China, where it was, and still is, used for medicinal purposes. It wasn't until the 17th century that it arrived in Europe and it wasn't widely used as a food until the mid 18th century.

There are 2 types of rhubarb: forced and outdoor rhubarb. Forced is grown in dark forcing sheds and is vibrant pink in colour, with thin, fine textured stalks and a sweeter more delicate flavour than outdoor rhubarb, which is coarser with stringy dark red and green stalks, and a much sharper flavour.

In the 1880s forced rhubarb started to be grown in Yorkshire, as the cold weather helped the plant to start growing earlier than in warmer areas of the country. The ready supply of coal from local pits was available to heat the forcing sheds and the soil suited the plant. The Wakefield triangle, between Leeds and Bradford, became home to the forced rhubarb industry. Unfortunately due to its intensive labour costs and increased competition with more exotic fruits, the popularity of rhubarb has waned, and the industry is much smaller than in previous years.

In America rhubarb is known as the 'Pie plant' simply because that's about all people used it for in Colonial days. These days rhubarb is used in both sweet and savoury dishes. It combines well with many flavours such as orange, ginger and apple but strawberries are probably rhubarb's most favoured companion. Strawberries and rhubarb go together like bacon and eggs! I'm not sure where the combination originated but strawberry and rhubarb pie is very popular in America, so it seems likely that it originated on the other side of the Atlantic.

Makes one 23cm (9 in) deep pie
Serves 6-8
Rich Short Crust Pastry (page 35)
450g (1lb) strawberries
450g (1lb) rhubarb

200g (7oz) caster sugar
3 tbsp cornflour
1/2 tsp ground cinnamon
Grated zest 1/2 lemon
2 tbsp granulated sugar

Preheat the oven to 190˚C, 170˚C fan oven, gas 5.

Prepare the pastry and rest it for 15 minutes in the fridge. Lightly grease a 23cm (9 in) diameter, 4cm (1 1/2 in) deep pie dish. Roll out just over half of the pastry on a lightly floured surface and use it to line the base of the pie dish. Do not trim the excess pastry at this stage. Lightly prick the base of the case. Rest the lined case and remaining pastry in the fridge for 20 minutes.

Wash, hull and halve the strawberries and put to one side.

Wash and chop the rhubarb into 2.5cm (1 in) pieces, put them into a medium pan with 100ml (3 1/2fl oz) water and 150g (5oz) caster sugar. Cover with a piece of buttered greaseproof paper or a pan lid and simmer gently for 4-5 minutes until the fruit is just tender. Mix the cornflour with 4 tablespoons of water and stir into the rhubarb, cook until the liquid thickens. Remove from the heat and stir through the strawberries. Add the cinnamon, lemon zest and remaining caster sugar to taste. Spoon the fruit into the pie dish.

Roll out the remaining pastry and dampen the pie edge with water. Using the rolling pin, lift the rolled pastry on top of the fruit and seal the edges. Make a small slit in the centre of the pie. Brush the pastry with a little water and sprinkle liberally with the granulated sugar. Bake the pie for 35-40 minutes until golden brown, if the pastry starts to colour too much, cover with foil. Serve warm with clotted cream.

TIP Decorate the pie with any leftover trimmings.

BLACKCURRANT AND APPLE PIE

Blackcurrants remain one of the few really tart fruits. These days so many fruits are grown exclusively as dessert fruits and are developed to be sweeter tasting. This is fine when you want to munch on an apple but not so good when it comes to cooking with them.

This fruit pie will awaken your taste buds to the joys of homemade fruit pies, made with Bramleys, a fine flavoured apple, and blackcurrants to give a really sharp tasting pie, packed with fruit flavour.

Makes one 19cm (7$^{1}/_{2}$ in) wide x 26cm (10$^{1}/_{4}$ in) long pie
Serves 4-6
Rich Short Crust Pastry (page 35)
700g (1lb 9oz) Bramley apples

50g (2oz) unsalted butter
200g (7oz) blackcurrants, washed, topped and tailed
50g (2oz) caster sugar
1 tbsp granulated sugar

Preheat the oven to 190°C, 170°C fan oven, gas 5.

Prepare the pastry and rest it for 15 minutes in the fridge.

Peel, core and thickly slice the apples. If cut too thinly they will break down too much when cooked. Heat the butter gently in a frying pan and add the sliced apples. Cook gently for 3-4 minutes then add the blackcurrants and caster sugar and cook for a further minute. Spoon the fruit into a 19cm (7$^{1}/_{2}$ in) wide x 26cm (10$^{1}/_{4}$ in) long pie dish.

Roll out the pastry a little larger than the pie dish. Brush the lip of the dish with water. Cut a strip from the edge of the rolled pastry to fit the width of the pie lip and press lightly onto the lip, dampen the pastry on the lip. Place the remaining pastry on top of the filling and seal the edges. Make a small slit in the centre of the pie. Brush with water and sprinkle with the granulated sugar. Bake for 25-30 minutes until the pastry is golden. Serve warm with cream.

BLACKBERRY AND APPLE PIE

The popularity of this autumnal fruit pie may have waned over the years but it really is a fantastic pie. I love the way the blackberries stain the apples to give a vibrantly marbled fruit pie.

Makes one 23cm (9 in) deep pie
Serves 6-8
Rich Short Crust Pastry (page 35)
Make 2 x pastry recipe
700g (1lb 9oz) Bramley apples
250g (9oz) blackberries
25g (1oz) caster sugar
1/4 tsp ground cinnamon
1 tbsp milk
1 tbsp granulated sugar

Preheat the oven to 190°C, 170°C fan oven, gas 5.

Lightly grease a 23cm (9 in) diameter, 4cm (1½ in) deep pie dish. Prepare the pastry and rest it for 15 minutes in the fridge. Roll out just over half of the pastry on a lightly floured surface and line the base of the pie dish. Lightly prick the base of the case. Do not trim the excess pastry. Rest it in the fridge whilst preparing the blackberry and apple filling.

Peel, core and slice the apples 6mm (1/4 in) thick and put into a mixing bowl. Add the blackberries and cinnamon and mix together. Spoon the mix into the lined pie dish.

Roll out the remaining pastry and dampen the pie edge with water. Lift the rolled pastry on top of the apples and seal the edges. Make a small slit in the centre of the pie. Brush with milk and sprinkle with granulated sugar. Bake the pie for 35-40 minutes until golden brown, if the pastry starts to colour too much cover with foil. Serve hot or cold.

RASPBERRY AND BASIL BRÛLÉE TARTS

I first tasted basil crème brûlée many years ago while holidaying in the Auvergne region of France. At the time is was an unusual dessert and one I had not come across before. It gave me the idea for these tarts. It does sound a little odd but the sweet basil flavour gives the custard a delicate, perfumed note that contrasts well with the sweet raspberries.

Other herbal infusions that also work well in custard-based tarts or crème brûlée include lemon grass, thyme and bay leaf.

Makes 6 small tarts
Sweet Short Pastry 3 (page 32)
Use 1/2 of the quantity, wrap and freeze the remaining pastry
284ml carton double cream
Small bunch fresh basil
4 egg yolks
75g (3oz) caster sugar
125g (4¹/₂oz) raspberries

Preheat the oven to 190˚C, 170˚C fan oven, gas 5.

Prepare the pastry and rest it for 15 minutes in the fridge. Roll out the pastry 3mm (¹/₈ in) thick and line six 12.5cm (5 in) diameter tartlet cases, lightly prick the bases and rest them in the fridge for 20 minutes or 10 minutes in the freezer.

Bake the pastry blind for 10-12 minutes, remove the baking beans and bake for a further 2-3 minutes. The pastry should be pale to golden in colour. Brush the pastry cases with a little of the egg yolk and bake for a further minute. Remove from the oven and allow to cool.

Reduce the oven temperature to 160˚C, 140˚C fan oven, gas 4.

Bring the cream to the boil in a small pan with the bunch of basil, remove from the heat and allow the basil to infuse the cream for a few minutes, before removing the basil leaves.

Mix together the egg yolks and all but 2 tablespoons of the sugar. Whisk in the cream and sieve the mixture. Pour the custard into the tartlet cases and drop the raspberries into the cases. Bake for 15-20 minutes until lightly set.

Sprinkle the tarts with the remaining sugar and either heat the grill to high and grill for 3-4 minutes until the sugar caramelises, taking care to cover the tart edges with foil or use a chef's blowtorch, to caramelise the sugar.

TIP These tarts are best served at room temperature and eaten within a few hours of making.

RASPBERRY AND LAVENDER TART

Roses, violets and other flowers were popular flavourings for sugar syrups in England in the 17th and 18th centuries and although they are no longer as fashionable as they once were, occasionally you will find desserts and confectionery flavoured with flowers.

I first came across lavender-flavoured desserts many years ago whilst holidaying in Provence. Initially I didn't enjoy eating what I thought tasted like perfumed cakes but lavender is now a firm favourite of mine. I particularly like to use it to flavour custards and ice creams and this recipe is one of my preferred lavender recipes.

Makes one 25.5cm (10 in) tart
Serves 8
Sweet Short Pastry 2 (page 32)
   Use 1/2 of the quantity of pastry, about
   350g (12oz), wrap and freeze the
   remaining pastry
750ml (11/4pt) milk
2 tsp lavender flowers

6 egg yolks
100g (31/2oz) caster sugar
50g (2oz) cornflour
750ml (11/4pt) milk
142ml carton double cream
450g (1lb) fresh raspberries
Fresh lavender and icing sugar to decorate

Preheat the oven to 190°C, 170°C fan oven, gas 5.

Prepare the pastry and rest it for 15 minutes in the fridge. Roll out the pastry 3mm (1/8 in) thick and line a 25.5cm (10 in) tart tin. Lightly prick the base and rest it for 20 minutes in the fridge or 10 minutes in the freezer.

Bring the milk and lavender to the boil in a heavy-based pan. Mix together 5 of the 6 egg yolks, and the sugar, and then add the cornflour. Sieve the milk onto the egg mixture to remove the lavender and then return the mixture to the pan. Cook the pastry cream mixture over a medium heat, whisking all the time for 3-4 minutes until the pastry cream is thick. Pour into a clean bowl and cover with a small piece of buttered greaseproof paper. Allow to cool and then refrigerate.

Bake the pastry blind for 10-15 minutes, remove the baking beans and bake for a further 4-5 minutes. The pastry should be pale to golden in colour. Brush the pastry cases with a little egg yolk and bake for a further minute. Remove from the oven and allow to cool.

Lightly whip the cream and fold it into the cold pastry cream. Spoon the mixture into the cooled pastry case and level the surface. Arrange the raspberries on top of the tart and decorate with fresh lavender and icing sugar.

TIP If you like you can use wafer thin layers of sponge on top of the pastry cream filling, as in the Strawberry Tart recipe (page 142), and drizzle this with eau de framboise (raspberry liqueur).

BERRY MERINGUE BARQUETTES

In 1840 the Duchess of Bedford decided that eight hours was too long to have to wait between meals, and asked her butler to bring her tea, bread and butter. She then began inviting her friends to join her and before long a social institution was born.

From the mid 1800s tea-rooms began to appear, and in 1894 the first Lyons teashop opened on London's Piccadilly, selling tea and cakes. These days one of the best places to take afternoon tea is in a high-end hotel. For a fixed price you can enjoy a selection of sandwiches, scones and clotted cream, a selection of pâtisserie and as much tea as you can drink.

I used to enjoy making pastries for afternoon tea; strawberry tartlets, chocolate éclairs, fresh fruit tartlets and gateau Opera were just some of my favourites. This is another great afternoon-tea pastry, adapted from a recipe given to me by Yolande Stanley, formerly pastry chef at the Ritz, now senior pastry-chef lecturer at Thames Valley University.

Makes 6 barquettes
Sweet Short Pastry 3 (page 32)
Use 1/2 of the quantity, wrap and freeze
    the remaining pastry
1 egg yolk
4 tbsp raspberry conserve
150g (5oz) caster sugar

3 egg whites
Pinch of cream of tartar
Pinch of egg white powder
200g (7oz) defrosted frozen raspberries
Fresh berries to serve

Sugar thermometer

Preheat the oven to 190˚C, 170˚C fan oven, gas 5.

Prepare the pastry and rest it for 15 minutes in the fridge. Roll out the pastry thinly and line six, 12.5cm (5 in) long and 2.5cm (1 in) wide, barquette cases. Alternatively if you don't have any barquette cases just use six, 12.5cm (5 in) diameter tartlet tins. Lightly prick the bases and rest them in the fridge for 20 minutes or 10 minutes in the freezer.

Bake the pastry blind for 10-12 minutes, remove the baking beans and bake for a further 2-3 minutes. The pastry should be pale to golden in colour. Brush the pastry cases with a little of the egg yolk and bake for a further minute. Remove from the oven and allow to cool.

Spoon a little raspberry conserve into the base of each barquette.

Place the sugar in a small pan with 50ml (2fl oz) water, heat gently to dissolve the sugar, then bring to the boil. Boil, without stirring, until the sugar thermometer reads 121˚C, 250˚F. Whilst the sugar is boiling whisk the egg whites in a large clean bowl with the cream of tartar and egg white powder, until they form soft peaks. When the temperature reaches 121˚C, 250˚F remove the sugar thermometer and place it in a jug of boiling water. Pour the sugar in a slow steady stream into the whisked egg whites whilst whisking on a low speed. Once the sugar has been added increase the speed and continue to whisk for about 5 minutes until the meringue has cooled slightly.

Fold the raspberries and the juice into the cooled meringue and pipe into the barquettes using a 1.5cm (3/4 in) plain nozzle. Bake the meringue for 2-3 minutes until the meringue turns a pale golden colour. Serve the barquettes with fresh berries on the side.

RASPBERRY AND PISTACHIO TARTS

These simple nutty tartlets are an adaptation of the classic French mirliton tart of Normandy. Mirliton tarts are small puff pastry-based almond tarts.

Makes 12 tarts
500g (1lb 2oz) puff pastry trimmings (see Tip page 27) or virgin Puff Pastry (page 30)
125g (4¹/₂oz) unsalted butter
125g (4¹/₂oz) caster sugar
2 eggs
50g (2oz) ground almonds
75g (3oz) ground pistachios
5 tbsp raspberry conserve
2 tbsp roughly chopped pistachios

Make the puff pastry the day before or have some trimmings ready in the freezer to defrost. If you haven't got any trimmings to hand simply roll out some virgin puff pastry to 3mm (1/8 in) thick, fold in half and in half again and refrigerate for 30 minutes then use as trimmings.

Preheat the oven to 220˚C, 200˚C fan oven, gas 7.

Roll out the pastry 2mm (less than 1/8 in) thick and cut out twelve, 10cm (4 in) rounds. Grease and line a 12-hole bun tin with the pastry rounds. Lightly prick the bases and rest them for 20 minutes in the fridge or 10 minutes in the freezer.

Cream the butter and sugar together, beat in the eggs and then stir in the ground almonds and ground pistachios. Spoon the raspberry conserve equally into the bottom of the pastry cases and then spoon the pistachio mix on top. Sprinkle with the chopped pistachios and bake for 15-20 minutes until the pastry is golden and the filling is firm to the touch. Dust with icing sugar and serve warm.

STRAWBERRY AND GRAND MARNIER TART

Although wild strawberries had been cultivated throughout Europe for many centuries it wasn't until the 17th century that an American variety, *F. Virginiana*, was introduced to Britain and helped pave the way for the modern strawberry. Developments continued slowly until the 19th century when two British men, Thomas Andrew Knight and Michael Keens developed the Downton and Elton and Keens seedling respectively from which most modern varieties are derived.

Although the English strawberry season has been extended by the use of polytunnels, strawberries are imported during the months when British strawberries are unavailable or when supply is insufficient to meet demand. Britain imports from Spain, Italy, France, Holland, Egypt, Israel and America to sustain the year-round demand for these fragrant fruits. Although I eat strawberries throughout the year I much prefer the more delicate, flavoursome English strawberries, available in the summer months and recommend that you make this tart using English strawberries for the best result.

Makes one 25.5cm (10 in) deep tart
Serves 8-10
Sweet Short Pastry 2 (page 32)
    Use 1/2 of the quantity of pastry,
    about 350g (12oz), wrap and freeze
    the remaining pastry
6 egg yolks
100g (3 1/2oz) caster sugar
50g (2 oz) cornflour
750ml (1 1/4pt) milk

1 vanilla pod, split lengthways
15g (1/2oz) unsalted butter
100g (3 1/2oz) white chocolate
142ml carton double cream
50g (2oz) vanilla sponge cake cut into
    wafer thin slices
4-5 tbsp Grand Marnier
900g (2lb) strawberries
150g (5oz) strawberry conserve

Preheat the oven to 190˚C, 170˚C fan oven, gas 5.

Prepare the pastry and rest it for 15 minutes in the fridge. Roll out the pastry on a lightly floured work surface to 3mm (1/8 in) thick and line a 25.5cm (10 in) tart case. Prick the base lightly with a fork and rest the pastry for 20 minutes in the fridge or 10 minutes in the freezer.

Mix together 5 of the 6 egg yolks, and the sugar, and then add the cornflour.

Bring the milk and vanilla pod to the boil in a heavy-based pan. Sieve the milk onto the egg mixture to remove the vanilla pod and then return the milk to the pan. Scrape the seeds from the pod into the milk.

Cook the pastry cream mixture over a medium heat, whisking all the time, for 3-4 minutes, until it is thick. Pour into a clean bowl and whisk in the butter. Cover with a small piece of buttered greaseproof paper. Allow to cool and then refrigerate.

Bake the pastry blind for 10-15 minutes, remove the baking beans and bake for a further 5 minutes. The pastry should be pale to golden in colour. Brush the pastry case with the remaining egg yolk and bake for a further minute. Remove the pastry case from the oven and allow to cool.

Chop the chocolate and place in a heatproof bowl over a pan of simmering water or heat in the microwave, on a low setting, until melted. Brush the melted chocolate over the base of the cooled pastry case and refrigerate for 5 minutes until the chocolate is set.

Fold the lightly whipped cream into the pastry cream to make crème diplomat and then spoon the mixture into the pastry case and level the surface. Lay the thin layers of sponge cake over the top and brush with the Grand Marnier. Hull the strawberries, place one large strawberry cut surface down onto the middle of the tart and cut the remaining strawberries in half.

Arrange the strawberry halves over the surface of the tart, starting in the centre and working out towards the edges. Gently heat the strawberry conserve and any remaining Grand Marnier in a small pan. Sieve the conserve and then brush the strawberries with the hot conserve. Dust the pastry edge of the tart with icing sugar and serve.

TIP The use of the sponge layer beneath the strawberries serves 2 purposes. It soaks up the Grand Marnier and it also provides a stable surface for the strawberries.

WILD STRAWBERRY AND WHITE CHOCOLATE TARTS

'Doubtless God could have made a better berry, but doubtless God never did' (Dr William Butler 17th century English writer, in reference to the strawberry.)

Wild strawberries or *fraise de bois* as they are usually known are wonderfully fragrant tiny fruits with a delicious flavour. They are not readily available but if you ever come across them be sure to try them.

Makes 6 small tarts
Sweet Short Pastry 3 (page 32)
Use 1/2 of the quantity, wrap and freeze the remaining pastry
150g (5oz) white chocolate
250g (9oz) mascarpone
1 vanilla pod, split lengthways and seeds scraped out
142ml carton whipping cream
200g (7oz) wild strawberries
3 tbsp redcurrant jelly
Mint leaves to decorate

Preheat the oven to 190˚C, 170˚C fan oven, gas 5.

Prepare the pastry and rest it for 15 minutes in the fridge. Roll out the pastry 3mm (1/8 in) thick and line six, 12.5cm (5 in) diameter, 2.5cm (1 in) deep tartlet tins. Lightly dock the bases and rest them for 20 minutes in the fridge or 10 minutes in the freezer.

Bake the pastry blind for 10-12 minutes, remove the baking beans and bake for a further 2-3 minutes. The pastry should be pale to golden in colour. Brush the pastry cases with a little egg yolk and bake for a further minute. Remove from the oven and allow to cool.

Chop the chocolate and place in a heatproof bowl over a pan of simmering water or heat in the microwave, on a low setting, until melted.

Lightly whip the cream and fold through the mascarpone and chocolate mixture.

Beat the mascarpone in a bowl to soften it and add the white chocolate and scraped vanilla seeds. Lightly whip the cream and fold through the mascarpone and chocolate mixture. Spoon the chocolate cream into the cooled cases and top with the wild strawberries. Melt the redcurrant jelly and drizzle over the tarts. Decorate with mint leaves and serve immediately.

RASPBERRY AND APPLE SOUFFLÉ TART

As the name suggests this tart has a light, airy filling that is made in the same way as a soufflé, by the addition of whisked egg whites to pastry cream. Fruit is then added to the mixture before the tart is baked. Apples and raspberries work well together but you could also make it with apples and blackberries.

This is one of those tarts that actually tastes just as good whether served chilled or at room temperature, so if there is any left you can enjoy it the next day, straight from the fridge!

Makes one 25.5cm (10 in) tart
Serves 8
Sweet Short Pastry 2 (page 32)
Use 1/2 of the quantity of pastry about
    350g (12oz), wrap and freeze the
    remaining pastry
300ml (1/2pt) milk (1 tbsp reserved for the
    egg wash)
3 eggs

75g (3oz) caster sugar
4 tbsp cornflour
2 tsp vanilla extract
1 egg yolk
200g (7oz) Bramley apples
125g (41/2oz) raspberries
Pinch cream of tartar
Pinch egg white powder

Preheat the oven to 190˚C, 170˚C fan oven, gas 5.

Prepare the pastry and rest it for 15 minutes in the fridge. Roll out the pastry 3mm (1/8 in) thick and line a 25.5cm (10 in) tart tin. Lightly prick the base and rest it in the fridge for 20 minutes or 10 minutes in the freezer.

Bring the milk to the boil in a small pan. Separate the eggs and put the whites to one side. Mix together 3 of the 4 egg yolks, and the sugar, and then add the cornflour. Whisk a little of the hot milk onto the egg mixture and then return the egg mixture to the milk in the pan. Cook the mixture over a medium heat, stirring all the time, for 3-4 minutes until the mixture has thickened, remove from the heat and pour the pastry cream into a clean bowl. Stir in the vanilla extract and cover with a piece of buttered greaseproof paper. Put to one side.

Bake the pastry blind for 10-15 minutes, remove the baking beans and bake for a further 4-5 minutes. The pastry should be pale to golden in colour. Brush the pastry cases with a little egg yolk and bake for a further minute.

Peel, core and chop the apples into 1cm (1/2 in) pieces.

Melt the butter in a pan and add the apples and cook gently for 4-5 minutes. Remove from the heat, stir through the raspberries and put to one side.

Whisk the egg whites stiffly with the cream of tartar and egg white powder and fold into the vanilla custard. Then fold in the fruit. Spoon the mixture into the pastry case and return to the oven, bake for 20-25 minutes until lightly browned on top. Allow to stand for 15 minutes before slicing.

RIBISELKUCHEN

The literal translation for this fabulous Austrian tart would be redcurrant cake but it is actually a redcurrant meringue pie. Redcurrants have been popular in Northern Europe since the 15th century and were domesticated in the 16th century. The creation of this tart probably dates from sometime in the early 19th century when the use of meringue became more widespread, although the exact date is unknown.

Makes one 25.5cm (10 in) tart
Serves 8
Sweet Short Pastry 2 (page 32)
Use 1/2 of the quantity of pastry, about 350g (12oz), wrap and freeze the remaining pastry
1 egg yolk

900g (2lb) redcurrants
300g (10oz) caster sugar
3 egg whites
Pinch of cream of tartar
Pinch of egg white powder

Sugar thermometer

Preheat the oven to 190˚C, 170˚C fan oven, gas 5.

Prepare the pastry and rest it for 15 minutes in the fridge. Roll out the pastry 3mm (1/8 in) thick and line a 25.5cm (10 in) tart tin. Lightly prick the base and rest it in the fridge for 20 minutes or 10 minutes in the freezer.

Bake the pastry blind for 10-15 minutes, remove the baking beans and bake for a further 4-5 minutes. The pastry should be pale to golden in colour. Brush the pastry cases with a little egg yolk and bake for a further minute.

Pick and top and tail the redcurrants. Wash and dry the fruits on kitchen paper and put them into a mixing bowl. Sprinkle over 115g (4oz) of the sugar and toss to mix the sugar through the berries.

Place the remaining sugar in a small pan with 100ml (31/2fl oz) water, heat gently to dissolve the sugar, then bring to the boil. Boil without stirring. Whilst the sugar is boiling whisk the egg whites in a large clean bowl with the cream of tartar and egg white powder until they form soft peaks. When the sugar reaches 121˚C, 250˚F remove the thermometer and place it in a jug of boiling water. Pour the sugar in a slow steady stream into the whisked egg whites whilst whisking on a low speed. Once the sugar has been added, increase the speed and continue to whisk for about 5 minutes until the meringue has cooled slightly.

Spoon the meringue over the fruit and bake in the oven for 4-5 minutes until lightly browned. Serve with cream.

BLACKCURRANT AND CINNAMON LATTICE TART

I really like pies that are made using the old style pie plate for the simple reason that there is usually a lot of fruit to pastry. The other good thing about pie plates is that because they are shallow the pastry cooks through more easily than in a deeper tart tin.

Makes one 23cm (9 in) tart
Serves 4-6
Rich Short Crust Pastry (page 32)
2 tsp ground cinnamon
Grated zest 1 lemon
300g (10oz) blackcurrants, topped and tailed
100ml (3½fl oz) crème de cassis or port
150g (5oz) caster sugar
3 tbsp cornflour
2 tbsp granulated sugar

Prepare the pastry with the addition of 1 teaspoon of cinnamon and grated zest of 1 lemon.

Lightly grease a 23cm (9 in) pie plate. Roll out half the pastry on a lightly floured surface, line the pie plate and lightly prick the base of the case. Rest the pastry and lined pie plate in the fridge for 20 minutes or 10 minutes in the freezer.

Put the blackcurrants in a pan with the crème de cassis or port and the sugar and simmer gently for 3-4 minutes. Mix the cornflour with 4 tablespoons of water and stir into the fruit. Stir gently until the liquid thickens. Put to one side.

Roll out the remaining pastry and cut into strips 2.5cm (1 in) wide. Lay 3 or 4 strips across the tart at intervals of about 2.5cm (1 in) and then more at right angles to each other, over the fruit, and seal them on the rim of the pie.
Mix together the remaining cinnamon and the granulated sugar. Brush the pastry lattice with water and sprinkle with the cinnamon sugar. Bake the tart for 25-30 minutes until golden. Serve warm with ice cream.

RASPBERRY, CHOCOLATE AND THYME MILLE FEUILLE

This dessert is a wonderful compilation of texture and flavour, with its layers of crispy, buttery puff pastry, creamy, chocolate mousse and plump, juicy fruit. Raspberry and dark chocolate make a surprisingly good combination but you need to use a strong bitter chocolate to stand up to the raspberry's sharp fruitiness.

The use of thyme in this dessert may surprise you but thyme is probably the most versatile of herbs and although generally used in savoury dishes, it has a natural affinity to chocolate. This recipe is based on a dessert I ate in a fantastic little restaurant called L'Almandier on the Cote d'Azur many years ago.

Makes 6

500g (1lb 2oz) puff pastry trimmings (see Tip page 27) or Puff Pastry (page 30)
200ml (7fl oz) milk (1 tbsp reserved for the egg wash)
4 sprigs thyme
2 tbsp cocoa powder
4 egg yolks
50g (2oz) caster sugar
2 tbsp cornflour
1 tsp vanilla extract
150g (5oz) dark chocolate
142ml carton double cream
200g (7oz) raspberries

Make the puff pastry the day before or have some ready in the freezer to defrost.

If you haven't got any trimmings to hand simply roll out some virgin puff pastry to 3mm (1/8 in) thick, fold in half and in half again and refrigerate for 30 minutes then use as trimmings.

Preheat the oven to 240°C, 220°C fan oven, gas 8.

Roll out the pastry 3mm (1/8 in) thick to give a 41cm (16 in) square. Heavily prick the pastry and rest it in the fridge for 20 minutes.

Bring the milk (less 1 tablespoon) and thyme to the boil in a small pan and whisk in the cocoa powder. Mix together 3 of the 4 egg yolks, and the sugar, and then add the cornflour. Remove the thyme from the chocolate milk and whisk a little of the hot milk onto the egg mixture and then return the egg mixture to the milk in the pan.

Cook the mixture over a medium heat, stirring all the time, for 3-4 minutes until the mixture has thickened, remove from the heat and pour the chocolate pastry cream into a clean bowl.

Chop the chocolate and place in a heatproof bowl over a pan of simmering water or microwave on a low heat setting until melted.

Stir the vanilla extract and melted chocolate into the pastry cream and cover with a piece of buttered greaseproof paper. Put to one side.

Mix together the remaining egg yolk and milk. Lay the pastry on a baking sheet and brush lightly with the egg wash. Bake the pastry for 10-12 minutes then lay a heavy tray on top of the pastry and continue to cook the pastry for a further

5-6 minutes until golden and cooked through. Remove the pastry from the oven and allow to cool.

Cut the pastry into 20 rectangles - 10cm (4 in) long and 5cm (2 in) wide. You will only need 18 but it is easier to cut 20 pieces and discard 2.

Lightly whip the cream and fold into the chocolate pastry cream. Using a 1.5cm (3/4 in) nozzle and piping bag, pipe the pastry cream onto 6 pastry rectangles and top them with raspberries. Place pastry rectangles on top of the raspberries and repeat. Finally top with the remaining pastry rectangles and dust with icing sugar. Refrigerate for up to an hour but preferably serve straight away.

BLUEBERRY PIE

Cultivated blueberries are a sweet fruit and need little sugar to sweeten them. The addition of cornflour in this pie helps to thicken the fruit filling during cooking so that when it cools it gels slightly and as you cut the pie, it retains its shape. You can of course use frozen berries for this recipe but if you do, you will need to double the quantity of cornflour.

Makes one 23cm (9 in) deep pie
Serves 6
Rich Short Crust Pastry (page 35)
Make 2 x pastry recipe
675g (1 lb 8oz) fresh blueberries

75g (3oz) caster sugar
2 tbsp cornflour
Grated zest and juice 1/2 lemon
1 tbsp milk
1 tbsp granulated sugar

Preheat the oven to 190°C, 170°C fan oven, gas 5.

Prepare the pastry and rest it for 15 minutes in the fridge. Lightly grease a 23cm (9 in) diameter, 4cm (11/2 in) deep pie dish. Roll out just over half of the pastry on a lightly floured surface and line the base of the pie dish. Lightly prick the base of the case. Do not trim the excess pastry.

Mix the berries, sugar, cornflour, grated lemon zest and juice in a bowl and then spoon into the lined pie dish.

Roll out the remaining pastry and dampen the pie edge with water. Using the rolling pin lift the rolled pastry on top of the blueberries and seal the edges. Make a small slit in the centre of the pie. Brush with milk and sprinkle with granulated sugar.

Bake the pie for 40-45 minutes, until golden brown, if the pastry starts to colour too much cover with foil. This pie is best eaten cold, so allow to cool for at least 2 hours.

BLUEBERRY AND LEMON TARTLETS

This flavour combination owes much to the Americans and many of my recipes are influenced by my travels around the various states. Home baking is so much more a part of family life in America than in the UK and every one seems to have their favourite pie, cake and cookie recipe.

New York institutions such as Dean & Deluca, Eli's, Graces and the Witch Bakery are just a small number of fantastic food shops that have helped provide food manufacturers in the UK with new product ideas. When I worked as a Development Chef for Sainsbury's, part of my job was to bring back new ideas into the business and help suppliers develop new product concepts. I visited numerous bakeries and food emporiums and ate my way through lots of cheesecake, cakes, pies, cookies and breads, in my search for potential commercial new product ideas and along the way I learnt a lot about American food.

This recipe is inspired by one of my favourite American flavour combinations. Try it for yourself, you'll not be disappointed.

Makes 6 small tarts
Sweet Short Pastry 3 (page 32)
Use 1/2 of the quantity, wrap and freeze
    the remaining pastry
200ml (7fl oz) milk (1 tbsp reserved for
    the egg wash)
1 vanilla pod, split lengthways

4 egg yolks
225g (8oz) caster sugar
3 tbsp cornflour
2 unwaxed lemons
142ml carton double cream
375g (13oz) blueberries

Preheat the oven to 190°C, 170°C fan oven, gas 5.

Prepare the pastry and rest it for 15 minutes in the fridge. Roll out the pastry 3mm (1/8 in) thick and line six, 12.5cm (5 in) diameter, 2.5cm (1 in) deep tartlet cases. Lightly prick the bases and rest them for 20 minutes in the fridge or 10 minutes in the freezer.

Bake the pastry blind for 10-12 minutes, remove the baking beans and bake for a further 2-3 minutes. The pastry should be pale to golden in colour. Brush the pastry cases with a little of the egg yolk and bake for a further minute.

Bring the milk and vanilla pod to the boil in a small pan. Mix together the remaining egg yolks and 50g (2oz) of the sugar and then add the cornflour. Remove the vanilla pod from the milk and scrape the seeds into the milk. Whisk a little of the hot milk onto the egg mixture and then return the egg mixture to the milk in the pan. Cook the mixture over a medium heat, stirring all the time, for 3-4 minutes until the mixture has thickened, remove from the heat and pour into a clean shallow bowl. Cover with a piece of buttered greaseproof. Allow to cool.

Thinly pare the zest from the lemons and remove any pith. Put the zest into a pan and cover with cold water. Bring to the boil, drain and refresh under cold running water. Then repeat the process. Julienne (thinly slice) the zest. Return the blanched zest to the pan and cover with 150ml (1/4pt) cold water and add 150g (5oz) of the caster sugar. Heat to dissolve the sugar then simmer very gently for 20 minutes, until the lemon is tender. Drain the lemon and spread the zest on a sheet of greaseproof paper sprinkled with half the remaining caster sugar. Sprinkle the zest with the remaining caster sugar.

When the pastry cream is cold, lightly whip the double cream and fold into the pastry cream.

Spoon the mixture into the pastry cases and top with the blueberries and candied lemon.

BERRY SOLEIL

The literal translation of this tart is 'berry sun' and the reason will become clear when you make it. The puff pastry case has a jagged appearance a bit like rays of sunlight. The tart is filled with crème diplomat, a mixture of crème pâtissière and whipped cream and then topped with fresh berries. Crème diplomat is so much more indulgent than a simple crème pâtissière that I love to use it to fill berry tarts.

I used to make this tart for the dessert trolley in the River Restaurant at The Savoy Hotel and as you can imagine it was a very popular summertime dessert.

Makes one 23cm (9 in) tart
Serves 6
Puff Pastry (page 30)
Use 1/2 recipe, wrap and freeze remaining pastry
200ml (7fl oz) milk (1 tbsp reserved for the egg wash)
1 vanilla pod, split lengthways
4 egg yolks
50g (3oz) caster sugar

3 tbsp cornflour
15g (1/2oz) unsalted butter
142ml carton double cream
125g (41/2oz) strawberries
125g (41/2oz) blackberries
125g (41/2oz) raspberries
2 tbsp redcurrant jelly
2 tbsp strawberry jam
2 tsp lemon juice

Preheat the oven to 240°C, 220°C fan oven, gas 8.

Make the puff pastry the day before or have some ready in the freezer to defrost.

Bring the milk (less the tablespoon) and vanilla pod to the boil in a small pan. Mix together 3 of the 4 egg yolks, and the sugar, and then add the cornflour. Remove the vanilla pod from the milk and scrape the seeds into the milk. Whisk a little of the hot milk onto the egg mixture and then return the egg mixture to the milk in the pan. Cook the mixture over a medium heat, stirring all the time, until the mixture has thickened, remove from the heat and pour into a clean shallow bowl. Stir in the butter and cover with a piece of buttered greaseproof. Allow to cool.

Mix together the remaining egg yolk and milk. Roll out the pastry to 3mm (1/8 in) thick on a lightly floured surface and cut out a 28cm (11 in) round. Cut a 2.5cm (1 in) strip from around the edge of the round. Brush the edge of the round with egg wash and lay the 2.5cm (1 in) strip on top cutting it to fit the base round. Press gently to seal the edges. Make 10-12 cuts 2.5cm (1 in) deep around the edge into the pastry. Turn back each cut to give a point and press down to seal.

Lay the pastry on a baking sheet, prick the base of the pastry and egg wash the pointed edges of the pastry. Bake for 15-20 minutes until golden and cooked through.

When the pastry cream is cold, lightly whip the double cream and fold them

both together. Spoon the pastry cream on top of the pastry case and top with the berries, except for the raspberries.

Heat the redcurrant jelly and strawberry jam with the lemon juice and 2 tablespoons of water and boil for 1 minute. Sieve the glaze then brush the berries with the hot glaze. Scatter over the raspberries and serve.

TIP It is easier to scatter the raspberries over after glazing the other berries. The fine hairs on the surface of the raspberry tend to prevent the raspberry from being glazed very easily.

1824 GOOSEBERRY PIE

This pie has been on the menu at the Athenaeum Club since 1824 when gooseberries were more widely used as a fruit pie filling than they are today. During the 18th century gooseberries were much revered and there were many clubs and societies devoted to growing and exhibiting the fruit, so much so that many considered it to be the primary English fruit. Its popularity continued into the 19th century and after the sugar tax was repealed in 1874 the demand for gooseberries increased even further. They remained popular until the increased availability of more exotic fruit varieties became commonplace.

During the time I produced the desserts at the Athenaeum Club I would use fresh gooseberries, when in season, but would have to resort to frozen berries at other times of the year. The Athenaeum gooseberry pie was made with just a top crust in a deep pie dish until one day when I unwittingly made it with pastry both top and bottom, not realising that the gooseberry pie was not for changing.

Makes one 19cm (7^1/$_2$ in) wide x 26cm (10^1/$_4$ in) long pie
Serves 6
Rich Short Crust Pastry (page 35)
1kg (2lb 2oz) fresh gooseberries, topped and tailed
200g (7oz) caster sugar
4 tbsp cornflour
100ml (3^1/$_2$fl oz) elderflower cordial
1 tbsp milk
1 tbsp granulated sugar

Preheat the oven to 190°C, 170°C fan oven, gas 5.

Prepare the pastry and rest it for 15 minutes in the fridge. Put the gooseberries into a large pan with 50ml (2fl oz) water and the sugar. Simmer the fruit gently for 5-10 minutes until just tender then drain the fruit. Retain the fruit juices.

Spoon the fruit into a 19cm (7^1/$_2$ in) wide x 26cm (10^1/$_4$ in) long pie dish. Mix the cornflour with 4-5 tablespoons of the fruit juices in a small bowl. Return the remaining fruit juices to the pan. Bring the fruit juices to the boil, reduce the heat, pour in the cornflour and stir until the liquid thickens. Then stir in the elderflower cordial. Pour the thickened juices over the gooseberries in the pie dish.

Brush the lip of the pie dish with water. Roll out the pastry a little larger than the dish. Cut a strip from the edge of the rolled pastry to fit the width of the pie lip and press lightly onto the lip, dampen the pastry on the lip. Place the remaining pastry on top of the gooseberries. Press to seal the edges and make a small slit in the centre of the pie, trim any excess pastry and decorate the pie with any leftover pastry. Brush the pastry with the milk and sprinkle with the granulated sugar. Bake for 35-40 minutes until the pastry is golden. Serve warm with custard or cream.

SUGAR & SPICE

It is very hard to imagine baking without sugar. Our diet might be healthier without it but life would also be far less pleasurable, especially for people like me who have a sweet tooth. I think that sugar, as with alcohol, should be consumed in moderation. Unfortunately there is so much sugar added to processed foods these days many people consume far more sugar than they realise.

However sugar is undoubtedly the most important ingredient in the production of sweet tarts and pies. It not only sweetens and enriches but also combines with other ingredients to form the structure of the dessert.

The vast majority of sugar used for baking purposes is granular although liquid sugars including honey, treacle and syrups are also used. Granular sugar can be divided into refined and unrefined. Refined sugars are 'white' sugars and unrefined sugars are brown in colour. Although it is important to check the labelling, as some brown sugars are refined sugars coloured by the addition of caramel and do not possess the flavourful characteristics of unrefined sugars.

Granular sugar is produced in different grades. Demerara is a type of coarsely ground sugar often sprinkled on cakes or breakfast cereal, granulated sugar is a little finer and is best used for jam making and sugar work because it gives a clearer jam, and the large crystals are less likely to crystallise sugar solutions. Caster sugar is more finely ground than granulated and dissolves more easily when creamed with butter or blended with other ingredients, giving cakes and pastries a lighter more even texture. Icing sugar is a powdered sugar and is ideal for sweetening cold mixes such as fruit sauces as it dissolves easily.

Unless a recipe specifies otherwise I recommend using refined caster sugar as it has the advantage of dissolving more easily than granulated in baked mixtures and will give the best end result when making pastry. Although I love the flavour of many unrefined sugars, such as muscovado, they can give pastries and pie fillings an undesirable brown appearance and the stronger tasting sugars can overpower the flavour of other ingredients. In some recipes such as a rich fruitcake, the use of unrefined sugar, such as dark muscovado sugar, is desirable' and I am not adverse to using golden caster sugar for pastry making or light muscovado to sweeten fruit or tart fillings.

Honey, treacle and syrup, are all forms of liquid sugar. Molasses, black treacle and golden syrup are all by-products of refined sugar cane. Although molasses and black treacle are often considered to be the same, molasses is obtained from the drainings of raw sugar and treacle is made from the syrup obtained from cooking the sugar. Golden syrup is made from the syrup during the first boiling of the sugar and black treacle is made from syrup from later boilings.

Honey is the oldest form of sugar, having been harvested for thousands of years. The Egyptians are thought to have been the first to keep bees for their honey over four thousand five hundred years ago. These days honey is produced all over the world and the styles of honey are numerous, ranging from Scottish heather honey to New Zealand manuka honey. I prefer to eat strongly flavoured honey but for cooking purposes clear, runny milder tasting honey is the best type to use unless the recipe specifies otherwise.

Maple syrup is a natural product produced from the sap of the American maple tree. It has a distinctive flavour and is available in different grades, which relate to its colour and flavour. It has a delicate but distinctive flavour and is less sweet than other syrups.

Corn syrup, another widely used American syrup, is produced from maize. There are 2 types of corn syrup: one comprises dextrins, maltose and dextrose, the other fructose and sucrose. The latter, known as high fructose corn syrup, is widely used in the manufacture of soft drinks and condiments. It is produced from genetically modified corn and genetically modified enzymes and should be avoided if at all possible. Corn syrup is not widely available in Britain and although it differs from honey and other liquid sugars, I have found that it is possible to substitute honey and golden syrup in recipes, such as pecan pie where the mixture is baked.

Arab traders were the first to introduce spices to the Europeans and along with the Venetians they controlled the Mediterranean trade from the 10th century until the Portuguese discovered the sea route to India in the 15th century. The Portuguese controlled the spice trade for a century until the Dutch took over in 1602, with the formation of the Dutch East India Company. Trading with Java and the Spice Islands, they established a monopoly on the trade of cloves and nutmeg. The British East India Company, established at around the same time, created a monopoly of trade with India from the middle of the 17th century and London became the spice capital of the world, a title it held for the next 200 years. Increased availability reduced the price and so people began to use spice more liberally, changing the flavour of British cooking.

Although popularity of spices has altered over the years the main spices used in baking sweet tarts and pies are vanilla, nutmeg, cinnamon, ginger and cloves, although allspice, saffron and cardamom are also used. Clove, nutmeg, allspice and cinnamon combine to form mixed spice, which is used in British baking but more often in cakes and bread products than tarts and pies.

TREACLE TART

Although considered by many to be an old fashioned British pudding, treacle tart did not exist in its current form until the 1880s when golden syrup was first sold in Britain. Recipes for treacle tart first began to appear in the early 1900s and Marguerite Patten sites treacle tart as being a recipe popular in the 1930s.

Treacle is the generic name given to all syrups produced during the refining of sugar cane but black treacle is generally referred to as treacle and light treacle as golden syrup. It was originally the name of a medicinal mixture used as an antidote against poisons, taken from the French *triacle*, over time this meaning died out and from the 17th century it took on its present day meaning.

There appear to be two styles of treacle tart; the most widely recognised version comprises breadcrumbs, golden syrup and lemon juice baked in a pastry case whereas the second version, Norfolk treacle tart, has the addition of egg and cream. In both cases the tart should be baked in a pie plate.

Makes one 23cm (9in) tart
Serves 4-6
Sweet Short Pastry 3 (page 32)
Use 1/2 of the quantity, wrap and freeze the remaining pastry
300g (10oz) golden syrup
50g (2oz) fresh white breadcrumbs
Grated zest and juice 1 lemon
Clotted cream to serve

Preheat the oven to 190°C, 170°C fan oven, gas 5.

Prepare the pastry and rest it for 15 minutes in the fridge. Lightly grease a pie plate. Lightly flour a clean work surface and roll out the pastry to 3mm (1/8in) thick.

Use it to line a 23cm (9in) pie plate and lightly prick the base of the case. Rest the pastry for 20 minutes in the fridge or 10 minutes in the freezer.

Warm the syrup in a small pan and stir through the breadcrumbs, lemon zest and juice. Spoon the breadcrumb mix onto the pie plate and level the surface.

Bake the treacle tart for 15-20 minutes until golden. Serve warm with clotted cream.

ECCLES CAKES

These fruity cakes originated in the town of Eccles in Lancashire - Eccles taking its name from the Greek word 'Ecclesia' meaning an assembly. An assembly or 'Wakes' took place annually at the church in Eccles and afterwards there was a fair at which small currant cakes were sold. The Puritans banned these little cakes in 1650 thinking they must be of pagan significance, on account of their exotic taste, but just over a century later a small shop in Eccles belonging to James Birch began selling them again.

They are surprisingly easy to make and taste wonderful if made with moist fruits and a good measure of spice.

Makes 6
Puff Pastry (page 30)
250g (9oz) puff pastry trimmings or virgin
    puff pastry, wrap and freeze remaining
    pastry
50g (2oz) unsalted butter
50g (2oz) soft brown sugar

40g (1^1/2oz) mixed peel, chopped
75g (3oz) currants
^{1}/2 tsp mixed spice
^{1}/4 tsp ground nutmeg
1 egg
1 tbsp milk
2 tbsp granulated sugar

Make the puff pastry the day before or have some ready in the freezer to defrost.

If you haven't got any trimmings to hand simply roll out some virgin puff pastry to 3mm (^{1}/8 in) thick, fold in half and half again and refrigerate for 30 minutes then use as trimmings.

Preheat the oven to 220°C, 200°C fan oven, gas 7.

Cream the butter and sugar and then mix in the fruit and spice.

Roll out the pastry 3mm (^{1}/8in) thick and cut out six, 12.5cm (5in) rounds.

Separate the egg and mix the yolk together with the milk, put the white to one side. Brush the edges with a little egg wash and place a little of the fruit mix in the centre of each pastry round. Bring together the edges to seal in the filling. Turn upside down so the seal is on the base and roll gently to flatten. Score 3 times on the top of each one with the back of a knife. Brush with egg white and sprinkle with granulated sugar. Put on a baking tray and bake for 18-20 minutes until golden.

SWEET POTATO PIE

This classic from the Deep South of America is a real find, so much nicer in my opinion than pumpkin pie. I first tasted sweet potato pie on a visit to New Orleans several years ago. The restaurant was a small self-service operation with formica topped tables serving po'boys, debris and other Creole specials – a very unassuming place.

I recommend using red sweet potatoes as they give both a better colour and flavour.

Makes one 23cm (9in) pie
Serves 6-8
Sweet Short Pastry 2 (page 32)
Use 1/3 of the quantity of pastry, about 250g (9oz), wrap and freeze the remaining pastry
500g (1lb 2oz) sweet potatoes, peeled and chopped

2 eggs
150g (5oz) light muscovado sugar
284ml carton double cream
1 tsp ground cinnamon
1/8 tsp ground nutmeg
1/8 tsp ground allspice
1 tbsp caster sugar
1 tsp vanilla extract

Preheat the oven to 190˚C, 170˚C fan oven, gas 5.

Prepare the pastry and rest it for 15 minutes in the fridge. Roll out the pastry on a lightly floured work surface to 3mm (1/8in) thick. Line a 23cm (9in) tart tin and lightly prick the base. Rest the pastry for 20 minutes in the fridge or 10 minutes in the freezer.

Bring a pan of water to the boil and add the sweet potatoes, cook until tender then drain. Blend in a food processor until smooth. Spoon the purée into a mixing bowl, add the eggs and muscovado sugar and mix well. Then stir in the spices and half the cream.

Meanwhile bake the pastry blind for 10-15 minutes, remove the baking beans and bake for a further 5 minutes. The pastry should be pale to golden in colour. Brush the pastry case with the egg yolk and bake for a further minute. Remove it from the oven. Reduce the oven temperature to 180˚C, 160˚C fan oven, gas 4.

Pour the potato mix into the pastry case and bake for 20-25 minutes until set. Remove from the oven and allow to cool.

Lightly whip the remaining cream, add the caster sugar and the vanilla extract and pipe the cream around the edge of the cooled pie.

RHUBARB AND GINGER PIE

Ginger partners rhubarb rather well. In this case the use of ginger syrup does much to soften the acidity of the rhubarb but it is the warm, aromatic nature of ginger that really makes this combination work. I always feel that rhubarb pie is best eaten with custard; the creaminess somehow foils the fruit's sharpness.

Makes one 23cm (9 in) deep pie
Serves 6-8
Rich Short Crust Pastry 2 (page 35)
with the addition of
1 tsp ground ginger
Grated zest 1 lemon
700g (1lb 10oz) rhubarb, trimmed and
    chopped

100ml (3^{1}/2fl oz) ginger syrup
4 tbsp cornflour
25g (1oz) stem ginger, finely chopped
1 tbsp milk
1 tbsp granulated sugar

Preheat the oven to 190˚C, 170˚C fan oven, gas 5.

Prepare the pastry with the ground ginger and lemon zest and rest it for 15 minutes in the fridge.

Put the rhubarb and 50ml (2fl oz) water in a pan. Cover the pan with a piece of greaseproof paper or a pan lid and simmer gently. When the rhubarb is just tender add the ginger syrup. Mix the cornflour and 4 tablespoons of water together and stir into the rhubarb. Stir until the liquid thickens. Pour the rhubarb into a shallow bowl to cool.

Lightly grease a 23cm (9 in) diameter, 4cm (1^{1}/2 in) deep pie dish. Roll out half the pastry to a thickness of 6mm (1/4 in) on a lightly floured surface and line the dish. Lightly prick the base of the case. Do not trim the excess pastry. Rest the pastry in the fridge for 20 minutes or in the freezer for 10 minutes.

Spoon the rhubarb into the lined pie dish. Roll out the remaining pastry and dampen the pie edge with water. Using a rolling pin, lift the rolled pastry on top of the rhubarb and seal the edges. Make a small slit in the centre of the pie. Brush with milk and sprinkle with granulated sugar. Bake the pie for 40-45 minutes until golden brown, if the pastry starts to colour too much cover with foil. Serve with custard.

BANBURY CAKES

It is thought that Crusaders returning from the Holy Land in the 13th century brought with them small, pastry envelopes, containing dried fruits and spice, that led to the creation eventually of the Banbury cake. These flat pastries, most often oval or rectangular in shape, owe their name to the market town of Banbury in Oxfordshire where they were sold in number and carried to different towns in England.

Makes 6

Puff Pastry (page 30)
250g (9oz) puff pastry trimmings (see Tip page 27) or virgin puff pastry, wrap and freeze remaining pastry
25g (1oz) unsalted butter
15g (1/2oz) plain flour
1/2 tsp mixed spice

50g (2oz) soft brown sugar
40g (11/2oz) mixed peel, chopped
75g (3oz) currants
2 tbsp rum
1 egg
1 tbsp milk
2 tbsp caster sugar

Make the puff pastry the day before or have some ready in the freezer to defrost. Use 250g (9oz) puff pastry trimmings, if you haven't got any trimmings to hand simply roll out some virgin puff pastry to 3mm (1/8 in) thick, fold in half and in half again and refrigerate for 30 minutes then use as trimmings.

Preheat the oven to 220°C, 200°C fan oven, gas 7.

Melt the butter, stir in the flour and spice and cook for a few minutes. Remove from the heat and stir in the sugar, fruit and rum.

Roll out the pastry 3mm (1/8in) thick and cut out six, 12.5cm (5in) rounds. Separate the egg and mix the yolk with the milk and put the white to one side. Brush the edges with a little egg wash and place a little of the fruit mix in the centre of each pastry round. Bring the edges together to seal in the filling. Turn upside down so the seal is on the base and roll out into a small rectangle or oval 12.5cm (5in) x 6.5cm (21/2in). Score 3 times on the top of each one with the back of a knife. Brush with the egg white and sprinkle with caster sugar bake for 18-20 minutes until golden.

PUMPKIN PIE

In the 1620s American settlers started making pumpkin pudding using hollowed out pumpkins, that were then filled with pumpkin flesh, milk, spices and honey. Over the next 50 years this pudding developed into the pumpkin pie that is now associated with Thanksgiving. Although the Americans may have had some help developing the recipe, as Norfolk's pilgrim fathers probably took the recipe with them in the form of 'million' pie, the old East Anglian name for a gourd. Recipes for pumpkin pie also appear in both *Le Vrai Cuisinier François* (The true French Cook) written by François Pierre La Varenne (1653) and *The Compleat Cook* written by Elise Fleming (1655), both some years before the first American pumpkin pies started to appear for Thanksgiving in the late 1600s.

If you have never eaten pumpkin pie and struggle to imagine how a vegetable could taste good cooked with sugar and spice, throw caution to the wind and try it anyway. I tend to use Libby's canned pumpkin purée as it is produced from a variety of pumpkin known for its rich colour and creamy texture but if you want to use fresh pumpkin, I recommend roasting rather than boiling the flesh so that it remains dry.

Makes one 23cm (9 in) deep pie
Serves 6-8
Sweet Short Crust Pastry 1 (page 31)
1 egg yolk
425g (14oz) pumpkin purée
2 eggs

150g (5oz) caster sugar
1 tsp ground cinnamon
1/2 tsp ground ginger
1/4 tsp ground cloves
284ml carton double cream

Preheat the oven to 190°C, 170°C fan oven, gas 5.

Prepare the pastry and rest it for 15 minutes in the fridge. Roll out the pastry on a lightly floured work surface to 3mm (1/8 in) thick. Lightly grease and line the base of a 23cm (9 in) diameter, 4cm (1 1/2 in) deep pie dish. Lightly prick the base of the case and rest the lined case in the fridge for 20 minutes.

Bake the pastry blind for 10-15 minutes, remove the baking beans and bake for a further 5 minutes. The pastry should be pale to golden in colour. Brush the pastry case with a little egg yolk and bake for a further minute. Remove the pastry case from the oven. Reduce the oven temperature to 180°C, 160°C fan oven, gas 4.

Mix together the pumpkin purée, eggs, any remaining yolk and sugar. Then stir in the spices and cream. Pour the mixture into the pie case and bake for 45-50 minutes until set. Refrigerate and serve cold.

ALMOND CRUSTED MINCE PIES

These days mince pies are sold in all shapes and sizes, individual, family and mini, topped with cherries, pecans and marzipan, filled with various mincemeats in a choice of pastry cases. With so much variety it's no wonder very few people bother making them.

When I worked at Blakes Hotel I used to make 3 different types of mince pies at Christmas, some with puff pastry, some with filo and some with sweet short crust. When Lady Weinburg complained the mincemeat was too sweet, I said I would buy a different variety, not realising that the head chef had told her that we made our own. Shortly after that incident I started making the mincemeat at Blakes!

Although I make my own mince pies, Fortnum & Mason's almond-topped mince pies are really very good. This is where I got the idea for this recipe. You can of course make your own mincemeat but if you haven't got time and you want a really full-flavoured mincemeat buy a standard variety and just add brandy to taste.

Makes 12 small pies
Sweet Short Pastry 3 (page 32)
Use 1/2 of the quantity, wrap and freeze the remaining pastry
75g (3oz) unsalted butter
25g (1oz) caster sugar
100g (3½oz) flour
50g (2oz) flaked almonds
300g (10oz) mincemeat
2 tbsp brandy

Preheat the oven to 190˚C, 170˚C fan oven, gas 5.

Prepare the pastry and rest it for 15 minutes in the fridge. Roll out the pastry 3mm (1/8 in) thick and cut out twelve, 10cm (4 in) rounds. Grease and line a 12-hole bun tin with the pastry rounds. Lightly prick the bases and chill for 20 minutes in the fridge or 10 minutes in the freezer.

Rub the butter and sugar together and then stir in the flour and the almonds. Put the mincemeat into a bowl and stir in the brandy, then spoon into the bases of the lined cases and sprinkle over the almond mixture. Bake the pies for 20 minutes until golden. Serve warm with cream or brandy butter.

SHOO-FLY PIE

With its origins in Amish Dutch Pennsylvania, Shoo-fly pie is an interesting, if very sweet pie. It has developed into an American-style coffee cake, with a crumb crust, as well as a gooey, molasses base in a pie shell. The sweet ingredients used to make it are thought to have attracted flies which were shooed away, hence its name.

Makes one 23cm (9in) deep pie
Serves 10-12
Rich Short Crust Pastry (page 35)
1 tsp bicarbonate of soda
125g (4$^{1}/_{2}$oz) black treacle
125g (4$^{1}/_{2}$oz) golden syrup
1 egg
300g (10oz) plain flour
150g (5oz) unsalted butter
100g (3$^{1}/_{2}$oz) soft brown sugar

Preheat the oven to 190°C, 170°C fan oven, gas 5.

Prepare the pastry and rest it for 15 minutes in the fridge. Grease a 23cm (9in) diameter 4cm (1$^{1}/_{2}$in) deep pie dish. Lightly flour a clean work surface and roll out the pastry to 6mm ($^{1}/_{4}$in) thick. Line the pie dish and lightly prick the base of the case. Rest the lined case in the fridge for 20 minutes.

Dissolve the bicarbonate of soda in 250ml (9fl oz) warm water and add the black treacle, golden syrup and egg. In a separate bowl rub the butter into the flour and stir in the sugar. Pour the treacle mix into the pastry case and sprinkle over the crumb mixture. Bake in the oven for 25 minutes, then reduce the oven temperature to 160°C, 140°C fan oven, gas 3 and bake for a further 30-35 minutes until lightly set.

Allow to cool for 1 hour before serving.

COFFEE AND CARDAMOM TART

The coffee plant originated in the mountains of Ethiopia and was bought back to the Yemen about 600 years ago. Yemen remained the centre of the coffee trade until Europeans decided to break Yemen's monopoly in the 1600s. Coffee plants were smuggled to Indonesia by the Dutch and to Nigeria and Jamaica by the British, so that they could exert more control over the industry. Today coffee is grown in over 50 countries worldwide.

The combination of coffee and cardamom can be traced back several centuries to Arabic cultures. A warm pungent spice with a note of eucalyptus, it complements coffee surprisingly well. The Arabs often ground and brewed it with coffee to give a perfumed drink and the wealthier you were the more cardamom you used because it was, and still is, an expensive spice.

I love cardamom's exotic flavour and thought it would work well with coffee in a tart. I liked the idea of coffee, walnuts and cardamom so I worked up this recipe. The coffee flavour isn't too over powering so you can appreciate the flavour of the walnuts as well.

Makes one 23cm (9 in) tart
Serves 6-8
Sweet Short Pastry 2 (page 32)
Use 1/3 of the quantity of pastry, about
    250g (9oz), wrap and freeze the
    remaining pastry
100g (31/2oz) unsalted butter
100g (31/2oz) dark brown sugar

2 eggs
50g (2oz) ground almonds
50g (2oz) ground walnuts
50g (2oz) plain flour
1 tbsp strong black coffee
15 cardamom pods, pods crushed, seeds
    removed and chopped
5 tbsp sieved icing sugar

Preheat the oven to 190°C, 170°C fan oven, gas 5.

Prepare the pastry and rest it for 15 minutes in the fridge. Roll out the pastry on a lightly floured work surface to 3mm (1/8 in) thick. Line a 23cm (9 in) tart tin and lightly prick the base. Rest the base in the fridge for 20 minutes or 10 minutes in the freezer.

Cream the butter and sugar together, beat in the eggs and then stir in the ground almonds and walnuts. Then add the flour, coffee and cardamom seeds. Spread the mix into the pastry case and bake the tart for 40-45 minutes until the sponge is firm to the touch.

Mix together the icing sugar with 1 tablespoon of boiling water and brush over the warm tart. Serve with ice cream or cream.

JAM TARTS

Whenever I think of jam tarts I think of the Queen of Hearts from the book *Alice in Wonderland* by Lewis Carroll.

'How about making us some nice tarts?' the King of Hearts asked the Queen of Hearts one cool summer day.

'What's the sense of making tarts without jam?' said the Queen furiously. 'The jam is the best part!'

'Then use jam.' said the King.

'I can't!' shouted the Queen. 'My jam has been stolen!'

You don't have to make your own jam for this recipe, if you haven't got time simply buy a jar.

Makes 12 small tarts
Sweet Short Pastry 3 (page 32)
Use 1/2 of the quantity, wrap and freeze the remaining pastry
450g (1lb) strawberries
375g (13oz) caster sugar
Juice 1 lemon
3 tbsp vanilla paste
1 egg yolk

Preheat the oven to 190°C, 170°C fan oven, gas 5.

Prepare the pastry and rest it in the fridge whilst you make the jam.

Crush half the strawberries and put into a large stainless steel or aluminium pan with 3 tablespoons of sugar, heat gently until the sugar dissolves, then add the rest of the fruit. Warm the remaining sugar for a few minutes, in the oven on a tray, then add to the fruit. Add 2 teaspoons lemon juice and boil rapidly for 15-20 minutes or until the jam sets. To test the jam put 2 tablespoons on a small plate and chill in the freezer for 3-4 minutes, if the jam crinkles when pushed, it is ready. Remove the jam from the heat and add the vanilla paste.

Roll out the pastry 3mm (1/8 in) thick and cut out twelve, 10cm (4 in) rounds. Grease and line a 12-hole bun tin with the pastry rounds. Lightly prick the bases and rest them for 20 minutes in the fridge or 10 minutes in the freezer.

Bake the pastry blind for 6-8 minutes, remove the baking beans and bake for a further 2-3 minutes. The pastry should be pale to golden in colour. Brush the pastry cases with a little egg yolk and bake for a further minute. Remove from the oven and half fill each case with the freshly made strawberry jam. Return to the oven for 5 minutes. Allow to cool slightly before serving the jam tarts.

LEMON CURD TARTS

Sugar first appeared in England in the late 13th century but it was expensive and considered a luxury item. Its popularity grew with the Elizabethans as they developed a taste for all things sweet, so it was probably during the reign of Elizabeth I that lemon curd was first made. British ports of the time were bustling with goods arriving from far-flung destinations, including sugar from the West Indies and lemons from the Mediterranean. It seems likely that an industrious farmer's wife combined locally produced eggs and butter with the imported lemons and sugar and created the rich lemon custard known as lemon curd.

There is nothing quite like warm, homemade lemon curd. It has a rich, buttery texture and tastes of real lemons, unlike so many commercial varieties that are merely day-glo-yellow spreads. It's easy to make and really worth trying.

Makes 12 small tarts
Sweet Short Pastry 3 (page 32)
Use 1/2 of the quantity, wrap and freeze the remaining pastry
125g (41/2oz) unsalted butter
Grated zest and juice of 3 lemons
225g (8oz) caster sugar
3 eggs

Preheat the oven to 190˚C, 170˚C fan oven, gas 5.

Put the butter, lemon zest, juice and sugar in a mixing bowl over a pan of simmering water. Strain the eggs into the melted butter. Stir every few minutes until the curd has thickened, this will take about 45 minutes.

Prepare the pastry and rest it for 15 minutes in the fridge. Roll out the pastry 3mm (1/8 in) thick and cut out twelve, 10cm (4 in) rounds. Grease and line a 12-hole bun tin with the pastry rounds. Lightly prick the bases and rest them for 20 minutes in the fridge or 10 minutes in the freezer.

Bake the pastry blind for 8-10 minutes, remove the baking beans and bake for a further 2-3 minutes. The pastry should be pale to golden in colour. Brush the pastry cases with a little egg yolk and bake for a further minute. Remove from the oven and allow to cool.

When the lemon curd is thick, spoon it into the tart cases. Refrigerate any that aren't eaten. Any leftover lemon curd can be stored in a glass jar in the fridge for a few days.

MANCHESTER TART

Manchester tart developed as a simpler version of Mrs Beeton's Manchester Pudding, the recipe for which appears in her *Book of Household Management* published in 1869. Manchester Tart became a popular school dinner dessert between the 1950s and 1970s and is now famous in its own right.

Makes one 23cm (9 in) tart
Serves 6
Sweet Short Pastry 2 (page 32)
Use 1/3 of the quantity of pastry about
    250g (9oz), wrap and freeze the
    remaining pastry
1 egg yolk

3 tbsp raspberry jam
5 tbsp desiccated coconut
450ml (3/4pt) milk
3 tbsp custard powder
50g (2oz) caster sugar
1 tsp vanilla extract
15g (1/2oz) unsalted butter

Preheat the oven to 190°C, 170°C fan oven, gas 5.

Prepare the pastry and rest it for 15 minutes in the fridge. Roll out the pastry on a lightly floured work surface to 3mm (1/8 in) thick. Lightly grease and line the base of a 23cm (9 in) tart tin. Lightly prick the base of the case and rest the lined case in the fridge for 20 minutes or the freezer for 10 minutes.

Bake the pastry blind for 10-15 minutes, remove the baking beans and bake for a further 5 minutes. The pastry should be pale to golden in colour. Brush the pastry case with a little egg yolk and bake for a further minute. Remove it from the oven.

Spread the jam over the base and sprinkle with half the coconut.

Mix 4 tablespoons of milk with the custard powder and bring the remaining milk to the boil in a pan. Pour the hot milk onto the custard powder then return to the pan and cook, stirring continuously, until the custard thickens. Remove from the heat, whisk in the sugar, vanilla extract and butter and pour into the pastry case.

Sprinkle with the remaining coconut and allow to cool before serving.

GYPSY TART

I can clearly remember eating gypsy tart when I was at school but have been unable to discover the origins of it. I came across several recipes, none of them containing eggs, but I found the tarts simply would not set, so I adapted a recipe to include eggs.

Makes one 25.5cm (10 in) tart
Serves 8
Sweet Short Pastry 1 (page 31)
Use 1/2 of the quantity of pastry, about
    350g (12oz), wrap and freeze the
    remaining pastry

1 egg yolk
410g can evaporated milk
350g (12oz) light muscovado sugar
2 eggs, lightly beaten
142ml carton whipping cream
2 tbsp grated dark chocolate

Preheat the oven to 190°C, 170°C fan oven, gas 5.

Prepare the pastry and rest it for 15 minutes in the fridge. Roll out the pastry on a lightly floured work surface to 3mm (1/8 in) thick. Lightly grease and line the base of a 25.5cm (10 in) tart tin. Lightly prick the base of the case and rest the pastry for 20 minutes in the fridge or for 10 minutes in the freezer.

Bake the pastry blind for 10-15 minutes, remove the baking beans and bake for a further 5 minutes. The pastry should be pale to golden in colour. Brush the pastry case with a little egg yolk and bake for a further minute. Remove the pastry case from the oven. Allow to cool. Reduce the oven temperature to 180°C, 160°C fan oven, gas 4.

Whisk together the evaporated milk and the sugar and then whisk in the eggs.

Pour the mix into the pastry case and bake for 15-20 minutes until lightly set. Allow the tart to cool completely, lightly whip the cream and pipe around the edge of the tart, sprinkle with the grated chocolate. Refrigerate before serving.

SPICED RICE AND PINE NUT TART

Torta di Riso or rice tart is a speciality of Siena. The filling is made with arborio rice, more often associated with risotto, but being round grain rice it is also ideal for making rice pudding.

Makes one 25.5cm (10 in) tart
Serves 6
Sweet Short Pastry 1 (page 31)
Use 1/2 of the quantity of pastry, about
    350g (12oz), wrap and freeze the
    remaining pastry
750ml (11/4pt) milk
50g (2oz) arborio rice

50g (2oz) caster sugar
4 egg yolks
1 tsp vanilla extract
284ml carton double cream
3 tbsp pine nuts
2 tbsp apricot jam
Raspberry sauce (page 37), to serve

Preheat the oven to 190°C, 170°C fan oven, gas 5.

Prepare the pastry and rest it for 15 minutes in the fridge. Roll out the pastry on a lightly floured work surface to 3mm (1/8 in) thick. Line the base of a 25.5cm (10 in) tart tin. Lightly prick the base of the case and rest it for 20 minutes in the fridge or 10 minutes in the freezer.

Bake the pastry blind for 10-15 minutes, remove the baking beans and bake for a further 5 minutes. The pastry should be pale to golden in colour. Brush the pastry case with a little egg yolk and bake for a further minute. Remove the pastry case from the oven and reduce the oven temperature to 180°C, 160°C fan oven, gas 4.

Bring the milk to the boil in a medium pan, reduce the heat and stir in the rice. Cook the rice, stirring frequently, for 20-25 minutes until tender. Remove from the heat and add the sugar, egg yolks, vanilla extract, cream and 1 tablespoon of the pine nuts.

Spread the base of the pastry case with the apricot jam and then pour the rice into the pastry case. Bake for 15-20 minutes until lightly set. Remove from the oven and allow to cool. Serve sprinkled with the remaining pine nuts and drizzled with raspberry sauce.

CUMBERLAND RUM NICKY

This tasty creation dates back to the early 18th century when the West Indies traded with Cumberland, and so the ports of Whitehaven, Workington and Maryport were at the centre of the British rum trade. Wool exported for carpet making was traded for spices from the Far East and spices such as ginger, pepper and nutmeg became part of Cumbrian cooking.

This recipe for Cumberland Rum Nicky is based on dried fruit but other versions make use of Cumbrian apples such as the Keswick codling.

Makes one 23cm (9 in) pie
Serves 4-6
Sweet Short Pastry 3 (page 32)
25g (1oz) preserved stem ginger, finely chopped
75g (3oz) dates, pitted and chopped
40g (1½oz) unsalted butter
40g (1½oz) caster sugar
2 tbsp dark rum

Preheat the oven to 190°C, 170°C fan oven, gas 5.

Prepare the pastry and rest it for 15 minutes in the fridge. Roll out the pastry on a lightly floured work surface to 3mm (⅛ in) thick. Lightly grease and line the base of a 23cm (9 in) pie plate with half the pastry. Lightly prick the base of the case and rest it in the fridge for 20 minutes or 10 minutes in the freezer.

Scatter the ginger and dates over the pastry. Cream the butter, sugar and rum together and spread over the ginger and dates.

Roll out the remaining pastry and cover the pie plate pressing gently to seal the edges.

Bake for 10 minutes then reduce the oven temperature to 180°C, 160°C fan oven, gas 4 and continue to bake for a further 25 minutes or until the pastry is golden.

Serve the Rum Nicky warm, with cream.

COCKTAIL MINCE PIES

Cocktail or mini mince pies are a bit fiddly to make but are great for Christmas parties, served as a sweet canapé. These mini mince pies are based on a cocktail-inspired mincemeat, hence their name. I thought it would be fun to make mincemeat based on a cocktail, using the corresponding dried fruits. Seabreeze cocktail, made with cranberry juice, seemed an appropriate choice given that cranberries are in season at this time of year and often feature in Christmas dishes but if you prefer simply use your favourite mincemeat.

It is best to make the mincemeat at least 2 weeks ahead of time, to allow the flavours to develop.

Makes 12 small tarts or 24 mini muffin size
Sweet Short Pastry 3 (page 32)
Seabreeze mincemeat:
250g (9oz) dried pineapple, roughly
    chopped
200g (7oz) luxury dried fruit
75g (3oz) dried cranberries, roughly
    chopped

50g (2oz) vegetable suet
Juice and grated zest of 1 lemon
125g (4$^{1}/_{2}$oz) dark muscovado sugar
125ml (4$^{1}/_{2}$fl oz) vodka
2 tbsp granulated sugar

To make the mincemeat simply mix all the ingredients together except the granulated sugar and ideally put the mincemeat into jars and allow to mature for 2 weeks before using.

Preheat the oven to 190°C, 170°C fan oven, gas 5.

Prepare the pastry and rest it for 15 minutes in the fridge. Roll out the pastry on a lightly floured work surface to 3mm ($^{1}/_{8}$ in) thick. Cut out rounds to fit the size of tin you are using. Grease and line a 12-hole bun tin or a 24-hole mini muffin tin with half the pastry. Lightly prick the bases and chill for 20 minutes in the fridge or 10 minutes in the freezer.

Place a spoonful of the mincemeat into each of the lined cases. Roll out the remaining pastry and cut lids to fit the pie cases. Brush the edge of the pastry with water and press the lids on gently to seal the edges. Brush with water and sprinkle with granulated sugar.

Bake for 15-20 minutes for cocktail mince pies and a little longer for full size mince pies.

NUTS

Nuts occur widely in pâtisserie, it is hard to imagine cooking without them since they are used in so many forms – ground nuts are used as a replacement for 'flour', adding flavour, richness and body to cakes and pastries, chopped nuts are used to add flavour but provide more texture than ground nuts and whole nuts are added for flavour, texture and are often used as a form of decoration. But these days, increasingly, nuts especially peanuts have fallen out of favour with food manufacturers and consumers because of the increasing number of allergy sufferers.

ALMONDS are the most widely used nut for culinary purposes is the sweet almond, although many people would probably be hard pressed to think of a culinary use beyond that of marzipan at Christmas.

The almond is thought to have evolved from the same stock as the peach along the desert fringes and lower slopes of the mountains that separate Central Asia from China. Wild almonds were discovered thousands of years ago and were spread by nomads who cast the stones along the way. Today Spain remains one of the world's key suppliers.

Almonds are used predominantly in sweet dishes and confectionery, in Europe, the Middle East and India. Throughout Europe they are used in the manufacture of sugared almonds, marzipan, macaroons and nougat, in the Middle East they are widely used in the production of sweet meats and pastries, and in India they are used in the production of desserts and sweetmeats. In European pâtisserie their most important use is as *crème d'amande*, almond cream or frangipane, as it is also known.

CHESTNUTS The sweet, or Spanish chestnut, also known as the European chestnut, originated in Asia Minor and was first cultivated by the Chinese 6,000 years ago. They are a delicate soft textured nut, highly prized and widely used throughout Europe especially by the French, Italians and Spanish. They are used as chestnut flour, preserved whole as *marrons glacés*, made into chestnut purée, sold whole, cooked and peeled in vac-packs, and in cans and jars. In Britain they are usually associated with Christmas but largely unused throughout the rest of the year which is a shame.

HAZELNUTS are my nut of choice when it comes to pairing chocolate and nuts. Other nuts such as brazils, almonds, chestnuts, walnuts and pecans have their place but none compare to the marriage of hazelnuts and chocolate.

Native to Europe, hazelnuts like almonds have been widely used since ancient times. Their history has been colourful: burned by priests to enhance clairvoyance, associated with the occult, used by herbalists to make remedies and as a marriage fertility symbol. Hazel comes from the Anglo-Saxon word for 'bonnet' and filbert, another name for the hazelnut, is from the English word 'full beard', on account of their appearance before being shelled.

Today they are used extensively in making chocolates and confectionery. The most famous hazelnut product is a rich, chocolate, hazelnut paste created by Pietro Ferrero in 1940. He called it *pasta gianduja* and it was made from cocoa, ground hazelnuts, cocoa butter and vegetable oil and the name is now applied to chocolates made in the same way. It was renamed Nutella in 1964 and remains the top selling 'spread' throughout Europe.

MACADAMIAS originated in subtropical eastern Australia but it wasn't until the 19th century that they were cultivated by John Macadam, from whom they take their name. Trees were taken to Hawaii and although not cultivated commercially until the 1920s, they have become the island's most important tree crop and Hawaii has become the world's largest producer. The nuts are very hard textured with a rich and creamy taste and although not widely used in Europe, they can be used in much the same way as other types of nut.

PEANUTS are thought to have originated in Brazil and arrived in the southern states of America from Africa where they were known as groundnuts or goobers from the African *nguba*.

Much American confectionery, desserts, cakes and cookies contain peanuts, often in the form of peanut butter, because it can be easily incorporated into a batter or dough. It was created by a physician as a soft protein substitute for people with poor teeth and in the early 20th century a mechanized process for making it was developed. Now more than half America's crop of peanuts is used to produce peanut butter.

Recently in New York I visited Peanut Butter & Co. on Sullivan Street in Greenwich Village. There were sandwiches, desserts, cookies and cakes all based around peanut butter – obviously not for everyone but worth a visit if you are a fan.

PECANS originated in central and eastern North America. Many American baked goods such as chocolate brownies, pecan pie and various types of cookie are now commonly found in Britain and pecans are now an everyday ingredient on the supermarket shelves. Due to the sweetness of the nut they have become a popular alternative to the slightly bitter walnut.

PINE NUTS or pine kernels are the seeds of pine trees. The Mediterranean or Italian pine nut (*pignoli*) comes from the stone pine and is used throughout the Mediterranean and Middle East. It is more costly than the Chinese variety, a shorter fatter nut with a stronger flavour, and is more widely grown than the Italian variety. Pine nuts are used in both sweet and savoury dishes; they are usually toasted and added to salads, pasta, fish and meat dishes, as well as being sprinkled over sweet tarts and biscuits before they are baked.

PISTACHIOS are native to Asia Minor and popular in Middle Eastern, Mediterranean countries and India, where they are prized as a delicacy due to their sweet flavour and colour, although this colour is often artificially accentuated. They are also a popular snack roasted and salted in their shells. Beware of pistachio 'flavoured' desserts and ice creams that have been made with cheap pistachio paste and lack real pistachio.

WALNUTS are regarded as the oldest tree food, dating back to the Neolithic period and are thought to have originated in Persia. Highly regarded by the Romans who called the walnut, the Royal Nut of Jove (Jove being the Roman king of their mythological gods), from the 4th century walnuts were cultivated in the Gresi-vaudan region of France but now most French walnuts are grown in the Périgord and Dauphiné, where they have an *appellation d'origen*.

Although largely used in making cakes and pastries, they also appear in the areas' regional dishes. Their complex flavour is suited to a wide range of applications including breads, cakes, pastries, oils, liqueur, pastas and pâtés. Personally I love walnuts and goat's cheese but there are so many wonderful walnut pairings it is hard to know where to start.

PEANUT BUTTER CREAM PIE

Peanuts arrived in America with the African slaves but were not widely grown until the Civil War years of 1861-1865, when they were needed to provide food. Mechanisation aided production and greater availability led to increased popularity. In 1904 peanut butter was first sold at the St. Louis Exposition, after which demand for it grew during the First World War, so that by the 1940s it had become an all-American favourite and is now considered to be a staple food!

Peanut butter is not to everyone's taste but if you are a fan you should try this recipe.

Makes one 23cm (9 in) pie
Serves 6-8
Sweet Short Pastry 3 (page 32)
Use 1/2 of the quantity, wrap and freeze
   the remaining pastry
1 egg yolk
75g (3oz) light muscovado sugar

200g (7oz) cream cheese
200g (7oz) smooth peanut butter
284ml carton double cream
2 tsp vanilla extract
2 medium bananas
Chocolate Sauce (page 38), to serve

Preheat the oven to 190°C, 170°C fan oven, gas 5.

Prepare the pastry and rest it for 15 minutes in the fridge. Lightly flour a clean work surface and roll out the pastry to 3mm (1/8 in) thick. Line a 23cm (9 in) tart tin and lightly prick the base. Rest the pastry for 20 minutes in the fridge or 10 minutes in the freezer.

Bake the pastry blind for 10-15 minutes, remove the baking beans and bake for a further 5 minutes. The pastry should be pale to golden in colour. Brush the pastry case with the egg yolk and bake for a further minute. Remove the pastry case from the oven and allow the case to cool.

Mix together the sugar, cream cheese and peanut butter. Lightly whip the cream and stir in the vanilla extract. Fold the cream through the peanut butter mix. Slice the bananas into the base of the pastry case and spread over the peanut butter cream. Refrigerate for 1 hour and freeze for 1/2 hour before serving. Serve straight from the freezer drizzled with chocolate sauce.

COCONUT CREAM PIE

Like so many American pie recipes this one originates from the Southern States where home-baked pies were extremely popular and very sweet. This recipe is based on one I ate and enjoyed in a Chicago restaurant a few years ago, though my version is a little less sweet.

I've topped the pie with Italian meringue but if you don't have a sugar thermometer then simply make standard French, or uncooked meringue, which will work just as well.

Makes one 23cm (9 in) deep pie
Serves 6-8
Rich Short Crust (page 35)
3 eggs
150ml (1/4 pt) milk

350ml (12fl oz) coconut milk
200g (7oz) caster sugar
50g (2oz) cornflour
Coconut shavings to serve

Preheat the oven to 190°C, 170°C fan oven, gas 5.

Prepare the pastry and rest it for 15 minutes in the fridge. Lightly flour a clean work surface and roll out the pastry to 3mm (1/8 in) thick. Grease and line a 23cm (9 in), 4cm (1 1/2 in) deep pie dish with the pastry. Lightly prick the base and then rest the pastry for 20 minutes in the fridge or 10 minutes in the freezer.

Bake the pastry blind for 10-15 minutes, remove the baking beans and bake for a further 5 minutes. The pastry should be pale to golden in colour. Separate the eggs and brush the pastry case with a little egg yolk and bake for a further minute. Remove it from the oven and allow to cool.

Bring the milk and coconut milk to the boil in a small pan. Mix together the egg yolks and 50g (2oz) of the sugar, and then add the cornflour. Whisk a little of the hot milk onto the egg mixture and then return the mixture to the milk in the pan. Cook the mixture over a medium heat, stirring all the time, for 3-4 minutes, until the mixture has thickened, remove from the heat and pour the coconut custard into the cooked pastry case.

Put the remaining sugar into a pan and add 100ml (3 1/2 fl oz) water, bring to the boil without stirring. Cook the sugar until the sugar thermometer reads 121°C, 250°F. Whilst the sugar is cooking whisk the egg whites. When the sugar reaches 121°C, 250°F pour the syrup slowly onto the egg whites in a steady steam whilst whisking on a low speed. Once the syrup has been added, increase the speed and whisk until the meringue is cool. Spoon the meringue over the custard and bake in the oven for 5-10 minutes until the meringue is golden brown. Sprinkle with coconut shavings and serve.

TIP If you like rum with your coconut add 1-2 tablespoons of white rum to the coconut custard once it has been cooked.

BAKEWELL TART

Medieval flathons or flans cooked in the 15th century were probably the precursors to the famous Bakewell Pudding, the first reference for which appears in 1826. The original pudding was an almond-custard affair, popular throughout the northern counties in the early 19th century. In the latter part of the century the pudding had evolved into a form more recognisable as the Bakewell Tart, as illustrated by Mrs Beeton's recipe of 1861, which contained ground almonds, and far less jam than earlier recipes, on a puff pastry base.

Although it is generally known as Bakewell Tart, in Bakewell and surrounding towns it is still known as Bakewell Pudding and may still be made using puff rather than short crust pastry.

Makes one 23cm (9 in) tart
Serves 6
Sweet Short Pastry 3 (page 32)
Use 1/2 of the quantity, wrap and freeze
    the remaining pastry
1 egg yolk
125g (4¹/2oz) unsalted butter

125g (4¹/2oz) light muscovado sugar
2 eggs
125g (4¹/2oz) ground almonds
50g (2oz) nibbed almonds
4-5 tbsp raspberry jam
6 tbsp icing sugar

Preheat the oven to 190˚C, 170˚C fan oven, gas 5.

Prepare the pastry and rest it for 15 minutes in the fridge. Lightly flour a clean work surface and roll out the pastry to 3mm (1/8 in) thick. Line a 23cm (9 in) tart tin with the pastry. Lightly prick the base and rest it for 20 minutes in the fridge or 10 minutes in the freezer.

Cream the butter and sugar together, beat in the eggs and then stir in the ground and nibbed almonds. Spread the jam over the base of the pastry and then spread over the almond mix. Bake the tart for 35-40 minutes, until the almond sponge is firm to the touch.

Mix the icing sugar with 1-2 tablespoons of boiling water and brush over the surface of the warm tart, serve warm.

COCONUT TART

Desiccated coconut is generally used in biscuit and cake making although the following recipe uses coconut cream in addition to desiccated coconut, to give a richer coconut flavour.

Makes one 23cm (9 in) tart
Serves 6
Sweet Short Pastry 3 (page 32)
Use 1/2 of the quantity, wrap and freeze
   the remaining pastry
2 egg yolks
1 egg
1 tbsp cornflour

75g (3oz) caster sugar
200ml (7fl oz) coconut cream
100g (3 1/2oz) desiccated coconut
1 tsp vanilla extract
3 tbsp raspberry jam
Icing sugar and Raspberry Sauce
   (page 37), to serve

Preheat the oven to 190°C, 170°C fan oven, gas 5.

Prepare the pastry and rest it for 15 minutes in the fridge. Lightly flour a clean work surface and roll out the pastry to 3mm (1/8 in) thick. Line a 23cm (9 in) tart tin and lightly prick the base. Rest pastry for 20 minutes in the fridge or 10 minutes in the freezer.

Bake the pastry blind for 10-15 minutes, remove the baking beans and bake for a further 5 minutes. The pastry should be pale to golden in colour. Brush the pastry case with a little of the egg yolk and bake for a further minute. Remove the pastry case from the oven and allow to cool. Reduce the oven temperature to 180°C, 160°C fan oven, gas 4.

Whisk together the egg yolk, eggs, cornflour and sugar. Then stir in the coconut cream, desiccated coconut and vanilla extract. Spread the jam over the pastry base and spoon over the coconut mixture. Bake the tart for 25-30 minutes until lightly set.

Just before serving dust with icing sugar and serve with the raspberry sauce.

DATE AND WALNUT PITHIVIERS

Gateau Pithiviers hails from the town of the same name in the Orléans region of France. The round puff pastry tart, traditionally made with scalloped edges and an almond cream filling, appears often with other fillings both savoury and sweet.

I came across a recipe for a Walnut Pithiviers and adapted it by adding the dates and orange. The addition of the sweet dates complement the bitter walnuts.

Makes one 20cm (8 in) round
Serves 4-6
Puff Pastry (page 30)
50g (2oz) unsalted butter
50g (2oz) light muscovado sugar
1 egg
25g (1oz) ground almonds
50g (2oz) ground walnuts

1 tsp grated orange zest
75g (3oz) no-soak or fresh dates, pitted
    and chopped
25g (1oz) chopped walnuts
1 egg yolk
1 tbsp milk
1 tbsp icing sugar

Make the puff pastry the day before or have some ready in the freezer to defrost.
    Preheat the oven to 220°C, 200°C fan oven, gas 7.
    Cut the pastry in 2, one piece slightly larger than the other. Roll out the larger piece and cut a round 23cm (9 in) in diameter. Roll out the smaller piece to 20cm (8 in) in diameter. Rest both in the fridge whilst making the filling.
    Cream the butter and sugar then gradually beat in the egg. Fold through the ground nuts then stir in the orange zest, dates and chopped walnuts. Mix together the egg yolk and milk.
    Lay the smaller round of pastry on a baking tray and brush the outer 2.5cm (1 in) edge with egg wash. Prick the centre of the pastry. Spread the date and walnut paste evenly over the pastry round, up to the egg washed edge. Lay the second piece of pastry on top and press lightly to seal the edges. Crimp with fingers or mark with a fork. Brush the top of the pastry with egg wash, taking care not to brush the cut pastry edge. Refrigerate for 10 minutes to set the egg wash.
    Using the back of a small knife etch a curved pattern from a central point to the crimped edge over the surface of the Pithiviers. Make a small incision at the central point to allow steam to escape. Knock up the edges of the pastry with a small knife and bake the Pithiviers for 35-40 minutes. When it is cooked remove it from the oven. Turn up the oven temperature to 240°C, 220°C fan oven, gas 8, sieve the Pithiviers with icing sugar and return it to the oven for 2-3 minutes until the icing caramelises and glazes the pastry. Serve warm with ice cream or vanilla sauce.

MAPLE PECAN PIE

A twist on an American classic, this recipe uses maple syrup instead of corn syrup. Corn syrup is not widely available here so if you come across recipes where it is listed substitute golden syrup or honey. Although golden syrup is heavier than corn syrup I've found that baked recipes work just as well. One type of corn syrup called high fructose corn syrup is produced from GM corn using GM enzymes and is very difficult for the body to digest, for this reason I prefer to use honey or maple syrup.

Makes one 25.5cm (10 in) pie
Serves 8-10
Sweet Short Pastry 1 (page 31)
Use 1/2 of the quantity of pastry, about 350g (12oz), wrap and freeze the remaining pastry
25g (1oz) unsalted butter

200g (7oz) dark brown sugar
150g (5oz) golden syrup
100g (3 1/2oz) maple syrup
200g (7oz) chopped pecans
5 eggs, lightly beaten
50g (2oz) pecan halves

Preheat the oven to 190°C, 170°C fan oven, gas 5.

Prepare the pastry and rest it for 15 minutes in the fridge. Lightly flour a clean work surface and roll out the pastry to 3mm (1/8 in) thick. Line a 25.5cm (10 in) tart tin with the pastry. Lightly prick the base and rest it for 20 minutes in the fridge or 10 minutes in the freezer.

Bake the pastry blind for 10-15 minutes, remove the baking beans and bake for a further 5 minutes. The pastry should be pale to golden in colour. Brush the pastry case with a little egg yolk and bake for a further minute. Remove the pastry case from the oven and allow to cool. Reduce the oven temperature to 170°C, 150°C fan oven, gas 3.

Melt the butter, sugar and golden syrup. Then add the maple syrup and chopped pecans. Allow the mix to cool slightly, then stir in the beaten eggs. Pour the mixture into the pastry case and arrange the pecan halves on top. Bake the pie for about 25 minutes until lightly set. Remove from the oven, dust with icing sugar and serve with ice cream.

MACADAMIA, HONEY AND LIME PIE

This recipe is adapted from a petits fours recipe I used to make called *Pain de Miel* or honey bread, the recipe for which was given to me by Allan Collier, when I was a student at Westminster Catering College. It is a very sweet tart, filled with buttery, soft toffee and crunchy nuts, with a back note of honey and lime and is extremely more-ish!

Makes one 23cm (9 in) pie
Serves 8-10
Sweet Short Pastry 3 (page 32)
Use 1/2 of the quantity, wrap and freeze
   the remaining pastry
1 egg yolk
225g (8oz) macadamia nuts, lightly
   roasted

115g (4oz) caster sugar
50g (2oz) honey
115g (4oz) unsalted butter
142ml carton double cream
Grated zest 3 limes

Sugar thermometer

Preheat the oven to 190°C, 170°C fan oven, gas 5.

Prepare the pastry and rest it for 15 minutes in the fridge. Lightly flour a clean work surface and roll out the pastry to 3mm (1/8 in) thick. Line a 23cm (9 in) tart tin with the pastry. Lightly prick the base and rest it in the fridge for 20 minutes or 10 minutes in the freezer.

Bake the pastry blind for 10-15 minutes, remove the baking beans and bake for a further 5 minutes. The pastry should be pale to golden in colour. Brush the pastry case with a little egg yolk and bake for a further minute. Remove the pastry case from the oven and allow to cool.

Whiz the macadamia nuts in a food processor for 30 seconds and put to one side.

Put the sugar, honey, butter and cream into a heavy-based large pan and using a sugar thermometer cook to medium ball (118°C, 240°F.) Whilst the sugar is cooking put the nuts on a tray and warm them in the oven for a few minutes. When the sugar mix reaches medium ball, remove the thermometer and place it in a jug of boiling water. Remove the pan from the heat and quickly stir in the warmed nuts and lime zest. Pour the mixture into the prepared pastry case and bake for 5 minutes. Remove from the oven and allow to stand until the mixture sets. This will take about 2 hours. Cut into thin slices and serve.

BAKLAVA

Baklava dates back to the 8th century when the Assyrians began making small sweet breads, comprising thin layers of bread dough, nuts and honey. It became popular and as the spice and silk routes developed, the recipe began crossing borders. It is thought that the Armenians were responsible for the addition of cinnamon and cloves, and that the Arabs adapted the recipes to include rosewater and cardamom. In fact every ethic group whose ancestry goes back to the Middle East makes a claim of ownership on baklava.

Makes one 23cm (9 in) x 33cm (13 in) tray
Makes 24 pieces
175g (6oz) caster sugar
1 cinnamon stick
2 tbsp honey
2 tsp orange flower water (optional)
2 tsp lemon juice
100g (3½oz) unsalted butter

15 sheets of filo pastry
150g (5oz) almonds, blanched and finely chopped
75g (3oz) pistachio, skinned and finely chopped
2 tsp ground cinnamon

Preheat the oven to 190°C, 170°C fan oven, gas 5.

Put 150g (5oz) of the caster sugar in a pan with 4 tablespoons of water, add the cinnamon stick and heat gently until the sugar dissolves, then simmer for 4-5 minutes. Add the honey, orange flower water, if using, and the lemon juice, and put to one side.

Melt the butter and brush the baking tray. Butter 5 sheets of filo and lay them on top of each other in the tray. Mix together the nuts, remaining sugar and cinnamon and spread half the mix over the filo sheets in the tin.

Butter another 5 sheets of filo and lay these on top of the nut mix. Then spread the remaining nut mix over the filo sheets. Butter the 5 remaining filo sheets and press these down on top of the nut mixture. Score the baklava into 24 small squares.

Bake the baklava for 25-30 minutes until golden. Remove from the oven. Remove the cinnamon stick from the syrup and pour over the warm baklava. Cut the baklava into small squares.

TIP Keep the filo pastry covered when not using it as it will dry out and become brittle.

If you like you can substitute other nuts such as walnuts.

WALNUT AND COFFEE CREAM TART

This recipe is similar to a pecan pie, both in appearance and texture, but the flavour is very different. The bitterness of the walnuts and coffee are balanced by the sugars, and the cream topping provides a contrasting texture to the filling. You could choose to serve it with a mid-morning coffee or as dessert.

Makes one 23cm (9 in) tart
Serves 6-8
Sweet Short Pastry 3 (page 32)
Use 1/2 of the quantity, wrap and freeze
   the remaining pastry
1 egg yolk
125g (4^1/$_2$oz) dark brown sugar
125g (4^1/$_2$oz) golden syrup

150g (5oz) chopped walnuts
3 tbsp strong black coffee
3 eggs
400ml (14fl oz) whipping cream
1 tsp vanilla extract
2 tbsp caster sugar
Chocolate shavings and cocoa powder to
   serve

Preheat the oven to 190°C, 170°C fan oven, gas 5.

Prepare the pastry and rest it for 15 minutes in the fridge. Lightly flour a clean work surface and roll out the pastry to 3mm (1/8 in) thick. Line a 23cm (9 in) tart tin and lightly prick the base. Rest it for 20 minutes in the fridge or 10 minutes in the freezer.

Bake the pastry blind for 10-15 minutes, remove the baking beans and bake for a further 5 minutes. The pastry should be pale to golden in colour. Brush the pastry case with a little egg yolk and bake for a further minute. Remove the pastry case from the oven and allow to cool. Reduce the oven temperature to 180°C, 160°C fan oven, gas 4.

Melt the sugar and golden syrup. Then add the chopped walnuts and coffee.

Allow the mix to cool slightly, then stir in the beaten eggs. Pour the mixture into the pastry case and bake the pie for about 20 minutes until firm to the touch. Allow the tart to cool.

Lightly whip the cream and add the vanilla extract and caster sugar and either swirl or pipe over the top of the cooled tart.

ALMOND AND POTATO TART

This is an unusual tart with a grainy texture and a delicate flavour. It probably originated as a peasant dish in the Garfagnana region of Tuscany where the best Italian potatoes are grown. Although usually served plain, I've chosen to add candied lemon and chocolate, to enliven an otherwise simple tart.

Makes one 25.5cm (10 in) tart
Serves 8-10
Sweet Short Pastry 2 (page 32)
Use 1/2 of the quantity of pastry, about
    350g (12oz), wrap and freeze the
    remaining pastry
1 egg yolk
500g (1lb 2oz) Maris Piper potatoes,
    peeled and chopped
125g (4 1/2 oz) caster sugar

75g (3oz) ground almonds
2 tbsp Marsala
Grated zest 2 lemons
Pinch salt
4 tbsp double cream
4 eggs
25g (1oz) unsalted butter, melted
3 tbsp candied lemon zest, finely chopped
25g (1oz) dark chocolate

Preheat the oven to 190°C, 170°C fan oven, gas 5.

Prepare the pastry and rest it for 15 minutes in the fridge. Lightly flour a clean work surface and roll out the pastry to 3mm (1/8 in) thick. Line a 25.5cm (10 in) tart tin with the pastry. Lightly prick the base and rest it for 20 minutes in the fridge or 10 minutes in the freezer.

Bake the pastry blind for 10-15 minutes, remove the baking beans and bake for a further 5 minutes. The pastry should be pale to golden in colour. Brush the pastry case with a little egg yolk and bake for a further minute.

Boil the potatoes and cook until tender. Drain and mash or rice to remove all lumps.

In a large bowl mix together the sugar, ground almonds, Marsala, lemon zest, salt and cream. Then add the potato and mix thoroughly. Add the eggs, gradually beating between each addition, then stir in the melted butter and beat well.

Pour the mix into the prepared case. Sprinkle with the candied lemon and bake for 20 minutes then reduce the oven temperature to 180°C, 160°C fan oven, gas 4 and cook for a further 20-25 minutes, until golden and firm to the touch. Remove and allow to cool.

Chop the chocolate and put into a heatproof bowl over a pan of simmering water or heat in the microwave on a low setting, until melted. Drizzle over the cool tart.

LINZER TART

More than just a jam tart, this Austrian pastry takes its name from the town of Linz. It is a simple combination of raspberry jam and nutty pastry and although plain, it is great tasting. Its popularity has spread throughout Northern Europe and it has lent its name to other items of pâtisserie including small tarts and biscuits.

Makes one 23cm (9 in) tart
Serves 6-8
Nut Pastry (page 36)
made with hazelnuts, 1/2 teaspoon of ground cinnamon and the grated zest of 1 lemon
300g (10oz) raspberry jam
1 tbsp milk
2 tbsp granulated sugar

Preheat the oven to 190˚C, 170˚C fan oven, gas 5.

Prepare the pastry with the hazelnuts, ground cinnamon and lemon zest and rest it for 15 minutes in the fridge. Lightly flour a clean work surface and roll out the pastry to 3mm (1/8 in) thick. Line a 23cm (9 in) tart tin with half the pastry. Lightly prick the base and rest it for 20 minutes in the fridge or 10 minutes in the freezer.

Spread the pastry with the raspberry jam. Roll out the remaining pastry and cut strips 2.5cm (1 in) wide. Lay 4 strips of pastry across the tart and 4 at right angles to the first strips, seal them on the edge of the tart tin. Brush the pastry lattice with milk and sprinkle with granulated sugar, bake the tart for 35-40 minutes until golden. Allow to stand for 30 minutes before serving.

CHESTNUT TART

Chestnuts are very popular in the northern regions of Italy, where chestnut purée is used in desserts and chestnut flour is used in baking. I've adapted a pastry recipe to include a little chestnut flour to give it more flavour but if you can't buy it locally don't worry simply use the standard sweet pastry recipe.

Makes one 25.5cm (10 in) tart
Serves 8-10
Sweet Short Pastry 2 (page 32)
Use $^1/_2$ of the quantity of pastry about 350g (12oz),
      wrap and freeze the remaining pastry
125g ($4^1/_2$oz) unsalted butter
125g ($4^1/_2$oz) light muscovado sugar
2 eggs
100g ($3^1/_2$oz) ground almonds
50g (2oz) chestnut purée
3 tbsp chestnut honey

Preheat the oven to 190°C, 170°C fan oven, gas 5.
    Prepare the pastry substituting 100g ($3^1/_2$oz) flour for chestnut flour and rest it for 15 minutes in the fridge. Lightly flour a clean work surface and roll out the pastry to 3mm ($^1/_8$ in) thick. Line a 25.5cm (10 in) tart tin and lightly prick the base. Rest it for 20 minutes in the fridge or 10 minutes in the freezer.
    Cream the butter and sugar then gradually beat in the eggs. Fold through the ground almonds and chestnut purée. Spoon the mixture into the prepared pastry case and bake for 25 minutes, then reduce the oven temperature to 180°C, 160°C fan oven, gas 4, and cook for a further 20-25 minutes until golden and firm to the touch. Remove the tart from the oven. Drizzle with the honey and serve warm with cream.

ALMOND JALOUSIE

A jalousie is a French term used to describe a puff pastry slice with horizontal cuts across its width, giving it a slatted appearance. Jalousie means Venetian blind in French. Traditionally the filling is frangipane (almond cream) but you can use fruit compote, jam or fresh fruit fillings. I particularly like raspberry jam and chocolate frangipane. If you want to try this add 50g (2oz) melted dark chocolate to the almond filling.

Makes one 30.5cm (12 in) x 12.5cm (5 in) slice
Serves 8
Puff Pastry (page 30)
100g (3½oz) unsalted butter
100g (3½oz) light muscovado sugar
2 eggs

125g (4½oz) ground almonds
1 tsp vanilla extract
3 tbsp raspberry jam
1 egg yolk
1 tbsp milk
Icing sugar to serve

Make the puff pastry the day before or have some ready in the freezer to defrost.

Preheat the oven to 220°C, 200°C fan oven, gas 7.

Cut the pastry in 2. Roll out both pieces of pastry on a lightly floured work surface to 30.5cm (12 in) x 12.5cm (5 in). Prick the centre of one of the puff pastry strips leaving a 2.5cm (1 in) border along each edge. This will be the base. Rest the pastry in the fridge for 20 minutes.

Cream the butter and sugar then gradually beat in the eggs. Fold through the ground almonds and vanilla extract.

Place the base strip on a baking tray and prick with a fork. Mix the egg yolk and milk and brush the border of the pastry with the egg wash. Spread the jam on the base pastry sheet, avoiding the egg washed edge. Then spread the almond cream over the jam.

Fold the top pastry strip in half lengthwise and make horizontal cuts 2.5cm (1 in) along the length of the strip leaving 2.5cm (1 in) from each end. Open the folded pastry onto the almond cream and seal the edges. Crimp or fork the edges.

Brush the top of the pastry with egg wash, taking care not to brush the cut pastry edge. Knock up the pastry edges with a small knife. Bake the jalousie for 25-30 minutes until golden. Remove from the oven and cut into slices, dust with icing sugar before serving.

CONVERSATION TARTS

I first made these little tarts at Westminster College many years ago but it wasn't until I started researching this book that I discovered their origin.

They were created at the end of the 18th century, taking their name from a piece of work by Madam d'Epinay titled *Les Conversations d'Emilie*. They are delicate, puff pastry tartlets, filled with rum-flavoured frangipane (almond cream) and covered with puff pastry and royal icing, which is marked in a criss-cross pattern.

Makes 12 small tarts
Puff Pastry (page 30)
Use 250g (9oz) trimmings
1 egg white
Pinch egg white powder
200g (7oz) icing sugar, sifted

125g (4^1/2oz) unsalted butter
125g (4^1/2oz) caster sugar
2 eggs
150g (5oz) ground almonds
1 tbsp rum
4 tbsp raspberry jam

Make the puff pastry the day before or have some trimmings ready in the freezer to defrost. If you haven't got any trimmings to hand simply roll out some virgin puff pastry to 3mm (1/8 in) thick, fold in half and in half again and refrigerate for 30 minutes, then use as trimmings.

Preheat the oven to 220˚C, 200˚C fan oven, gas 7.

Cream the butter and sugar then gradually beat in the egg. Fold through the ground almonds and rum.

Roll out the pastry 2mm (less than 1/8 in) thick and cut out twelve, 10cm (4 in) and 12 x 7.5cm (3 in) rounds. Grease and line a 12-hole bun tin with the larger pastry rounds. Lightly prick the bases and rest them for 20 minutes in the fridge or 10 minutes in the freezer.

In a small bowl whisk the egg white and egg white powder together and then gradually add the icing sugar. Whisk until mixture is stiff and smooth.

Roll out the remaining pastry and cut lids to fit the tarts.

Cream the butter and sugar, then gradually beat in the eggs. Fold through the ground almonds and vanilla extract. Spoon a little jam into each pastry case and then 3/4 fill with almond mixture.

Brush the pastry edge with water and lay the lids on top. Seal the edges. Refrigerate the tarts to firm up the pastry. When the pastry is firm, carefully spread a thin layer of royal icing over the pastry. Score the top of the tarts, in a criss-cross pattern and bake the tarts for 15-20 minutes until golden and cooked through.

PISTACHIO TART

Pistachio trees are widely grown throughout the Mediterranean and these sweet delicate nuts are used in both sweet and savoury dishes. Unfortunately their green colour is often accentuated artificially and many confectioners rely on pistachio pastes that taste absolutely horrible. Not so this pistachio tart, this is the real deal. The pistachio flavour is complemented, but not overwhelmed by, the raspberry jam and bitter chocolate, to give a tart with a balance of texture and flavours.

Makes one 23cm (9 in) tart
Serves 6
Sweet Short Pastry 3 (page 32)
Use 1/2 of the quantity, wrap and freeze
    the remaining pastry
1 egg yolk
125g (41/2oz) unsalted butter
125g (41/2oz) light muscovado sugar

2 eggs
75g (3oz) ground almonds
75g (3oz) roughly ground pistachios
2 tbsp raspberry jam
1 tbsp pistachio nuts, roughly chopped
25g (1oz) dark chocolate
Icing sugar to dust

Preheat the oven to 190°C, 170°C fan oven, gas 5.

Prepare the pastry and rest it for 15 minutes in the fridge. Lightly flour a clean work surface and roll out the pastry to 3mm (1/8 in) thick. Line a 23cm (9 in) tart tin with the pastry. Lightly prick the base and rest it for 20 minutes in the fridge or 10 minutes in the freezer.

Cream the butter and sugar together, beat in the eggs and then stir in the ground almonds and pistachios. Spread the jam over the base of the pastry and then spread over the nut mix. Sprinkle with chopped pistachio nuts. Bake the tart for 30 minutes and then lower the oven temperature to 180°C, 160°C fan oven, gas 4 and bake for a further 10 minutes, until firm to the touch.

Chop the chocolate and put in a heatproof bowl over a pan of simmering water or heat in the microwave on a low setting, until melted. When cool drizzle with melted chocolate and dust with icing sugar.

DAIRY

Man has been consuming dairy products for thousands of years. Neolithic man is known to have milked animals and converted milk to butter and cheese as early as 2000 BC in parts of Britain. It is thought the skills were introduced to Britain from the area known as the 'Fertile Crescent' which lies between the Euphrates and the Tigris in Iraq.

Butter, milk and milk products had become an important part of the British diet by the medieval period and were used throughout the country and so from the middle of the 16th century the Elizabethans regularly enjoyed milk puddings and custards.

Milk and cheese production continued on a small scale throughout the country until the 19th century but it was the Industrial Revolution, and in particular the development of the railways, that changed the face of the British dairy industry, when it became possible to transport milk long distances, from the areas of rural production, to the growing towns. That, and the advent of pasteurisation, refrigeration and bottled milk enabled households to have greater access to better quality dairy products for general consumption, as well as baking.

I am especially passionate about the quality of dairy products used in pâtisserie, and abhor the use of margarine. **Butter** must be unsalted. If you want to spread butter on your bread, salted is fine, but don't try cooking with it. Some salted butters contain so much salt they simply destroy the flavour of desserts and cakes, this is why recipes stipulate the use of unsalted. Butter is by far the most important fat used for pastry making. Although other fats such as margarine, lard, shortening and plasticized fat, made from hydrogenated vegetable fat, and to a lesser extent oil, are used, butter should be the fat of choice unless a recipe stipulates otherwise. Strudel pastry is one such recipe where oil gives the best results. The simple reason butter makes the best pastry is because it has the best flavour, as well as producing a pastry with a good flaky crust.

Neither would I advocate the use of skimmed **milk** in an attempt to save on a few calories. Though we are now a nation of semi-skimmed milk drinkers and although semi-skimmed can be used successfully in making pâtisserie, why not simply eat less of the full fat, full flavour version? Milk is used extensively for making tart and pie fillings, the most important of which is crème pâtissière or pastry cream, a flour thickened egg custard which can be used to fill tarts and pies served either hot or cold. It is also used as the basis for making crème diplomat (crème pâtissière and whipped cream) and crème Chiboust (crème pâtissière and meringue lightly set with gelatine). Milk is also used as the basis for baked egg custard mixtures, which were one of the earliest known tart fillings or flathons, as they were known in the 15th century.

Cream is used both in its liquid and also aerated, or whipped, form and contains a higher percentage of butterfat than milk; it is this quality that enables cream to be whipped. In order to whip cream it needs to contain a butterfat content between 35% (whipping cream) and 48% (double cream). Clotted cream with a butterfat content of 55% is unsuitable for whipping, as is single cream, with its butterfat content of just 18%. In its liquid form cream enriches, but once whipped, it also adds volume and lightness to a mixture.

Crème fraîche originated in Normandy, it is a lightly-soured, thick cream and is widely used throughout France and other parts of Europe. Traditionally it was produced from unpasteurized cream and was thickened by naturally occurring bacteria. These days pasteurised cream is generally used and a bacterial culture is added to thicken the cream. It has been available in Britain for about 10 years now and has become a popular substitute for sour cream and cream. Unlike sour cream, crème fraîche doesn't curdle when heated and can also be whipped. It can be used in hot and cold recipes and also makes a great accompaniment to a wide variety of sweet and savoury dishes.

Yoghurt is also a cultured dairy product originating thousands of years ago in Eastern Europe and Western Asia. There are numerous types of yoghurt and the differences in style are down to the type of milk and the type of bacterial culture used to produce the yoghurt. It is not widely used in making pâtisserie, although it is used in Austria and Germany to a greater extent than in Britain and France. It is sometimes added in place of cream to lower the fat content of desserts.

Soft cheeses are used as fillings for tarts and pies. Most tend to be fresh or 'unripened' cheese. These include cream and curd cheese, ricotta, mascarpone and goat's cheese. Soft fresh cheeses have long been used to form part of dessert. The ancient Greeks and Romans would serve cheese with fruits and honey, and although the earliest recipe for a cheesecake, or cheese tart, dates back to the 14th century there is evidence to suggest the Romans made a type of cheese tart as far back as the 2nd century BC.

PASTEL DE NATA

These delicious Portuguese custard tarts are absolutely divine little mouthfuls of creaminess, best served mid-morning or at the end of a meal with coffee. The most famous are the *Pastéis de Belém,* baked to a secret recipe. Each weekday 10,000 are sold from the Belém Bakery and Café in Lisbon, and on Sundays they sell a staggering 25,000. They are served warm with a sprinkling of ground cinnamon and dusted with icing sugar.

If like me you have not been fortunate enough to enjoy them direct from the Belém Bakery and you do not have a Portuguese café or bakery near by, why not try making this recipe.

Makes 12 tarts
Puff Pastry (page 30)
Use 250g (9oz) trimmings
3 egg yolks
50g (2oz) caster sugar
2 tbsp custard powder

300ml (1/2pt) milk
142ml carton double cream
1 vanilla pod, split lengthways
1 tsp vanilla extract
Icing sugar and ground cinnamon to serve

Make the puff pastry the day before or have some trimmings ready in the freezer to defrost. If you haven't got any trimmings to hand simply roll out some virgin puff pastry to 3mm (1/8 in) thick, fold in half and in half again, and refrigerate for 30 minutes then use as trimmings.

Preheat the oven to 220°C, 200°C fan oven, gas 7.

Mix together the yolks and sugar and then add the custard powder. Add 4 tablespoons of the milk and mix to a paste.

Bring the remaining milk and cream to the boil with the split vanilla pod and then pour half of the boiled liquid onto the custard paste. Return the mixture to the pan, with the remaining milk and cream, and cook gently, stirring all the time, for 2-3 minutes, until the custard has thickened, taking care not to let it boil. Remove from the heat, pour into a clean mixing bowl, cover with a round of buttered greaseproof and allow to cool.

Roll out the pastry 2mm (less than 1/8 in) thick and cut out twelve, 10cm (4 in) rounds. Grease and line a 12-hole bun tin with the pastry rounds. Lightly prick the bases and rest them for 20 minutes in the fridge or 10 minutes in the freezer.

Spoon the custard into the pastry cases and bake for 20 minutes until golden. Dust with icing sugar and serve warm.

YORKSHIRE CURD TART

Also known as Yorkshire cheesecake, this tart dates back over 250 years. It originated in the Yorkshire Dales as a by-product from the dairy industry; fresh curds leftover from the cheese making were baked with egg, sugar and a little rosewater, in a pastry case, the result is a mild creamy tart with a slightly grainy texture. These days the rosewater is absent from the recipe and the tart is speckled with currants.

My friend Liz, a fellow pastry chef, gave me this recipe. At one time we were both working in gentleman's clubs in London's Pall Mall; I was at the Athenaeum and Liz was at the Army and Navy, after work we'd meet up and exchange recipe ideas over cups of coffee.

Makes one 23cm (9 in) tart
Serves 6-8
Sweet Short Pastry 1 (page 31)
Use 1/3 of the quantity of pastry, about
    250g (9oz), wrap and freeze the
    remaining pastry
1 egg yolk
400g (14oz) curd cheese

125g (41/2oz) caster sugar
2 eggs
2 whites
Grated zest 1 lemon
100ml (31/2 fl oz) milk
2 tsp nutmeg
75g (3oz) currants

Preheat the oven to 190°C, 170°C fan oven, gas 5.

Prepare the pastry and rest it for 15 minutes in the fridge. Lightly flour a clean work surface and roll out the pastry to 3mm (1/8 in) thick. Line a 23cm (9 in) tart tin with the pastry. Lightly prick the base and then rest it for 20 minutes in the fridge or 10 minutes in the freezer.

Bake the pastry blind for 10-15 minutes, remove the baking beans and bake for a further 5 minutes. The pastry should be pale to golden in colour. Brush the pastry case with the egg yolk and bake for a further minute. Remove it from the oven. Reduce the oven temperature to 180°C, 160°C fan oven, gas 4.

Mix together the curd cheese, sugar, eggs and remaining egg yolk. Then add the lemon zest, milk and spice. Whisk the whites until stiff and fold through the cheese mixture. Carefully stir through the currants, then pour the mix into the pastry case. Bake for 15-20 minutes until lightly set. Serve at room temperature.

CUSTARD TART

This is probably one of the oldest of British tarts, dating back several centuries. These days custard tarts are flavoured with vanilla and nutmeg, but earlier versions were often flavoured with cinnamon and rosewater, as well as nutmeg.

I like my custard tarts rich and creamy, with a good measure of vanilla but not too sweet. I'd recommend tasting the custard mixture, unless you shouldn't or don't like the idea of eating raw egg, to check whether you'd prefer the mixture a little sweeter.

Makes one 23cm (9 in) tart
Serves 6-8
Sweet Short Pastry 2 (page 32)
Use 1/3 of the quantity of pastry, about 250g (9oz), wrap and freeze the remaining pastry
3 eggs
2 yolks

50g (2oz) caster sugar
350ml (12fl oz) milk
284ml carton double cream
1 tsp vanilla extract
Pinch grated nutmeg

Preheat the oven to 190˚C, 170˚C fan oven, gas 5.

Prepare the pastry and rest it for 15 minutes in the fridge. Lightly flour a clean work surface and roll out the pastry to 3mm (1/8 in) thick. Line a 23cm (9 in) tart tin with the pastry. Lightly prick the base and rest it for 20 minutes in the fridge or 10 minutes in the freezer.

Bake the flan case blind for 10-15 minutes, remove the baking beans and bake for a further 5 minutes. The pastry should be pale to golden in colour. Brush the pastry case with some of the egg yolk and bake for a further minute. Remove from the oven. Reduce the oven temperature to 160˚C, 150˚C fan oven, gas 3.

Lightly beat together the eggs, egg yolks and sugar. Add the milk, cream and vanilla extract. Strain the mix and pour into the baked case. Sprinkle with the nutmeg and bake for 25-30 minutes until lightly set.

TIP Make sure that the pastry is thoroughly cooked before the custard is poured into the case because the base of the case won't cook any further once you've added a wet filling.

KENTISH PUDDING PIE

I first came across this recipe when reading Mary Norwak's book *English Puddings*. It's a hearty, old-fashioned pudding made during Lent when meat pies couldn't be eaten. It makes a deep pie and looks great made in an old-style enamel pie dish. Add a good measure of fruit and spice to the filling though or it can taste a little bland.

My version is richer than early recipes as I like a creamier filling.

Makes one 19cm (7¹/2 in) wide x 26cm (10¹/4 in) pie
Serves 6
Rich Short Crust (page 35)
750ml (1¹/4pts) milk
125g (4¹/2oz) ground rice

100g (3¹/2oz) unsalted butter
75g (3oz) caster sugar
3 eggs
142ml carton double cream
¹/2 tsp ground nutmeg
75g (3oz) currants

Preheat the oven to 180°C, 170°C fan oven, gas 4.

Prepare the pastry and rest it for 15 minutes in the fridge. Lightly flour a clean work surface and roll out the pastry to 3mm (¹/8 in) thick. Line the 19cm (7¹/2 in) wide x 26cm (10¹/4 in) pie dish with the pastry and lightly prick the base. Rest the case in the fridge whilst making the filling.

Pour the milk into a pan and stir in the ground rice. Bring to the boil and simmer for 3-4 minutes, stirring continuously. Remove from the heat.

Cream together the butter and sugar and then gradually add the eggs, beating between each addition. Stir the creamed mix into the milk and ground rice. Add the cream, spice and currants and pour into the lined pie dish. Bake for 35-40 minutes until golden and firm to the touch. Serve hot or cold.

GATEAU PARIS BREST

Although the British understanding of the French word gâteau is 'cake', in France it has a much wider application. It is used to describe pancakes, sweet and savoury puddings, as well as tarts, so although Gateau Paris Brest doesn't resemble a typical tart I decided to include it in the book because it is such a famous choux pastry dessert. It was created to mark the Paris to Brest bicycle race of 1891, by a Parisian pâtissier whose shop was close to the route of the race. It is now popular throughout Paris and Brest.

This recipe uses praline-flavoured fresh cream but some versions may use a cooked butter cream, 'crème au beurre', that is heavier and richer.

Makes one 25.5cm (10 in) round
Serves 6-8
Choux Pastry (page 36)
7 egg yolks
225g (8oz) caster sugar
3 tbsp cornflour
300ml (1/2pt) milk

200g (7oz) blanched hazelnuts
1 egg yolk
1 tbsp milk
2 tbsp flaked almonds
284ml carton double cream
Icing sugar to serve

Preheat the oven to 220°C, 200°C fan oven, gas 7. Brush a 30.5cm (12 in) square baking tray with melted butter and chill it in the freezer.

Mix together the yolks and 75g (3oz) of the sugar and then add the cornflour. Add 4 tablespoons of milk and mix to a paste.

Bring the remaining milk to the boil and then pour half of the boiled liquid onto the egg mixture. Return this to the pan, with the remaining milk, and cook gently for 3-4 minutes, stirring all the time, until the pastry cream has thickened. Remove from the heat, pour into a clean mixing bowl. Cover with a piece of buttered greaseproof paper and allow to cool.

Put the hazelnuts onto a baking tray and toast them in the oven for 2-3 minutes, until golden. Oil a 25.5cm (10 in) wide piece of foil and lay the foil on the work surface. Put the remaining sugar into a clean dry pan and cook gently over a low heat. If the sugar starts to cook unevenly move the sugar slightly with a wooden spoon, resisting the temptation to stir the sugar. Cook the sugar until it turns a pale golden colour. Add the nuts to the pan and coat the nuts in caramel. Pour the caramel-coated nuts onto the oiled foil and spread them out so they will cool more quickly.

Prepare the choux pastry. The pastry should be pipeable but also hold its own shape. Using a piping bag and 1.5cm (3/4 in) nozzle, pipe a large ring 5cm (2 in) wide, 25.5cm (10 in) in diameter on the chilled baking tray. Over pipe the remaining choux pastry on top of the ring.

Mix together the egg yolk and milk and brush the choux pastry with egg wash. Sprinkle with flaked almonds and bake for about 20-25 minutes until golden brown.

Remove from the oven and allow to cool.

Break the praline (caramel nuts) into pieces and put them in a food processor. Whiz the praline for 1- 2 minutes until finely ground. Lightly whip the cream and fold the praline into the cream. Fold the praline cream into the pastry cream.

Slice the choux ring in half horizontally, spoon the hazelnut cream onto the bottom half of the choux ring and top with the remaining half. Refrigerate for 1 hour before serving, dust with icing sugar and serve.

PROFITEROLES ROYALE

Unlike cream-filled profiteroles, Profiteroles Royale are filled with vanilla ice cream and served with hot chocolate sauce. You could try filling them with a selection of flavours; I particularly like filling them with a mixture of caramel and chocolate ice creams. They make a stunning special occasion dessert, piled high on a stemmed cake stand, and drizzled with chocolate sauce.

Makes about 30 profiteroles
Serves 6-8
Choux Pastry (page 36)
1 egg yolk
1 tbsp milk
284ml carton double cream
1 tsp vanilla extract
200g (7oz) dark chocolate
1 tbsp brandy (optional)
500ml tub good quality dairy vanilla ice cream

Make the choux pastry. The pastry should be pipeable but also hold its own shape. Pipe bulbs of choux pastry using a 1.5cm (3/4 in) plain nozzle onto greased and chilled baking trays 1.5cm (3/4 in) apart.

Mix together the egg yolk and milk and brush the choux pastry with egg wash and bake at 220°C, 200°C fan oven, gas 7 for about 15 minutes, until golden brown. Allow to cool.

Melt the chocolate in a bowl over a pan of simmering water or on a low heat in the microwave. Heat the remaining cream in a small pan, bringing it almost to the boil, pour slowly into the melted chocolate, stirring continuously. Add the brandy if using.

Use a small knife and cut each profiterole in half, fill each profiterole with a dessert spoon or two of ice cream, return the profiteroles to the freezer in batches. Just before serving chill the serving dish in the freezer for 5 minutes, then pile the profiteroles into the dish and drizzle over the chocolate sauce. Serve immediately.

PROFITEROLES WITH CHOCOLATE SAUCE

Choux pastry has an interesting history. When Catherine de Medici left Florence to marry the Duke of Orléans, who later became King Henry II of France, she took with her several chefs. It was her head chef, Panterelli, who is credited with inventing choux pastry in 1540, although at that time it was called *Pâte à Panterelli*.

Over the years the original recipe changed and in the Middle Ages it was known as *Pâte à Popelini*; it wasn't until the 18th century it became known as *Pâte à Choux*. In 1760, a pâtissier named Avice created choux buns or profiteroles, so called because the little buns resembled *petits choux* or cabbages. Antoine Carême went on to perfect the recipe in the 19th century and it is this recipe that forms the basis for choux pastry today.

Makes about 30 profiteroles
Serves 6-8
Choux Pastry (page 36)
1 egg yolk
1 tbsp milk

850ml double cream (1pt 9fl oz)
2 tbsp caster sugar
1 tsp vanilla extract
200g (7oz) dark chocolate
1 tbsp brandy (optional)

Preheat the oven to 220°C, 200°C fan oven, gas 7. Brush 2 baking trays with melted butter and chill them in the freezer.

Prepare the choux pastry. The pastry should be pipeable but hold its own shape. Pipe bulbs of choux pastry using a 1.5cm (3/4 in) plain nozzle onto the chilled baking trays, 1.5cm (3/4 in) apart. Mix together the egg yolk and milk, and brush the profiteroles with egg wash. Bake for about 20 minutes until golden brown. Remove from the oven and allow to cool.

Whilst the choux buns are in the oven, lightly whip 600ml (1pt) of the cream, add the remaining sugar and the vanilla extract, and refrigerate.

Melt the chocolate in a bowl over a pan of simmering water or on a low heat in the microwave. Heat the remaining cream in a small pan bringing it almost to the boil. Slowly pour the cream into the melted chocolate stirring continuously. Add the brandy if using.

Use a small knife and make a small hole in the base of each profiterole. Using a 6mm (1/4 in) nozzle, fill a piping bag with the lightly whipped cream and fill the profiteroles. At this point the profiteroles can be refrigerated but they are best eaten within an hour or two. Divide the profiteroles between the plates and drizzle over the chocolate sauce. Serve immediately.

TIP Profiteroles can be successfully frozen (unfilled). Simply defrost before use and crisp them in a hot oven for 2-3 minutes then allow them to cool before filling them.

CHEESECAKE PIE

I adapted this recipe from one of Adrianna Rabowitz's recipes. Adrianna is the person behind Little Red Barn Brownies, and other American biscuits, and I first came across her products while I was working at Sainsbury's. I thought her products were fantastic, so I set up a meeting for her with the bakery buying team, and helped her get some of her brownies and biscuits into the supermarket's stores.

I baked several recipes from her book and particularly liked a fruit-based cheesecake that was topped with a pastry crust. This is my version of the recipe.

Makes one 23cm (9 in) pie
Serves 10-12
Sweet Short Pastry 2 (page 32)
Use ½ of the quantity of pastry, about
    350g (12oz), wrap and freeze the
    remaining pastry
4 tbsp flour
2 tbsp butter
200g (7oz) caster sugar

500g (1lb 2oz) cream cheese
Pinch salt
3 tbsp cornflour
2 eggs
2 egg yolks
200ml crème fraîche
2 tsp vanilla extract
300g (10oz) strawberry preserve

Preheat the oven to 190˚C, 170˚C fan oven, gas 5. Prepare the pastry and rest it for 15 minutes in the fridge. Grease a 23cm (9 in) springform tin.

Roll out the pastry on a lightly floured work surface to about 6mm (¼ in) thick. Line the base and ¾ of the way up the sides of the pan. Lightly prick the base and then rest the pastry for 20 minutes in the fridge or 10 minutes in the freezer.

Bake the pastry blind for 10-12 minutes, then remove the baking beans and bake for a further 4-5 minutes.

Rub together the 4 tablespoons of flour, 2 tablespoons of butter and 2 tablespoons of the sugar and put to one side.

Beat the cream cheese until soft and smooth. Add the salt, cornflour and remaining sugar and beat for 1 minute. Add the eggs and yolks, gradually beating well to combine. Stir through the crème fraîche and vanilla.

Pour the mix into the prepared case and then stir through the strawberry preserve. Sprinkle with the crumb mixture and bake for 50-55 minutes until lightly set. After 20 minutes reduce the oven temperature to 150˚C, 130˚C fan oven, gas 2. Turn off the oven and allow the pie to cool in the oven for 30 minutes. Cool the cheesecake to room temperature, remove from the pan, cover with foil and refrigerate until cold.

RICOTTA, LEMON AND SULTANA TART

This light textured continental-style tart is an adaptation of *crostata di ricotta* or Italian ricotta tart, of which there are many different regional versions.

Ricotta tart is one of many desserts associated with the festival, *Madonna del Carmine*, that is celebrated throughout Italy, on July 16th, each year. The festival celebrates the prophet Elias's first vision of the Madonna on the Karmel Mountain.

Ricotta, made from the whey of milk be it cow's, ewe's, goat's or buffalo, is a medium-fat, soft cheese, that is ideal for cooking. It is a key ingredient in many Italian desserts such as *cannoli*, *cassata Siciliana* and ricotta pudding.

Makes one 23cm (9 in) tart
Serves 6-8
Sweet Short Pastry 2 (page 32)
Use 1/3 of the quantity of pastry, about 250g (9oz), wrap and freeze the remaining pastry
1 tbsp brandy

75g (3oz) sultanas
500g (1lb 2oz) ricotta cheese
75g (3oz) caster sugar
1 egg
2 egg yolks
Grated zest 1 lemon

Preheat the oven to 190°C, 170°C fan oven, gas 5.

Gently warm the brandy and add the sultanas. Leave to soak.

Prepare the pastry and rest it for 15 minutes in the fridge.

Roll out the pastry on a lightly floured work surface to 3mm (1/8 in) thick. Line a 23cm (9 in) tart tin with the pastry. Lightly prick the base and then rest the pastry for 20 minutes in the fridge or 10 minutes in the freezer.

Bake the pastry blind for 10-15 minutes, remove the baking beans and bake for a further 5 minutes. The pastry should be pale to golden in colour. Brush the pastry case with a little egg yolk and bake for a further minute. Remove the pastry case from the oven. Reduce the oven temperature to 180°C, 160°C fan oven, gas 4.

Mix together the ricotta, caster sugar, egg, egg yolk, and the grated lemon zest. Fold through the sultanas. Spoon the mixture into the pastry case and level the surface with the back of the spoon. Bake the tart for 20 minutes or until lightly set. Remove the tart from the oven and allow to cool for at least 30 minutes before serving.

AMARETTO TART

While I was training at Westminster College I met Penny, a very talented pastry chef. For many years she worked at Orso's Italian restaurant in London's Covent Garden, creating beautiful Italian desserts - this recipe of hers is a personal favourite of mine. I'm not sure if it is authentic, I doubt it is, but who cares when it tastes so good!

Makes one 23cm (9 in) tart
Serves 6-8
Sweet Short Pastry 2 (page 32)
Use 1/3 of the quantity of pastry, about 250g (9oz),
     wrap and freeze the remaining pastry
6 egg yolks
75g (3oz) caster sugar
450ml (3/4pt) double cream
3 tbsp Amaretto di Saronno
12 large amaretti biscuits

Preheat the oven to 190°C, 170°C fan oven, gas 5.

Prepare the pastry and rest it for 15 minutes in the fridge. Roll out the pastry on a lightly floured work surface to 3mm (1/8 in) thick. Line the tart tin with the pastry. Lightly prick the base and then rest the pastry for 20 minutes in the fridge or 10 minutes in the freezer.

Bake the pastry blind for 10-15 minutes, remove the baking beans and bake for a further 5 minutes. The pastry should be pale to golden in colour. Brush the pastry case with some of the egg yolk and bake for a further minute. Remove the pastry case from the oven. Reduce the oven temperature to 160°C, 150°C fan oven, gas 3.

Lightly beat together the egg yolks and sugar. Add the cream and Amaretto and sieve the mix. Crush 4 of the biscuits and add them to the custard mix. Pour the custard into the baked case. Arrange the remaining 8 amaretti, evenly on top of the tart and bake for 20-25 minutes, until lightly set. Serve at room temperature.

DOUBLE-CRUSTED CUSTARD PIE

This American-style custard pie is so called because a standard American pie is an open topped affair, unlike the British counterpart, which always has a pastry top and sometimes a bottom pastry layer as well. Each year the American Pie Council sponsors a national championship, where the country's pie makers bake their favourite recipes, in an attempt to win the prestigious Pie Maker of the Year Award.

Makes one 23cm (9 in) deep pie dish
Serves 6-8
Rich Short Crust (page 35)
Make 2 x pastry recipe
8 egg yolks
175g (6oz) caster sugar
75g (3oz) cornflour

450ml (3/4pt) milk
284ml carton double cream
1 vanilla pod, split lengthwise
15g (1/2oz) unsalted butter
1 tsp vanilla extract
1 tbsp granulated sugar

Preheat the oven to 190°C, 170°C fan oven, gas 5.

Prepare the pastry and rest it for 15 minutes in the fridge. Lightly grease a 23cm (9 in) diameter x 4cm (11/2 in) deep pie dish. Roll out half the pastry to a thickness of 3mm (1/8 in) and line the pie dish. Lightly prick the pastry case. Do not trim the excess pastry. Rest the pastry in the fridge while you make the custard filling.

Mix together the yolks and sugar and then add the cornflour. Add 4 tablespoons of milk and mix to a paste.

Bring the remaining milk, less 1 tablespoon, and the cream, to the boil with the split vanilla pod and then pour half of the boiled liquid onto the custard paste. Pour the custard into the pan with the remaining milk and cream, cook gently for 2-3 minutes until the custard has thickened, taking care not to let it boil. Remove from the heat and pour into a clean mixing bowl. Whisk in the butter and vanilla extract, cover with a piece of buttered greaseproof and allow to cool.

Spoon the cooled custard into the lined pie dish and roll out the remaining pastry to a thickness of 3mm (1/8 in). Dampen the pie edge with water. Using a rolling pin, lift the rolled pastry on top of the custard. Seal the edges and crimp or fork to decorate. Make a small slit in the centre of the pie. Brush with milk and sprinkle with granulated sugar.

Bake the pie for 35 minutes and then lower the temperature to 180°C, 160°C fan oven, gas 4 and bake for a further 15-20 minutes until golden brown. Remove the pie from the oven and allow the pie to cool for an hour before serving.

GOAT'S CHEESE AND LEMON TART

I was given the idea for this tart by one of my students when I was teaching at Thames Valley University. He was a young Frenchman who mentioned that he had made one similar while working in a Parisian restaurant.

The acidity of the goat's cheese gives a subtle tang to the flavour, but you need to make sure the cheese is fresh tasting, otherwise it will overpower the other ingredients.

Makes one 23cm (9 in) tart
Serves 6-8
Sweet Short Pastry 2 (page 32)
Use 1/3 of the quantity of pastry, about
    250g (9oz), wrap and freeze the
    remaining pastry
250g (9oz) ricotta cheese

250g (9oz) soft fresh goat's cheese
75g (3oz) caster sugar
2 eggs, separated
1 egg yolk
Grated zest 2 lemons
Fresh Raspberry Sauce (page 37),
    to serve

Preheat the oven to 190°C, 170°C fan oven, gas 5.

Prepare the pastry and rest it for 15 minutes in the fridge. Roll out the pastry on a lightly floured work surface to 3mm (1/8 in) thick. Line a 23cm (9 in) tart tin, lightly prick the base and then rest the pastry for 20 minutes in the fridge or 10 minutes in the freezer.

Bake the pastry blind for 10-15 minutes, remove the baking beans and bake for a further 5 minutes. The pastry should be pale to golden in colour. Brush the pastry case with a little egg yolk and bake for a further minute. Remove the pastry case from the oven. Reduce the oven temperature to 180°C, 160°C fan oven, gas 4.

Mix together the ricotta, goat's cheese, sugar and egg yolks including any remaining egg yolk and the grated lemon zest. Whisk the egg whites and fold through the mixture.

Spoon the mixture into the pastry case, level the surface with the back of the spoon. Bake the tart for 20 minutes or until lightly set. Remove the tart from the oven and allow to cool for at least 30 minutes before serving. Serve with raspberry sauce.

CREAM CHEESE STRUDEL

Cream cheese strudel is an Austrian speciality, although many other countries including Hungary, Germany and Switzerland, have their own versions. This recipe flavoured with lemon and rum-soaked fruits is my favourite but cherries also go well with the cream cheese filling.

Makes one strudel
Serves 8-10
Strudel Pastry (page 33)
4-5 tbsp dark rum
100g (3½oz) raisins
600g (1lb 5oz) cream cheese

Grated zest 2 lemons
½ tsp ground cinnamon
100g (3½oz) caster sugar
1 egg
1 egg yolk
75g (3oz) melted unsalted butter

Preheat the oven to 200°C, 180°C fan oven, gas 6.

Gently warm the rum and soak the raisins in it.

Prepare the strudel pastry and rest it in a warm place – it's easier to use when it's warm.

Mix the cream cheese with the lemon zest, cinnamon, sugar and egg and egg yolk until smooth.

Roll the dough out to a rectangle on a lightly floured work surface, until it is about 30.5cm (12 in) long and 20cm (8 in) wide. Then using the rolling pin, lift the dough onto a clean, lightly floured tea towel. Using the backs of your hands stretch the dough out further, taking the rectangle to the edges of the kitchen cloth or until the dough becomes paper-thin. The rectangle will be about 41cm (16 in) long and 30.5cm (12 in) wide.

Brush the dough with half the melted butter. Spread the cream cheese mixture evenly over the dough leaving about 2.5cm (1 in) around the edge. Scatter the rum soaked raisins over the cream cheese mixture. Then using the tea towel roll the strudel up along one of its longer sides. It is easier to do this by rolling it away from you. Use the kitchen cloth to help transfer the strudel to a greased baking tray. Shape the strudel into a horseshoe shape and brush with more of the melted butter. Bake for 25 minutes until golden brown. Half way through cooking, brush with the remaining butter. Dust with icing sugar and serve warm.

SEMOLINA TART

The word semolina is derived from Italian and denotes 'fine flour', whereas in English semolina is taken to mean a more coarsely ground wheat. Semolina is used to make a number of sweet and savoury dishes, including gnocchi, halva, milk puddings and cakes. When cooked it produces an interesting grainy texture but because it is made from hard, durum wheat it doesn't break down when cooked.

Although milk puddings are not to everyone's taste, this warmly spiced tart is surprisingly good.

Makes one 25.5cm (10 in) tart
Serves 8
Sweet Short Pastry 1 (page 31)
Use 1/2 of the quantity of pastry about
    350g (12oz), wrap and freeze the
    remaining pastry
750ml (11/4pt) milk
115g (4oz) semolina
25g (1oz) unsalted butter
75g (3oz) caster sugar

2 eggs
2 egg yolks
6 tbsp double cream
3/4 tsp mixed spice
Grated zest 1 lemon
75g (3oz) sultanas
25g (1oz) candied peel, very finely
    chopped
1/4 tsp ground nutmeg

Preheat the oven to 190°C, 170°C fan oven, gas 5.

Prepare the pastry and rest it for 15 minutes in the fridge. Roll out the pastry to 3mm (1/8 in) thick and line a 25.5cm (10 in) tart tin. Lightly prick the base and then rest the pastry for 20 minutes in the fridge or 10 minutes in the freezer.

Bake the pastry blind for 10-15 minutes, remove the baking beans and bake for a further 5 minutes. The pastry should be pale to golden in colour. Brush the pastry case with some of the egg yolk and bake for a further minute. Remove it from the oven. Reduce the oven temperature to 180°C, 160°C fan oven, gas 4.

Pour the milk into a pan and stir in the semolina. Bring to the boil and simmer for 5 minutes, stirring continuously. Remove from the heat.

Cream together the butter and sugar and then gradually add the eggs, beating between each addition. Stir the creamed mix into the milk and ground rice. Add the cream, spice, lemon zest and dried fruit and pour into the tart case. Sprinkle with the nutmeg and bake for 20-25 minutes, until firm to the touch. Serve hot or cold.

CREAM CHEESE AND CHERRY FILO PIE

I love the crispness of filo pastry and it contrasts so well with the creamy, cheesecake-like filling of this recipe. Ready-made filo pastry is very easy to use but there are just two simple rules to follow. The first is to keep any filo pastry you are not using covered, to stop it drying out, as it quickly becomes brittle, and the second rule is to brush the filo liberally with melted unsalted butter, to give the pastry a good colour and flavour.

Makes one 25.5cm (10 in) pie
Serves 10
75g (3oz) unsalted butter
1 tsp ground cinnamon
10 sheets filo pastry
500g (1lb 2oz) cream cheese
125g (4¹/₂oz) caster sugar
1 egg
2 egg yolks
100ml (3¹/₂oz) crème fraîche
2 tsp vanilla extract
3 tbsp cornflour
425g tin pitted black cherries, drained
4 tbsp clear honey
2 tbsp toasted flaked almonds

Preheat the oven to 190°C, 170°C fan oven, gas 5. Lightly grease a 25.5cm (10 in) tart tin.

Melt the butter and stir in the cinnamon. Lay 1 sheet of filo pastry in the tart tin and brush with the melted butter. Lay another on top at a different angle so the edges start to overlap the edge of the tart tin and brush this with butter. Repeat using 7 sheets of filo.

Mix together the cream cheese, sugar, egg and egg yolks until smooth. Add the crème fraîche, vanilla extract, cornflour and cherries and spoon into the pastry case. Level the surface with the back of a spoon.

Lift the edges of the filo over the top of the cream cheese filling. Butter the remaining filo sheets, crumple these and place on top of the tart. Bake the tart for 45-50 minutes until golden and remove from the oven. Warm the honey and pour over the pie, sprinkle with toasted flaked almonds and serve.

MAIDS OF HONOUR

These tartlets were created during the reign of Henry VIII and were popularised by the King, whom it was said, was very fond of them. It is not known for certain who first baked them, whether it was Catherine of Aragon's French pastry cook, or Anne Boleyn, when she was maid of honour to Catherine. Nevertheless they remain popular to this day. There are many variations of these famous, little almond tarts, some flavoured with lemon, others like this one, with brandy.

The Original Maids of Honour Shop opposite Kew Gardens is said to produce the only truly authentic tarts; the original recipe having been passed to an ancestor of the family in the mid 19th century.

Makes 12 tarts
Puff Pastry (page 30)
Use 500g (1lb 2oz) puff pastry trimmings
50g (2oz) unsalted butter
50g (2oz) caster sugar
200g (7oz) curd cheese, sieved
2 eggs
2 tbsp brandy
50g (2oz) coarsely ground almonds

Make the puff pastry the day before or have some trimmings ready in the freezer to defrost. If you haven't got any trimmings to hand, simply roll out some virgin puff pastry to 3mm (1/8 in) thick, fold in half and in half again and refrigerate for 30 minutes, then use as trimmings.

Preheat the oven to 220˚C, 200˚C fan oven, gas 7.

Roll out the pastry 2mm (less than 1/8 in) thick and cut out twelve, 10cm (4 in) rounds. Grease and line a 12-hole bun tin with the pastry rounds. Lightly prick the bases and rest them for 20 minutes in the fridge or 10 minutes in the freezer.

Cream together the butter and sugar and then beat in the cheese. Add the eggs and brandy, then stir in the ground almonds.

Half fill each pastry case with the curd mixture and bake the tarts for 15-20 minutes until golden and firm to the touch.

TIP If you want to, you could also put a teaspoonful of jam in the base of each base before adding the curd cheese filling, to make them a little sweeter.

RHUBARB AND CUSTARD CREAM PIE

Rhubarb or the 'Pie plant', as it is commonly known in America, is very popular, especially in and around the area of Utica, Michigan, which is the self-styled rhubarb capital of the world. Of the many rhubarb pie recipes that I have come across I like this one very much. Rhubarb is a sharp tasting fruit and the rich creamy custard in this recipe balances its tartness.

Makes one 23cm (9 in) deep pie
Serves 8
Rich Short Crust (page 35)
500ml (18fl oz) milk
4 egg yolks
225g (8oz) caster sugar
50g (2oz) cornflour

15g (1/2oz) unsalted butter
1 tsp vanilla extract
200g (7oz) rhubarb
3 tbsp clear honey
2 tsp grated orange zest

Sugar thermometer

Preheat the oven to 190°C, 170°C fan oven, gas 5.

Prepare the pastry and rest it for 15 minutes in the fridge. Roll out the pastry on a lightly floured work surface to 3mm (1/8 in) thick. Line a 23cm (9 in), 4cm (11/2 in) deep pie dish with the pastry. Lightly dock the base and then rest the pastry for 20 minutes in the fridge or 10 minutes in the freezer.

Bake the pastry blind for 10-15 minutes, remove the baking beans and bake for a further 5 minutes. The pastry should be pale to golden in colour. Brush the pastry case with a little egg yolk and bake for a further minute. Remove the pastry case from the oven and allow to cool.

Bring the milk to the boil in a small pan. Mix together the egg yolks and 75g (3oz) of the sugar and then add the cornflour. Whisk a little of the hot milk onto the egg mixture and then return the mixture to the milk in the pan. Cook the mixture over a medium heat, stirring all the time, for 3-4 minutes, until the mixture has thickened. Remove from the heat and pour the pastry cream into a clean bowl. Stir through the butter and vanilla extract and cover with a piece of buttered greaseproof.

Put the rhubarb in a pan with 2 tablespoons of water, the honey and orange zest and poach lightly for 5 minutes until tender.

Put the remaining sugar into a pan and add 100ml (31/2fl oz) water, bring to the boil without stirring. Cook the sugar until the sugar thermometer reads 121°C, 250°F. Whilst the sugar is cooking whisk 3 of the 4 egg whites. When the sugar reaches 121°C, 250°F pour the syrup slowly onto the egg whites in a steady steam, whilst whisking on a low speed. Once the syrup has been added, increase the speed and whisk until the meringue is cool.

Drain the rhubarb and stir the rhubarb through the custard. Spoon the custard into the pastry case. Spoon the meringue over the custard and bake in the oven for 5-10 minutes until the meringue is golden brown. Allow to cool for 1 hour before serving.

ICE-CREAM PIE

The original American ice-box pies probably date back to the early 1900s, when electric refrigerators began to be mass-produced. As the name suggests they are often no-bake desserts made from the contents of the fridge or freezer. This truly amazing pie is a fun dessert that you can personalise with your choice of favourite ice creams, and is guaranteed to impress.

Makes one 23cm (9 in) tart
Serves 6-8
Sweet Short Pastry 3 (page 32)
Use 1/2 of the quantity, wrap and freeze the remaining pastry
1 egg yolk
200g (7oz) dark chocolate
284ml carton double cream
500ml tub good quality dairy caramel ice cream
500ml tub good quality dairy vanilla ice cream
25g (1oz) soft amaretti or biscuits of your choice

Preheat the oven to 190°C, 170°C fan oven, gas 5.

Prepare the pastry and rest it for 15 minutes in the fridge. Roll out the pastry on a lightly floured work surface to 3mm (1/8 in) thick. Line the tart tin with the pastry. Lightly prick the base and then rest the pastry for 20 minutes in the fridge or 10 minutes in the freezer.

Bake the pastry blind for 10-15 minutes, remove the baking beans and bake for a further 5 minutes. The pastry should be pale to golden in colour. Brush the pastry case with the egg yolk and bake for a further minute. Remove it from the oven and allow the case to cool.

Chop the chocolate and put into a heatproof bowl, over a pan of simmering water or heat gently in the microwave, until melted. Brush the pastry case with a little of the melted chocolate and pop the pastry case in the fridge for 10 minutes. Boil 125ml (4 1/2 fl oz) of the cream and stir the boiled cream into the remaining melted chocolate. Put to one side. Lightly whip the remaining cream and put to one side.

Remove the ice cream from the freezer and alternately scoop some of each flavour into the base of the pastry case until all the ice cream has been used. Put the ice cream pie into the freezer for 15-20 minutes, to firm up before serving.

Remove the pie from the freezer, spoon over the whipped cream, crumble the amaretti, or biscuits, over the cream, and pour over the chocolate sauce. Serve immediately.

GATEAU BASQUE

The Pays Basque region is in the south-west corner of France, bordering the much larger Spanish Basque region. Basque cake, or *Pastiza*, as it is known locally, is found throughout the region in bakeries, market stalls and in restaurants. The original recipe was made using a yellow cherry preserve but nowadays they are usually filled with crème pâtissière and maybe a dash of rum and some candied lemon.

Makes one 23cm (9 in) pie
Serves 6
450g (1lb) plain flour
215g (7¹/₂oz) unsalted butter
300g (10oz) caster sugar
2 eggs
5 egg yolks
1 sachet dried yeast

25g (1oz) cornflour
150ml (¹/₄pt) milk
142ml carton double cream
75g (3oz) ground almonds
Grated zest 2 lemons
1 tsp vanilla extract
Icing sugar to serve

Preheat the oven to 180°C, 160°C fan oven, gas 4.

Sieve the flour into a bowl and rub in 200g (7oz) of the butter. Make a well in the centre and add the beaten eggs, 225g (8oz) of the sugar, 2 of the 5 egg yolks and the dried yeast. Knead the ingredients for at least 5 minutes to form a smooth dough. Lightly grease a mixing bowl and place the dough in it. Refrigerate the dough for 1 hour.

Mix together the remaining yolks and sugar and then add the cornflour and 4 tablespoons of milk and mix to a smooth paste.

Bring the remaining milk and cream to the boil and then pour half of the boiled liquid onto the custard paste. Pour the custard into the pan with the remaining milk and cream, and cook gently, stirring all the time, for 2-3 minutes, until the custard has thickened. Add the ground almonds and lemon zest and cook for a further minute.

Remove from the heat, pour into a clean mixing bowl and whisk in the remaining butter and the vanilla extract. Cover with a piece of buttered greaseproof and allow to cool.

Lightly grease a 23cm (9 in) shallow cake tin. Roll out approximately ²/₃ of the dough to a thickness of 6mm (¹/₄ in) and line the tin. Trim the excess dough. Lightly prick the base. Spoon the almond custard into the lined tin and roll out the remaining dough. Dampen the pie edge with water and lift the rolled dough on top of the custard, and seal the edges. Make a small slit in the centre of the pie. Bake the pie for 25-30 minutes until golden brown. Remove from the oven and allow to cool, dust with icing sugar before serving. Refrigerate any leftover pie.

CARAMEL CUSTARD TARTS

Dulce de Leche is a rich caramel cream made from condensed milk, that you can use to make cakes, pastries and ice creams. I've combined it in this recipe with rich orange custard but it would work equally well with a vanilla or chocolate custard.

Each tart is a delectable sweet indulgence so go ahead and indulge!

Makes 12 small tarts
Sweet Short Pastry 3 (page 32)
Use 1/2 of the quantity, wrap and freeze
   the remaining pastry
3 egg yolks
75g (3oz) caster sugar

2 tbsp custard powder
350ml (12fl oz) milk
1 tsp grated orange zest
100ml (3½fl oz) double cream
6 tbsp *Dulce de Leche*
Icing sugar to serve

Preheat the oven to 190°C, 170°C fan oven, gas 5. Prepare the pastry and rest it for 15 minutes in the fridge.

Roll out the pastry 2mm (less than 1/8 in) thick and cut out twelve, 10cm (4 in) rounds. Grease and line a 12-hole bun tin with the pastry. Lightly prick the bases and rest them for 20 minutes in the fridge or 10 minutes in the freezer.

Mix together the yolks and half the sugar and then add the custard powder. Add 4 tablespoons of milk and mix to a paste.

Put the remaining sugar in a pan and heat gently until the sugar caramelises then pour in the milk and cream and add the orange zest. Bring to the boil, stirring to dissolve the caramel. Pour half the caramel milk onto the custard paste then return this to the pan with the remaining caramel milk and cook gently, stirring all the time, for 2-3 minutes until the custard has thickened, taking care not to let it boil. Remove from the heat, pour into a clean mixing bowl and cover with a round of buttered greaseproof paper and allow to cool.

Spoon the *Dulce de Leche* into the bottom of the pastry cases and then top with the caramel custard. Bake the pastry cases for 15-20 minutes until golden. Dust with icing sugar and serve warm.

CHOCOLATE

Chocolate is the one food I would find it very difficult to live without. It is an ingredient like no other; evoking passion through its aroma, taste, smooth silky texture and melting quality.

The chocolate required for making tarts, pies and other pâtisserie needs to be a good quality chocolate. Forget the likes of Bournville, which is far too sweet and lacks real chocolate flavour, I'm talking about the continental-style bars. I buy my chocolate, or couverture, in kilo-sized slabs from a supplier to the catering trade but for the majority of people it's much easier just to buy it from your local shop. Couverture is a French term meaning 'covering', but it is also the term used to describe quality chocolate, used in professional kitchens.

In simple terms chocolate is categorized into 3 types: namely dark, milk and white. Dark chocolate is the most flavourful of the types because it contains the highest proportion of cocoa solids. Roast cocoa nibs, collected from the dried cocoa beans, are ground to produce cocoa solids, also known as cocoa mass, and it is the variety, quality, roasting and blending of the cocoa beans that gives a chocolate its distinctive, flavour characteristics.

Milk chocolate contains a lower proportion of cocoa solids and some milk solids, and white chocolate contains no cocoa solids, only cocoa butter and milk solids. In addition to cocoa solids, milk solids and cocoa butter, with the exception of block cocoa, used exclusively in making pâtisserie, all chocolate also contains sugar. Some chocolates also contain flavourings and lecithin, a stabiliser.

In order for dark chocolate to be classified as such, it needs to contain a minimum of 46% cocoa solids, and milk chocolate, a minimum of 20% cocoa solids. Chocolate bars and confectionery produced for the British market containing added vegetable fat, a high sugar content and a relatively low cocoa solid content make them unsuitable for pastry work (desserts). But there are now some good quality, dark chocolates with more respectable cocoa solid contents, that are readily available. Most supermarkets offer own label brands of continental-style that double as top-end eating chocolate, and are also suitable for use in pastry making. The dark varieties offer a minimum of '70% cocoa solids'. Unfortunately this has become the quality threshold for dark chocolate giving people the impression that chocolate with levels lower than this are inferior, but this is not the case. There are some good quality, dark chocolates with cocoa solids levels between 60-70%.

Milk chocolate is used to a lesser extent than dark chocolate in pastry making because once added to other ingredients, the chocolate flavour becomes too diluted. White chocolate is used to a greater extent than milk chocolate and although it doesn't possess a true chocolate flavour, because it contains no cocoa solids, it is often used in ice creams and mousse-type desserts to give a sweet, buttery, vanilla flavour.

Other chocolate products, including bakers chocolate and modelling chocolate, are used in professional kitchens. These products do not need tempering and make the products ideal for enrobing. Tempering is the process applied to melted chocolate, to ensure the crystals realign when they set, to give the chocolate sheen and a brittle texture. If chocolate is incorrectly tempered, a white streaky 'bloom' may appear on the surface, and the chocolate will not 'snap' when broken. Chocolate needs to be tempered when making chocolates and chocolate decorations, but not when chocolate is used for baking purposes.

CHOCOLATE FUDGE BROWNIE PIE

This recipe elevates the humble brownie from coffee-shop cake to dessert. I have simply taken my favourite chocolate brownie recipe and baked it in a crisp pastry case. Serve topped with vanilla ice cream and drizzled with hot fudge sauce for a sensational chocolate experience!

Makes one 23cm (9 in) tart
Serves 6-8
Sweet Short Pastry 1 (page 31)
Use ⅓ of the quantity of pastry, about
    250g (9oz), wrap and freeze remaining
    pastry
1 egg yolk
115g (4oz) unsalted butter

200g (7oz) dark chocolate, chopped
175g (6oz) unrefined light brown sugar
Pinch of salt
1 tsp vanilla extract
2 eggs, beaten
40g (1½oz) plain flour
150g (5oz) pecans, coarsely chopped

Preheat the oven to 190˚C, 170˚C fan oven, gas 5.

Prepare the pastry and rest it for 15 minutes in the fridge. Lightly flour a clean work surface and roll out the pastry to 3mm (⅛ in) thick. Line a 23cm (9 in) tart tin and lightly prick the base. Rest the pastry for 20 minutes in the fridge or 10 minutes in the freezer.

Bake the pastry blind for 10-15 minutes, remove the baking beans and bake for a further 5 minutes. The pastry should be pale to golden in colour. Brush the pastry case with a little of the egg yolk and bake for a further minute.

Melt the butter and chocolate together in a heatproof bowl, over a pan of simmering water or in the microwave on a low heat. Stir through the sugar, salt and vanilla extract. Add the beaten eggs and then fold in the flour and half the nuts. Spoon the mixture into the prepared pastry case and sprinkle over the remaining nuts. Bake the tart for 20 minutes until the pastry is golden in colour and the tart is a little soft to the touch.

Serve warm with Hot Fudge Sauce (page 37) and Vanilla Ice Cream (page 39) or as the Americans would say *à la mode*.

TIP As when making brownies, the trick is not to over bake, so the filling stays soft and moist.

FIG AND CHOCOLATE BRIOCHE TART

This recipe uses brioche, an enriched bread dough, rather than pastry as its base. A type of brioche was probably first made as early as the 15th century although it wasn't until the 17th century that it arrived in Paris. Brioche can be made with varying ratios of butter to flour; the higher the ratio of butter to flour, the richer the brioche, but the richer the brioche the more difficult it becomes to work. Although I usually like to prove my dough overnight, as this helps develop the flavour and also allows time for the butter to firm, this recipe can be made and used straight away.

Makes one 25.5cm (10 in) tart
Serves 8-10
For the brioche:
1 tsp dried yeast
300g (10oz) plain flour
Pinch of salt
75g (3oz) caster sugar
3 eggs
2 egg yolks
150g (5oz) unsalted butter, softened and
    cut into small pieces

For the topping:
300ml (1/2pt) milk
1 tbsp cocoa powder
3 egg yolks
75g (3oz) caster sugar
2 tbsp cornflour
2 tsp vanilla extract
100g (31/2oz) dark chocolate, melted
5-6 large ripe figs, thickly sliced
Icing sugar to serve

Preheat the oven to 200˚C, 180˚C fan oven, gas 6.

Grease a 25.5cm (10 in) tart tin. To make the brioche, dissolve the yeast in 125ml (41/2oz) warm water and add 2 tablespoons of flour, place somewhere warm until the yeast has produced a frothy liquid (about 10 minutes).

Sift the remaining flour and salt into the mixing bowl of a food mixer and stir through the sugar. When the yeast is ready pour the liquid into the remaining flour, salt and sugar. Using a dough hook, beat in the eggs and egg yolks. Then beat in the butter. Mix the dough for at least 2-3 minutes after incorporating the butter. Cover the dough with a clean damp cloth and allow it to prove for 1 hour in a warm place, or until it has doubled in size.

Bring the milk (less 1 tablespoon) and the cocoa powder, to the boil in a small pan. Mix together 2 of the 3 egg yolks and the sugar, then add the cornflour and mix to a smooth paste. Whisk a little of the hot milk onto the egg mixture and then return the egg mixture to the milk in the pan. Cook the mixture over a medium heat, stirring all the time for 3-4 minutes until the mixture has thickened, remove from the heat and pour the pastry cream into a bowl.

Chop the chocolate and place in a heatproof bowl over a pan of simmering water or heat in the microwave on a low setting until melted. Then stir the vanilla extract and melted chocolate into the pastry cream. Cover with a small piece of buttered greaseproof paper.

Mix the reserved tablespoon of milk and remaining egg yolk together. Knock back the dough in the mixing bowl, put into the tart tin and push to the edge of the tin. Brush the dough with egg wash. Carefully spread the pastry cream over the top of the brioche dough, leaving 2.5cm (1 in) of dough uncovered around the outer edge. Arrange the fig slices on top. Allow the dough to prove for 15-30 minutes and then bake for 20-25 minutes until the crust is golden. Dust the crust with icing sugar and serve the tart warm, with coffee.

CHOCOLATE AND CARAMEL TART

Rich and full flavoured, balancing bitterness and sweetness, this tart packs a punch. As with all chocolate tarts, the better, the chocolate the better the tart.

Makes one 23cm (9 in) tart
Serves 6-8
Sweet Short Pastry 1 (page 31)
Use 1/3 of the quantity of pastry, about 250g (9oz), wrap and freeze the remaining pastry
1 egg yolk

150g (5oz) caster sugar
284ml carton double cream
100g (3 1/2oz) unsalted butter, chopped into small pieces
200g (7oz) dark chocolate, chopped
4 tbsp milk
1 egg, beaten

Preheat the oven to 190°C, 180°C fan oven, gas 5.

Prepare the pastry and rest it for 15 minutes in the fridge. Lightly flour a clean work surface and roll out the pastry to 3mm (1/8 in) thick. Line a 23cm (9 in) tart tin and lightly prick the base. Rest the pastry for 20 minutes in the fridge or 10 minutes in the freezer.

Bake the pastry blind for 10-15 minutes, remove the baking beans and bake for a further 5 minutes. The pastry should be pale to golden in colour. Brush the pastry case with a little egg yolk and bake for a further minute. Remove from the oven and allow to cool. Reduce the oven temperature to 170°C, 150°C fan oven, gas 3.

Put the sugar and 75ml (3fl oz) water into a pan and heat gently until the sugar caramelises and turns a golden brown, do not allow the sugar to become too dark or the caramel will taste bitter. Remove the pan from the heat and whisk in 100ml (3 1/2fl oz) cream. Then gradually whisk in the butter. Allow the caramel to cool.

Put the chocolate in a heatproof bowl over a pan of simmering water or heat in the microwave on a low setting, until melted. Bring the remaining cream and the milk to the boil. Gently stir the cream and milk into the melted chocolate and allow the mix to cool before adding the beaten egg and any remaining yolk.

Spoon the caramel into the pastry case and pour in the chocolate. Swirl the mixtures together with the tip of a knife and bake the tart for 20-25 minutes, until lightly set. Allow to cool, then refrigerate for 2 hours before serving.

CHOCOLATE SILK PIE

This rich, chocolate American pie looks and tastes as impressive as it sounds, with its dark chocolate interior topped with folds of mallowy white meringue. It's not hard to guess how the name for it came about since 'smooth as silk' is a commonly used descriptive phrase.

Although I have used Italian, or cooked meringue, for the topping, if you don't have a sugar thermometer you can make French, or uncooked, meringue. Simply whisk the egg whites until soft peaks form then add the sugar gradually whisking between each addition of sugar until the meringue is thick and glossy.

Makes one 23cm (9 in) pie
Serves 8
Rich Short Crust Pastry (page 35)
4 eggs
500ml (18fl oz) milk
2 tbsp cocoa powder
225g (8oz) caster sugar

50g (2oz) cornflour
200g (7oz) dark chocolate
15g (1/2oz) unsalted butter
Pinch of cream of tartar
Pinch of egg white powder

Sugar thermometer

Preheat the oven to 190°C, 170°C fan oven, gas 5.

Prepare the pastry and rest it for 15 minutes in the fridge. Lightly flour a clean work surface and roll out the pastry to 3mm (1/8 in) thick. Line a 23cm (9 in), 4cm (11/2 in) deep, pie dish with the pastry. Lightly prick the base and then rest the pastry for 20 minutes in the fridge or 10 minutes in the freezer.

Bake the pastry blind for 10-15 minutes, remove the baking beans and bake for a further 5 minutes. The pastry should be pale to golden in colour. Separate the eggs into 2 mixing bowls. Brush the pastry case with a little of the egg yolk and bake for a further minute. Remove the pastry case from the oven and allow to cool. Turn off the oven.

Bring the milk to the boil in a small pan with the cocoa powder. Mix together the egg yolks and 50g (2oz) of the sugar and then add the cornflour. Whisk a little of the hot chocolate milk onto the egg mixture and then return the mixture to the milk in the pan. Cook the mixture over a medium heat, stirring all the time until the mixture has thickened, remove from the heat and pour the pastry cream into a clean bowl.

Chop the chocolate and place in a heatproof bowl over a pan of simmering water or heat in the microwave on a low setting, until melted. Stir the melted chocolate into the pastry cream with the butter, and mix until incorporated. Pour the chocolate pastry cream into the pastry case, put a piece of buttered greaseproof paper over the chocolate custard and allow to cool.

Place the remaining sugar in a small pan with 125ml (41/2fl oz) water, heat gently to dissolve the sugar then bring to the boil and boil without stirring until the sugar thermometer reads 121°C, 250°F. Whilst the sugar is boiling whisk the egg whites in

a large clean bowl with the cream of tartar and egg white powder until they form soft peaks. When the sugar reaches 121°C, 250°F remove the sugar thermometer and place it in a jug of boiling water and pour the sugar in a slow steady stream into the whisked egg whites, whilst whisking on a low speed. Once the sugar has been poured onto the egg whites, increase the speed and continue to whisk for about 5 minutes until the meringue has cooled slightly.

Preheat the oven to 190°C, 170°C fan oven, gas 5.

Spoon the meringue on top of the pie filling and brown the meringue in the oven for about 5 minutes.

CHOCOLATE AND RASPBERRY TART

The basis of this recipe is a light textured chocolate mousse that you could also use as a filling for sponge cakes, or add a dash of brandy or Grand Marnier and serve on its own with dessert biscuits.

Makes one 23cm (9 in) tart
Serves 6-8
Sweet Short Pastry 3 (page 32)
Use 1/2 of the quantity, wrap and freeze
    the remaining pastry
200g (7oz) dark chocolate, chopped

4 egg yolks
142ml carton double cream
6 egg whites
25g (1oz) caster sugar
250g (9oz) fresh raspberries

Preheat the oven to 190°C, 180°C fan oven, gas 5.

Prepare the pastry and rest it for 15 minutes in the fridge. Lightly flour a clean work surface and roll out the pastry to 3mm (1/8 in) thick. Line a 23cm (9 in) tart tin and lightly prick the base. Rest the pastry for 20 minutes in the fridge or 10 minutes in the freezer.

Bake the pastry blind for 10-15 minutes, remove the baking beans and bake for a further 5 minutes. The pastry should be pale to golden in colour. Brush the pastry case with a little egg yolk and bake for a further minute. Remove it from the oven and allow to cool.

Chop the chocolate and put in a heatproof bowl over a pan of simmering water or heat in the microwave on a low setting, until melted, allow to cool slightly then stir in the egg yolks.

Lightly whip the cream and carefully fold into the chocolate mixture. Whisk the egg whites until they are stiff and whisk in the sugar. Fold the egg whites into the chocolate mixture followed by half the raspberries and spoon the chocolate mixture into the prepared pastry case. Arrange the remaining raspberries on top. Refrigerate the tart for 45 minutes before serving.

TARTE MONMARTRE

This is a bold statement of a tart and so perhaps it is named after the Parisian district, famed for its artists, because of its contrast in both flavour and colour.

I used to simply enjoy chocolate on its own or chocolate desserts accompanied by vanilla sauce or ice cream; it is only in recent years that I have started to enjoy chocolate paired with fruit flavours. Here is one. Chocolate and lemon is a much less obvious, and far more daring combination, than chocolate and orange. The acidity of the lemon fights the bitterness of the chocolate, so the balance is more difficult to achieve but if you use a good quality dark chocolate, the lemon should not undermine the chocolate.

Makes one 25.5cm (10 in) tart
Serves 10-12
Sweet Short Pastry 1 (page 31)
Use 1/2 of the quantity of pastry, about 350g (12oz), wrap and freeze the remaining pastry
4 egg yolks

5 eggs
200g (7oz) caster sugar
Grated zest and juice 3 lemons
142ml carton double cream
175g (6oz) dark chocolate, melted
1 tbsp cocoa powder, sifted
250ml (9oz) crème fraîche

Preheat the oven to 190°C, 180°C fan oven, gas 5.

Prepare the pastry and rest it for 15 minutes in the fridge. Lightly flour a clean work surface and roll out the pastry to 3mm (1/8 in) thick. Line a 25.5cm (10 in) tart tin and lightly prick the base. Rest the pastry for 20 minutes in the fridge or 10 minutes in the freezer.

Bake the pastry blind for 10-15 minutes, remove the baking beans and bake for a further 5 minutes. The pastry should be pale to golden in colour. Brush the pastry case with a little of the egg yolk and bake for a further minute. Remove the pastry case from the oven and allow to cool. Reduce the oven temperature to 150°C, 130°C fan oven, gas 2.

Whisk the yolks, 3 of the 5 eggs and 125g (4 1/2oz) sugar with the lemon juice and zest, in a bowl, over a pan of simmering water until the mixture resembles lemon curd. Then stir through the cream. Spread the mix over the base of the pastry case.

Whisk the remaining eggs and sugar in a bowl until the mixture is thick and creamy. Then fold in the chocolate, cocoa powder and crème fraîche. Carefully spread the chocolate over the lemon mixture and bake the tart for 20-25 minutes until lightly set. Allow to stand for 30 minutes before serving.

CHOCOLATE AND BOURBON PECAN PIE

While I was working as a development chef for Sainsbury's I was fortunate to visit America on a number of occasions in search of new food concepts. I journeyed across several states visiting bakeries, specialist food stores and restaurants. This pie is based on one I ate at Rick Bayless's restaurant, Topolobampo, in Chicago. This is one of my top tarts and it is divine!

Makes one 25.5cm (10 in) pie
Serves 8-10
Sweet Short Pastry 1 (page 31)
Use 1/2 of the quantity of pastry about
    350g (12oz), wrap and freeze the
    remaining pastry
25g (1oz) unsalted butter

200g (7oz) dark brown sugar
250g (9oz) golden syrup
150g (5oz) dark chocolate, chopped
3 tbsp bourbon
150g (5oz) chopped pecans
6 eggs, beaten

Preheat the oven to 190°C, 170°C fan oven, gas 5.

Prepare the pastry and rest it for 15 minutes in the fridge. Lightly flour a clean work surface and roll out the pastry to 3mm (1/8 in) thick. Line a 25.5cm (10 in) tart tin and lightly prick the base. Rest it in the fridge for 20 minutes or 10 minutes in the freezer.

Bake the pastry blind for 10-15 minutes, remove the baking beans and bake for a further 5 minutes. The pastry should be pale to golden in colour. Brush the pastry case with a little of the egg yolk and bake for a further minute. Remove it from the oven and allow to cool. Reduce the oven temperature to 170°C, 150°C fan oven, gas 3.

Melt the butter, sugar and golden syrup in a medium pan. Put 100g (3½oz) of the chocolate in a heatproof bowl over a pan of simmering water or heat in the microwave on a low setting, until melted. Then add the melted chocolate, bourbon and 100g (3½oz) of the chopped pecans to the melted butter mixture.

Allow the mix to cool slightly, then stir in the beaten eggs and remaining chopped chocolate. Pour the mixture into the pastry case and scatter the remaining pecans on top. Bake the pie for about 25 minutes, until lightly set. Allow the pie to stand for 30 minutes before slicing. Dust with icing sugar and serve with ice cream.

CHOCOLATE AND HAZELNUT CREAM PIE

Hazelnuts were very popular with the Victorians and by the end of the 19th century there were 7,000 acres of hazelnut orchards, or 'plats', in the county of Kent. The Kentish cobnut, or filberts, as they were then known, remains our most important variety. However from the beginning of the 20th century, production here began to decline due to the cost of labour and changing agricultural practices, so that now sadly, there are as few as 250 acres of plats remaining. Today when you buy hazelnuts they will most likely be of Turkish origin - despite the Italian regions of Piedmont and Campagna being famous for growing them, Turkey is the world's largest producer providing over 70% of the world's supply.

Here is a recipe for my favourite chocolate-nut combination, chocolate and hazelnut pie. In my opinion the milky, sweet flavour of the hazelnut blends perfectly with the flavours of good dark chocolate.

Makes one 25.5cm (10 in) pie
Serves 8-10
Nut Pastry (page 36)
1/2 recipe quantity using ground hazelnuts
500ml (18fl oz) milk
1 tbsp cocoa powder
4 egg yolks
50g (2oz) caster sugar

50g (2oz) cornflour
150g (5oz) dark chocolate
3 tbsp chocolate hazelnut paste such as
    Green & Blacks or Nutella
284ml carton whipping cream
1 tbsp brandy
White chocolate shavings and cocoa
    powder to serve

Preheat the oven to 190˚C, 170˚C fan oven, gas 5.

Prepare the pastry and rest it for 15 minutes in the fridge. Lightly flour a clean work surface and roll out the pastry to 3mm (1/8 in) thick. Line a 25.5cm (10 in) tart tin and lightly prick the base. Rest the pastry for 20 minutes in the fridge or 10 minutes in the freezer.

Bake the pastry blind for 10-15 minutes, remove the baking beans and bake for a further 5 minutes. The pastry should be pale to golden in colour. Brush the pastry case with a little of the egg yolk and bake for a further minute. Remove it from the oven and allow to cool.

Bring the milk to the boil in a small pan with the cocoa powder. Mix together the egg yolks and 40g (1½oz) of the sugar and then add the cornflour. Whisk a little of the hot chocolate milk onto the egg mixture and then return the mixture to the milk in the pan. Cook the mixture over a medium heat, stirring all the time for 3-4 minutes until the mixture has thickened, remove from the heat and pour the pastry cream into a clean bowl.

Put the chocolate in a heatproof bowl over a pan of simmering water or heat in the microwave on a low setting, until melted. Stir the melted chocolate and the chocolate hazelnut paste into the pastry cream and pour into the pastry case. Put a piece of buttered greaseproof paper over the chocolate pastry cream and allow to cool, then refrigerate for 30 minutes.

When the chocolate pastry cream is cool, lightly whip the cream, add the remaining sugar and brandy and spoon over the chocolate. Decorate with white chocolate shavings and cocoa powder.

CHOCOLATE TRUFFLE TART

This tart is similar to a cocoa-dusted, chocolate truffle. It's a straight forward recipe to master and produces a tart with a wonderfully smooth, mousse-like filling. The recipe, and others like it, are much used throughout professional kitchens and the use of glucose, a liquid sugar produced from potato or maize starch, helps create the silky finish.

Makes one 23cm (9 in) tart
Serves 6-8
Sweet Short Pastry 3 (page 32)
Use 1/2 of the quantity, wrap and freeze
    the remaining pastry
150g (5oz) dark chocolate

1 leaf (or 4g powdered) gelatine
25g (1oz) liquid glucose
25g (1oz) water
2 tsp brandy
1 tsp strong black coffee
284ml carton whipping cream

Preheat the oven to 190°C, 180°C fan oven, gas 5.

Prepare the pastry and rest it for 15 minutes in the fridge. Lightly flour a clean work surface and roll out the pastry to 3mm (1/8 in) thick. Line a 23cm (9 in) tart tin and lightly prick the base. Rest the pastry for 20 minutes in the fridge or 10 minutes in the freezer.

Bake the pastry blind for 10-15 minutes, remove the baking beans and bake for a further 5 minutes. The pastry should be pale to golden in colour. Brush the pastry case with a little egg yolk and bake for a further minute. Remove the pastry case from the oven and allow to cool.

Chop the chocolate and place in a heatproof bowl over a pan of simmering water or heat in the microwave on a low setting until melted.

Soak the leaf gelatine in cold water. If using powdered gelatine sprinkle into 1 tablespoon of hot water and stir to dissolve. Put the glucose in a pan with the water, bring to the boil then remove from the heat. Squeeze any excess water from the leaf gelatine. Add the gelatine to the hot glucose and water and stir to dissolve. If using powdered gelatine heat it gently in the microwave for 15-20 seconds to make sure it is completely dissolved. Add the brandy and coffee to the gelatine mixture and then stir the melted chocolate into the gelatine mixture.

Lightly whip the cream and fold the cream into the chocolate. Spoon the chocolate into the prepared pastry case. Refrigerate the tart for 45 minutes and dust with cocoa before serving.

CHOCOLATE AND ORANGE TARTLETS

Chocolate and orange is a very commercial flavour combination, just think of Terry's chocolate orange and the orange Kit Kat that was introduced as a limited edition flavour. There is no doubt it is a fantastic pairing but you need to make sure you don't add too much orange or it can overpower the chocolate.

A French master pastry chef gave me this indulgent, chocolate tart recipe. The filling is made using ganache, a rich chocolate cream, that forms the basis for many chocolates and chocolate desserts. Like so many discoveries ganache was made accidentally by an apprentice pâtissier in Paris in the 19th century. The boy knocked some boiling cream into a pot of melted chocolate and the owner of the shop called him *un ganache*, an imbecile. The owner, hoping to find some use for the mixture, found that the chocolate liquid was silky smooth and on cooling set to a soft luxurious paste. Ganache comprises chocolate and cream sometimes with the addition of butter and flavouring.

Makes 12 small tarts or one 23cm
(9 in) tart
Sweet Short Pastry 3 (page 32)
Use 1/2 of the quantity, wrap and freeze
the remaining pastry
1 egg yolk

300g (10oz) dark chocolate, chopped
225ml (8fl oz) double cream
5 tbsp milk
Grated zest 1/2 orange
2 eggs, beaten
Candied orange pieces to decorate

Preheat the oven to 190°C, 180°C fan oven, gas 5.

Prepare the pastry and rest it for 15 minutes in the fridge. Lightly flour a clean work surface, roll out the pastry to 3mm (1/8 in) thick and cut out twelve, 10cm (4 in) rounds. Grease and line a 12-hole bun tin with the pastry. Lightly prick the bases and then rest them for 20 minutes in the fridge or 10 minutes in the freezer.

Bake the pastry blind for 6-8 minutes, remove the beans and bake for a further 2-3 minutes. The pastry should be pale to golden in colour. Brush the pastry cases with a little of the egg yolk and bake for a further minute. Remove from the oven and reduce the oven temperature to 170°C, 150°C fan oven, gas 3.

Chop the chocolate and place in a heatproof bowl over a pan of simmering water or heat in the microwave on a low setting until it has melted. Boil the cream and the milk together in a small pan with the orange zest. Gently stir the cream and milk into the melted chocolate and allow the mix to cool slightly, before adding the beaten eggs and any remaining yolk.

Pour the chocolate mixture into the pastry cases and bake the tarts for 15-20 minutes until lightly set. Allow to stand for 15 minutes before serving. Decorate with candied orange just before serving.

WHITE CHOCOLATE AND PASSION FRUIT TARTS

I used to make a white chocolate and passion fruit mousse at Blakes Hotel, that was very popular, so I took the concept and translated it into this creamy, fruit tart.

Made from cocoa butter, milk solids and sugar, and flavoured with vanilla, white chocolate has a much sweeter, more milky flavour than either milk or dark chocolate and as a result combines well with a wide range of flavours.

Makes 6 small tarts
Sweet Short Pastry 3 (page 32)
Use 1/2 of the quantity, wrap and freeze
    the remaining pastry
200g (7oz) white chocolate
175ml (6fl oz) milk (1 tbsp reserved for the
    egg wash)
1 vanilla pod, split lengthways

3 egg yolks
2 tbsp caster sugar
2 tbsp cornflour
8 large passion fruits
284ml carton double cream
Tropical fruits or Raspberry Sauce
    (page 37), to serve

Preheat the oven to 190°C, 170°C fan oven, gas 5.

Prepare the pastry and rest it for 15 minutes in the fridge. Lightly flour a clean work surface and roll out the pastry to 3mm (1/8 in) thick. Use it to line six, 12.5cm (5 in) diameter x 2.5cm (1 in) deep tartlet tins, lightly prick the bases and then rest them in the fridge for 20 minutes or 10 minutes in the freezer.

Bake the pastry blind for 10-12 minutes, remove the baking beans and bake for a further 2-3 minutes. The pastry should be pale to golden in colour. Brush the pastry cases with a little egg yolk and bake for a further minute. Remove from the oven and allow to cool.

Chop the chocolate and place in a heatproof bowl over a pan of simmering water or heat in the microwave on a low setting until melted.

Bring the milk and vanilla to the boil in a heavy-based pan. Mix together the egg yolks and the sugar and then add the cornflour. Pour half the milk onto the egg mixture, remove the vanilla pod and return the egg and milk to the pan. Cook the pastry cream over a medium heat, whisking all the time, for 3-4 minutes until the mixture is thick. Pour into a clean bowl. Scrape the seeds from the vanilla pod and stir into the pastry cream. Then stir in the melted chocolate. Cover with a small piece of buttered greaseproof paper and allow to cool.

Cut 6 of the 8 passion fruit in half and scoop the seeds into a blender or food processor. Whiz the passion fruit juice and seeds for 10 seconds and then sieve the juice. Lightly whip the cream and stir the passion fruit juice into the cream.
Fold the passion fruit cream into the pastry cream and then pile the mixture into the tart cases. Spoon the seeds from the remaining fruits over the tops of the tarts. Serve the tarts with tropical fruits or a raspberry sauce.

PIEDMONT TART

Piedmont in Northern Italy is renowned for producing some of the best hazelnuts in the world and since 1856 when Gianduja, a blend of hazelnuts and chocolate, was first created in the region it has been inextricably linked to chocolate and hazelnut confections. This recipe is based on one given to me by Penny, a very talented pastry chef, who used to cook at Orso's Italian restaurant in London.

Makes one 25.5cm (10 in) tart
Serves 8
Sweet Short Pastry 1 (page 31)
Use 1/2 of the quantity, wrap and freeze
   the remaining pastry
1 egg yolk

125g (41/2oz) unsalted butter
125g (41/2oz) caster sugar
2 eggs
225g (7oz) ground hazelnuts
125g (4oz) dark chocolate
25g (1oz) white chocolate

Preheat the oven to 190°C, 170°C fan oven, gas 5.

Prepare the pastry and rest it for 15 minutes in the fridge. Lightly flour a clean work surface and roll out the pastry to 3mm (1/8 in) thick. Use it to line a 25.5cm (10 in) tart tin and lightly prick the base. Rest it for 20 minutes in the fridge or 10 minutes in the freezer.

Bake the pastry blind for 10-15 minutes, remove the baking beans and bake for a further 5 minutes. The pastry should be pale to golden in colour. Brush the pastry case with a little of the egg yolk and bake for a further minute. Remove from the oven and allow to cool. Reduce the oven temperature to 180°C, 160°C fan oven, gas 4.

Chop the dark chocolate and place in a heatproof bowl over a pan of simmering water or heat in the microwave on a low setting, until melted.

Cream the butter and sugar together, beat in the eggs and then stir in the ground hazelnuts and 3/4 of the melted dark chocolate. Spread the chocolate mix over the cooled pastry case and bake the tart for 20-25 minutes until the hazelnut sponge is firm to the touch. Allow to cool.

Chop the white chocolate and place in a small heatproof bowl over a pan of simmering water or heat in the microwave on a low setting, until melted.

Drizzle the remaining dark chocolate liberally over the top of the tart and then drizzle over the white chocolate. Refrigerate for 5 minutes to set the chocolate before serving.

GLOSSARY

ACIDULATED: with the addition of a little lemon juice or vinegar. Acidulated water is used to make puff pastry.

BRISÉE: a short crust pastry that can be both sweet or savoury.

CRÈME PÂTISSIÈRE: a rich egg custard thickened with flour used to fill tarts and small pâtisserie. Also known as pastry cream and confectioners custard.

CRÈME D'AMANDE: an almond cream that is baked to give an almond sponge filling.

CRÈME DIPLOMAT: a mix of crème pâtissiere and whipped cream.

DETREMPE: the dough from which puff pastry is made.

DEMI-FEUILLETAGE: 'half puff' pastry is a quick-method puff pastry that doesn't have the same degree of flakiness or rise as full butter puff.

DOUBLE OR BOOK TURN: the name given to one of two methods used in the folding of the pastry during its lamination. The double or book turn is folded in half then each half is folded in on itself so it resembles a book.

FEUILLETAGE: full butter puff pastry.

FRANGIPANE: a common name for crème d'amande.

PÂTE FROLLE: rich sweet pastry made with ground almonds.

GLAZE: this refers to the finish given to a tart or pastry which can be achieved by a number of different methods. Most often by brushing with a mixture of boiled apricot jam, water and lemon juice (apricot glaze.) Other glazes include caramelised sugar, sugar syrup and chocolate glaze.

GLIADIN: one of the two proteins found in flour from which gluten is formed.

GLUTENIN: the other protein found in flour from which gluten is formed.

HYDROGENATED FAT: a type of hard fat produced by heat-treating liquid fat. The structure of the fat is altered and the fats are converted to saturated and trans fats.

LAMINATION: the formation of layers made during the rolling and turning of puff pastry. The layers comprise fat layers and dough layers. Air is also trapped within the layers of dough during lamination.

PÂTE: paste or pastry.

PÂTISSERIE: the name given to small cakes and confections sold in French pastry shops.

PLASTICIZE: the action used to work butter in order to bring it to the same consistency as the detrempe in puff pastry making.

REST: the action of allowing dough or pastry to recover from being worked (rolled, plied, or kneaded) usually at a cool temperature.

PÂTE À CHOUX: or choux pastry is first cooked in a pan before being piped into shape and baked. Its texture is very different to other pastry.

PÂTE SABLÉE: a delicate sweet pastry made by the rubbing in method

SAUCE ANGLAISE: a rich custard made using eggs without the addition of flour.

PÂTE SUCRÉE: sweet pastry made using the creaming method, it is more robust than Pâte Sablée.

PÂTE TATIN: Tatin pastry is a type of rich Brisée.

SFOGLIA: the Italian name for puff pastry and also the name of a specific triangular-shaped pastry from Campania.

SHORT: refers to the crumbly texture of pastry.

SINGLE TURN: the name given to one of two methods used in the folding of the pastry during its lamination. The single turn is straightforward, the dough is folded into 3, the bottom third is folded up over the middle third and then the top third folded down.

SOFT FLOUR: flour with a protein content between 6-10%. This range encompasses what would have been the ranges for weak and medium flours.

STAMEN: stamen is the plural of stigma. Saffron stigma is the orange red thread taken from the centre of the crocus flower.

STRONG FLOUR: flour with a protein content from 12-14%.

BIBLIOGRAPHY

Allen, Gray & Haas, Jenni, *The Almond People,* Blue Diamond growers

Ayrton, Elizabeth, *English Provincial Cooking*, Penguin Books Ltd

Baker, Jenny, *Kettle Broth to Gooseberry Fool*, Faber & Faber 1997

Bianchi, Anne, *Italian Festival Food*, Macmillan Publishing

Davidson, Alan, *The Penguin Companion to Food*, Penguin Books 2002

Grafton, Gillian, articles on apples and pears

Hanneman, L.J. *Pâtisserie*, Heinemann 1986

Jaworsk, Stephanie, www.joyofbaking.com

Jayne-Stanes, Sara, *Chocolate: the definitive guide*, Grub Street 1999

Larousse Gastronomique, Hamlyn 2001

Lehndorff, John, *As American as Apple Pie*, American Pie Council

Mason, Laura & Brown, Catherine, *Traditional Foods of Britain A Regional Inventory*, Prospect Books 2004

Nicolello, L.G. *Basic Pastrywork Techniques*, Arnold 1987

Norwak, Mary, *English Puddings Sweet & Savoury*, Grub Street 1996

Overton, Mark, *Agricultural Revolution in England 1500-1850*, Cambridge University Press

Spry, Constance & Hume, Rosemary, *The Constance Spry Cookery Book*, Grub Street 2004

Stradley, Linda, *What's Cooking America*, Threeforks Books 2000

www.walnuts.org

INDEX